The Amazing World of Englishes

The Amazing World of Englishes

A Practical Introduction

by
Peter Siemund
Julia Davydova
Georg Maier

De Gruyter Mouton

ISBN 978-3-11-026645-0
e-ISBN 978-3-11-026646-7

Library of Congress Cataloging-in-Publication Data

A CIP catalog record for this book has been applied for at the Library of Congress.

Bibliographic information published by the Deutsche Nationalbibliothek

The Deutsche Nationalbibliothek lists this publication in the Deutsche Nationalbibliografie;
detailed bibliographic data are available in the Internet at http://dnb.dnb.de.

© 2012 Walter de Gruyter GmbH & Co. KG, Berlin/Boston

Printing: Hubert & Co. GmbH & Co. KG, Göttingen
∞ Printed on acid-free paper

Printed in Germany

www.degruyter.com

Table of contents

Introduction

The amazing world of Englishes

This book is the result of an academic enterprise undertaken by three people fascinated by the English language, its diverse forms, histories, and cultures. We believe that anyone taking their first step into the ever-growing world of Englishes is likely to ask the question: "Why is it important to study English?"

This question may be answered in different ways. Firstly, English boasts a fascinating history going back to the 5th century AD, when some of the Germanic tribes crossed the North Sea to set foot on what is now known as Great Britain. Secondly, English has incorporated many structural properties from other languages that make it difficult to recognise its Germanic origin. Thirdly, English has made itself at home almost everywhere in the world – in the New World of North America, on the buzzing streets of Lagos, Cape Town, New Delhi, Mumbai, Hong Kong, Manila or Singapore, in the never-sleeping cities of Beijing, Shanghai or Moscow, and along the scorched vistas of Australia. Thus, it is not surprising that English is one of the most widely distributed languages in terms of its speakers.

One of the repercussions of this extensive spread of English is that it has diversified into a variety of different forms – Indian English, Singapore English, Nigerian English, Irish English, South African English, etc. in addition to the standard varieties of British and American English – that over time have become the object of extensive academic enquiry. These diverse forms of English have been shaped by local cultures and languages and, of course, the people who adopted it. In other words, English has been localised.

Another consequence of the global spread of English is that it has become a means of communication amongst people who do not share a common language. As people need to get their message across irrespective of their linguistic and cultural background, they need a form of English that is understood by everyone. It is in this sense that English has been globalised.

Moreover, English spoken in dynamic metropolitan areas is often different from English spoken in traditional rural areas. English spoken by native speakers is not the same as English spoken by non-native speakers. Furthermore, there are distinct forms of English spoken by specific social or ethnic groups. Finally, we can single out Pidgin and Creole Englishes that emerge in contact situations when people do not share a common language.

Structure of the book

The diversification of English into many different – and sometimes even mutually unintelligible – forms raises some important questions: Who are native speakers of English? Who are non-native speakers of English? How can a distinction between native and non-native speakers of English be plausibly drawn and maintained given that English today is acquired in a variety of different contexts? Who speaks standard varieties of English? To what extent are regional varieties of English different from standard dialects and what exactly are these differences? Our book addresses these important questions by drawing on an empirical-inductive approach, offering a wide range of activities and an extended set of exercises.

Following Kachru's (1985) concentric circle model, this book is divided into three major parts, marked by different colours. The first part deals with those regions where English is spoken as the dominant native language – the so-called 'inner-circle' varieties (Chapters 2–5).

The second part discusses the Englishes in countries where English was adopted as an official or co-official language and is used as a link language for interethnic communication. This group is referred to as the 'outer-circle' (Chapters 6–8).

Finally, the third part focuses on forms of English in countries where English plays an important role in international communication, but not for historical or administrative reasons. This is the so-called 'expanding circle' (Chapter 9). The book is rounded off by an introductory chapter (Chapter 1) and a concluding section in which fundamental concepts are introduced and the major issues are summarised.

Target audience

In view of the fact that English has developed so many different forms spoken all around the world, the question arises as to how the astounding linguistic heterogeneity inherent in modern English can be made accessible to those audiences that have no training in linguistics and are perhaps only intuitively aware of the contemporary diversification of the English language. This textbook has been specifically designed to address this issue. In so doing, it caters to the needs of secondary school and undergraduate university students demonstrating upper-intermediate and advanced levels of proficiency in English. The textbook is also of interest, however, to a more general public interested in issues related to the expansion of English, English diversity, and varieties of English. While assuming a sound command of English, the textbook does not require previous knowledge of linguistics or linguistic terminology.

Guidelines for students

The approach of the book is empirical-inductive. This means that we aim to familiarise you with the characteristics of the different varieties of English with the help of authentic audio, video, and text materials from the regions discussed in the textbook in order for you to discover the specifics of these varieties yourselves.

Each chapter is introduced by a general **Introduction**, which provides you with the necessary background information on the given variety.

In the individual chapters, all materials deal with different sociocultural and linguistic aspects of the variety at hand. The individual source materials are presented in the form of various activities such as **Reading Comprehension**, **Listening Comprehension**, and **Viewing Comprehension**. Listening and Viewing Comprehension activities are accompanied by references to websites on which the corresponding sound and video files can be found or alternative instructions on how to find them.

Each text, video or audio file is accompanied by a number of **Comprehension** and **Analysis Exercises**, and most of them also by **Discussion** or **Creative Writing** tasks. In addition to this, the textbook features **Role-Playing Games** and **Self-Study** exercises. The Role-Playing Games deal with issues related to society and culture and are aimed at triggering and facilitating in-class discussions on the role of English and the specific features in the respective variety.

Many activities follow a distinct pattern consisting of pre-X exercises, while-X exercises, and post-X exercises. This aims to provide a target-oriented introduction to and discussion of the presented variety-specific features. In general, our exercises allow for a step-by-step training of particular lexical and morphosyntactic features.

Vocabulary-building exercises accompany texts and transcripts. Building on the learners' knowledge of academic language, the exercises introduce basic terminology used in academic discourse to talk about language and linguistics. These exercises also intend to familiarise students with culture-specific notions and variety-specific lexis. All lexical items appearing under **Vocabulary** and **Definitions** are typically set in bold face in the texts.

For reviewing vocabulary and variety-specific content, we included **Memory** and **Taboo** games. They may be copied from the book and then cut into individual cards.

Finally, all materials exhibit varying levels of difficulty. Reading Comprehension materials can be generally regarded as most straightforward in terms of delivering the message about the diversity of English. Listening and Viewing Comprehension activities are often more demanding, as here the learner is asked to rely largely on their auditory perception in order to reconstruct variety-relevant features.

Acknowledgements

The book has grown out of a research project on the teaching of varieties of English in undergraduate university courses and high school classroom settings. The project ran from 2007–2010 as part of the Collaborative Research Centre on Multilingualism (*Sonderforschungsbereich* 538). The financial support of the German Research Foundation and the University of Hamburg is herewith gratefully acknowledged.

We also benefited substantially from the advice given by the Hamburg Teacher Training Institute (especially Christiane Fraedrich) and the feedback we received from the many teachers and instructors who used and tested a prototype of our book.

We are especially thankful to Kirk Hazen, Martina Hoffmann, Larisa M. Khokhlova, Ute Niemeyer, Katrin Sie-mund, Peter Trudgill, and Florian Zieger. The overall quality of the book benefited greatly as a result of their thoughtful comments and suggestions.

We are grateful to all authors, publishers, archives, libraries, and other copyright holders who granted us permission to reproduce their material.

A special word of gratitude goes to Isabel Peters, who designed the layout of the book. Leonie Fölsing and Audrey MacDougall proved indispensable proofreaders. We also appreciate the technical support rendered by Pagona Nassery and Maria Schröder at various stages of the project.

Last but not least, we would like to acknowledge the technical support we received from Mouton de Gruyter's editorial team: Birgit Sievert, Julie Miess, and Jens Lindenhain.

Disclaimer

Every effort has been undertaken by the authors to obtain and supply all copyright information and clearances for the texts, pictures, images, and other media included in this book. In the case that the information provided should be incomplete or erroneous, the copyright owners are requested to contact the authors and the publisher so that necessary actions can be taken and corrections made. The contents from the external sources do not necessarily reflect our own point of view. We do not assume any responsibility for the contents provided by the external Internet links contained in this book.

Accompanying website

We offer some of our contents for download at the following website:

www.awe.uni-hamburg.de
userid: awe2012
password: amazing

REFERENCES AND FURTHER READING

Kachru, Braj B. 1985. Standards, codification and sociolinguistic realism: the English
    language in the outer circle. In: Quirk, Randolph and Henry G. Widdowson (eds.),
    English in the World. Teaching and Learning the Language and Literatures.
    Cambridge: Cambridge University Press and the British Council.

Kachru, Braj B. 1988. The sacred cows of English. *English Today* 4:4, 3–8.

Kachru, Braj B. 1997. World Englishes and English-using communities. *Annual Review of
    Applied Linguistics* 17, 66–87.

Circles of English

Chapter 1

English as a global language

Introduction

Within the past few decades, English has become a truly global language. A quick glance at the world map makes it clear that there are few places on this planet where English is not spoken.

Great Britain, North America, and Australia are places where English is the mother tongue of the vast majority of people living there.

In South and Southeast Asia, as well as in many parts of Africa, English has established itself as a link language besides the indigenous languages. Having been introduced during the colonial era by missionary schools or in face-to-face encounters, English plays an important role in education and administration in countries like India, Singapore, Sri Lanka, Nigeria, Ghana, Kenya, and Tanzania. In these countries, English developed in an environment where indigenous (or local) languages were dominant.

For instance, India boasts 22 national languages, many of which belong to different language families. Thus, Hindi, Bengali, and Punjabi are Indo-European languages, whereas Kannada, Malayalam, and Tamil are Dravidian languages. In this highly complex linguistic situation, English is used as a glue stick, a language link that unites all.

As English emerged in situations where local languages prevailed, it has acquired some lexical and grammatical features that stem from those languages. For example, the discourse particle *lah* in Singapore English, as in *I mean you can choose lah* [#i], is of Chinese origin. Many words are borrowed from local languages into a newly emerging variety of English. *Masaala*, *daal*, and *goshth* are all Hindi words that people feel comfortable using while speaking English.

English is also the official language or one of the official languages in these countries. To give an example, there are nine official languages in Nigeria, of which English is one: Edo, Efik, Adamawa Fulfulde, Hausa, Idoma, Igbo, Central Kanuri, Yoruba, and English. [#ii]

English is also used for creative writing in countries where it has a second-language status. Vikram Seth is one notable example: The author received an advance worth £250,000 for his 1,350-page long epos *A Suitable Boy*; he collected £1.4 million for publishing *Two Lives*. [#iii]

In large parts of Europe, China and Russia, and in countries of South America, English is taught as a first foreign language in school because it is believed to be an important international language. English is not an official language in these countries; it is not used in administration, although its role in education has started to increase.

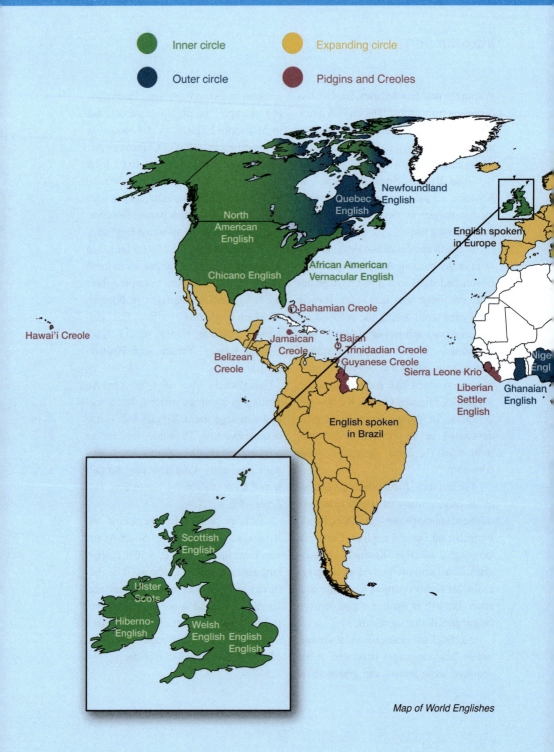

Inner circle

Expanding circle

Outer circle

Pidgins and Creoles

Newfoundland English

Quebec English

North American English

English spoken in Europe

Chicano English

African American Vernacular English

Bahamian Creole

Hawai'i Creole

Jamaican Creole

Bajan

Trinidadian Creole

Belizean Creole

Guyanese Creole

Sierra Leone Krio

Nige Engl

Liberian Settler English

Ghanaian English

English spoken in Brazil

Scottish English

Ulster Scots

Hiberno-English

Welsh English English English

Map of World Englishes

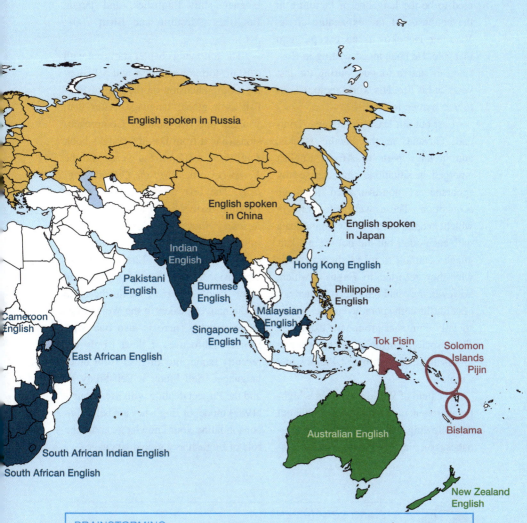

English spoken in Russia

English spoken in China

English spoken in Japan

Indian English

Hong Kong English

Pakistani English

Burmese English

Philippine English

Malaysian English

Singapore English

Cameroon English

Tok Pisin

Solomon Islands Pijin

East African English

Bislama

South African Indian English

South African English

Australian English

New Zealand English

BRAINSTORMING

Discuss the role of English as a global language in pairs or in groups. Make sure to answer the following questions:

1. Who speaks English today? Where is English spoken today?
2. When do you speak English?
3. Why do we call English a global language today?
4. What is standard English? Who speaks standard English?

English is traditionally not considered to be the language of literature in the countries of the expanding circle. Vladimir Nabokov is an exception to that rule. He abandoned writing in Russian, his native tongue, during the last years of his life. His world famous *Lolita* was written in English.

Last but not least, in Jamaica, Trinidad, Guyana, in the Pacific Islands, and in large parts of Africa, English emerged in situations characterised by spontaneous, non-instructed language acquisition. These were situations in which people needed to communicate with each other but did not share a language common to all of them. This is why they resorted to English, which, however, they had only very limited access to (through sporadic contact with a socially dominant group, for example). These sociolinguistic contexts gave rise to so-called English-based Pidgins and Creoles.

The field of World Englishes is highly heterogeneous, but we can single out the following forms: metropolitan Englishes, colonial Englishes, regional dialects, sociolects, immigrant Englishes, language-shift Englishes, and jargon Englishes (Mesthrie and Bhatt 2008: 3–6).

The following chapter starts out with a Brainstorming exercise and a Listening Comprehension on the role of English as a global language. After that, you can find two Reading Comprehensions (a text from David Crystal's book *English as a Global Language* and the *Newsweek* article *Not the Queen's English*). The text excerpt from Jennifer Jenkins' textbook *World Englishes: A Resource Book for Students* looks at the role that English plays in Europe. The ensuing Project and Listening Comprehension (*Learn English by learning other people's stories*) tackle the issue of the native speaker in the World Englishes debate. There is also one Mini Project that focuses on those words that recently came into English from other languages. Self-Study I, Self-Study II, and the Project dealing with McArthur's (1987) model of Englishes are helpful in consolidating your knowledge about the role of English as a global language.

 LISTENING COMPREHENSION

1. Explore the website of the International Dialects of English Archive (http://web.ku.edu/~idea/) and listen to speakers from different parts of the English-speaking world!
2. On YouTube you can find video clips featuring the current heads of state of Great Britain, the United States, Australia, and Ireland. Who in your opinion speaks standard English?

 READING COMPREHENSION

The circles of English

The following text describes the gradual emergence of English as an international lingua franca. Read the text and pay close attention to the graphic presented below.

The present-day world status of English is primarily the result of two factors: the **expansion** of British colonial power, which peaked towards
5 the end of the nineteenth century, and the **emergence** of the United States as the leading economic power of the twentieth century. It is the
10 latter factor which continues to explain the world position of the English language today [...]. The USA has nearly 70 per cent of all English mother-tongue
15 speakers in the world (excluding **creole varieties**). Such dominance, with its political/economic **underpinnings**, currently gives America a controlling interest in the way the language is likely
20 to develop.

How then may we summarize this complex situation? The US linguist Braj Kachru has suggested that we think of the spread of English around the world
25 as three **concentric** circles, representing different ways in which the language has been acquired and is currently used. Although not all countries fit neatly into this model, it has been widely regarded
30 as a helpful **approach**.

Circles of English

The *inner circle* refers to the traditional bases of English, where it is the **primary** language: it includes the USA, UK, Ireland, Canada, Australia and New Zealand. 35

The *outer* or *extended circle* involves the earlier phases of the spread of English in non-native settings, where the language has become part of a country's chief institutions, and plays an 40 important 'second language' role in a **multilingual setting**: it includes Singapore, India, Malawi and over fifty other territories.

45 The *expanding* or *extending circle* involves those nations which recognize the importance of English as an international language, though they do not have a history of colonization by members 50 of the inner circle, nor have they given English any special administrative sta-

tus. It includes China, Japan, Greece, Poland and (as the name of this circle suggests) a steadily increasing number of other states. In these areas, English is 55 taught as a foreign language.

[David Crystal 2003: 59–60. #1; bold face added]

Vocabulary

Look up the following words in a monolingual English dictionary: expansion, emergence, underpinnings, concentric, approach, and primary.

Definitions

Try to find definitions for the terms "creole varieties" and "multilingual setting".

COMPREHENSION

Now that you have read the text about the expansion of English as a global language, answer the following questions:

1. Why has English become a global language? Give two possible explanations.
2. Braj Kachru, an American linguist, talks about the three circles of English. What are they?
3. Which role does English play in each of the characterised circles?
4. Which circle could your home country be placed in and why?

ANALYSIS AND DISCUSSION

1. Describe the differences and similarities between the inner and outer circles of English.
2. Discuss the advantages (or disadvantages) of being a native speaker of English.

CREATIVE WRITING

Imagine that you spend your summer holidays in a summer school in England where you share rooms with students from France, Spain, Nigeria, and Singapore. Comment on the English they use in an email to your friends at home. Give examples of the language you heard.

Summer school

 READING COMPREHENSION

The rapid growth of English around the globe has recently been highlighted in some important mass media outlets. In her feature *Not the Queen's English*, Carla Power, a *Newsweek* correspondent, provides some lively images of the ever-expanding world of English.

Not the Queen's English

by Carla Power

The name – Cambridge School of Languages – **conjures images** of spires and Anglo-Saxon aristocrats conversing in the Queen's English. But this Cambridge
5 is composed of a few **dank rooms** with **rickety chairs** at the edge of a **congested** Delhi **suburb**. Its rival is not stately Oxford but the nearby Euro Languages School, where a three-month English
10 course costs $16. "We tell students you need two things to succeed: English and computers," says Chetan Kumar, a Euro Languages manager. "We teach one. For the other" – he points to a nearby Inter-
15 net stall – "you can go next door."

The professors back in Cambridge, England, would no doubt question the schools' pedagogy. There are few books or tapes. Their teachers pronounce "*we*"
20 as "*ve*" and "*primary*" as "*primmry*." And yet such **storefront shops** aren't merely the **ragged** edge of the massive English-learning industry, which in India alone is a $100 million-per-year
25 business. They are the front lines of a global revolution in which hundreds of millions of people are learning English, the planet's language for commerce, technology – and, increasingly, empow-
30 erment. Within a decade, 2 billion people will be studying English and about half the world – some 3 billion people – will speak it, according to a recent report from the British Council.

35 From Caracas to Karachi, parents keen for their children to achieve are forking over tuition for English-language schools. China's English fever – elevated to epidemic proportions by
40 the country's recent accession to the World Trade Organization and the coming 2008 Olympics – even has its own **Mandarin** term, *Yingwen re*. And governments from Tunisia to Turkey are
45 pushing English, recognizing that along with computers and mass migration, the language is the **turbine engine of globalization**. As one 12-year-old self-taught English-speaker from China's
50 southwestern Sichuan province says, "If you can't speak English, it's like you're deaf and dumb."

Linguistically speaking, it's a whole new world. Non-native speakers of English now outnumber native speakers 3 to 1, according to English-language expert David Crystal, whose numerous books include "English as a Global Language." "There's never before been a language that's been spoken by more people as a second than a first," he says. In Asia alone, the number of English-users has topped 350 million – roughly the combined populations of the United States, Britain and Canada. There are more Chinese children studying English – about 100 million – than there are Britons.

The new English-speakers aren't just passively absorbing the language – they're shaping it. New Englishes are mushrooming the globe over, ranging from "Englog," the Tagalog-infused English spoken in the Philippines, to "Japlish", the **cryptic** English

Multilingual society

poetry beloved of Japanese copywriters ("Your health and loveliness is our best wish," reads a candy wrapper. "Give us a chance to realize it"), to "Hinglish", the mix of Hindi and English that now crops up everywhere from fast-food ads to South Asian college campuses. "**Hungry kya?**" ("Are you hungry?"), queried a recent Indian ad for Domino's pizza.

In post-**apartheid** South Africa, many blacks have adopted their own version of English, **laced with indigenous** words, as a sign of freedom – in contrast to **Afrikaans**, the language of oppression. "We speak English with a Xhosa accent and a **Xhosa** attitude," veteran actor John Kani recently told the BBC.

All languages are works in progress. But English's globalization, **unprecedented** in the history of languages, will revolutionize it in ways we can only begin to imagine. In the future, suggests Crystal, there could be a tri-English world, one in which you could speak a local English-based dialect at home, a national variety at work or school, and international Standard English to talk to foreigners. With native speakers a **shrinking minority** of the world's **Anglophones**, there's a growing sense that students should stop trying to **emulate Brighton** or **Boston English**, and embrace their own local versions. Researchers are starting to study non-native speakers' "mistakes" – "She look very sad," for example – as structured grammars. In a generation's time, teach-ers might no longer be correcting stu-dents for saying "a book who" or "a per-son which." Linguist Jennifer Jenkins, an expert in world Englishes at King's College London, asks why some Asians, who have trouble pronouncing the "th" sound, should spend hours trying to say "thing" instead of "sing" or "ting." In-ternational pilots, she points out, already pronounce the word "three" as "tree" in radio dispatches, since "tree" is more widely comprehensible.

Not everyone is as open-minded about English, or its advance. The Web site of the Association for the Defence of the French Language displays a "mu-seum of horrors" – a series of digital pic-tures of English-language signs on Pa-risian streets. But others say such defen-siveness misses the point. "This is not about English swamping and **eroding** local identities," says David Graddol, author of the British Council report. "It's about creating new identities – and about making everyone bilingual."

Indeed, English has become the **common linguistic denominator**. Whether you're a Korean executive on business in Shanghai, **a German Euro-crat hammering out laws in Brussels** or a Brazilian biochemist at a confer-ence in Sweden, you're probably speak-ing English. And as the world adopts an international brand of English, it's na-tive speakers who have the most to lose.

Cambridge **dons** who insist on speak-ing the Queen's English could be met with giggles – or blank stares. British or American business **execs** who **jabber** on in their own idiomatic **patois**, with-out understanding how English is used by non-natives, might lose out on deals.

To achieve fluency, non-native speakers are learning English at an ever-younger age. Last year primary schools in major Chinese cities began offering English in the third grade, rather than middle school. A growing number of parents are enrolling their preschool-ers in the new crop of local English courses. For some mothers-to-be, even that's not early enough; Zhou Min, who hosts several English programs at the Beijing Broadcasting Station, says some pregnant women speak English to their fetuses. At Prague's Lamea children's English-language school, 3-year-olds sing songs about snowmen and chant colors in English. Now 2-year-olds have a class of their own, too.

For the traditional custodians of English – the British and, more recently, the Americans – this means money. The demand for native English-speakers is so huge that there aren't enough to go around; China and the Middle East are starting to import English teachers from India. The average price of a four-day business-English course in London for a French executive runs 2,240 euro. Despite – or perhaps because of – all the new Englishes cropping up, it's the American and British versions that still carry prestige, particularly with tuition-paying parents. Australia and Britain, in particular, have invested heavily in branding themselves as destinations for learning English. More than 400 foreign English-teaching companies are trying to break into China. On a visit to Beijing last week, British Chancellor Gordon Brown said the Chinese thirst to acquire the language was "a huge opportunity for Britain," which already boasts a 1.3 billion pound English-teaching industry. Says Jenkins, "Owning English is very big business."

To see big business in action, one need only walk down London's busy Oxford Street, where ads **hawk instant access to** the language of success: DOES YOUR ENGLISH EMBARRASS YOU? BUSINESS ENGLISH FOR BEGINNERS; LEARN ENGLISH IN JUST 10 WEEKS! Above clothing stores, bustling English-language schools are packed with eager twenty-somethings from around the world. Ben Beaumont, a **buoyant** 28-year-old Briton, presides over a class that includes a South Korean business manager, a nurse from rural Japan and an Italian law student. "Do you want a lot of homework or a little?" he asks. The class is unequivocal: "A lot!"

Why such enthusiasm? In a word, jobs. A generation ago, only elites like diplomats and CEOs needed English for work. "The ante on what's needed is going up year by year," says Graddol. "Throughout organizations, more people need more English." In China, the Beijing Organizing Committee for the 2008 Olympics is pushing English among staff, guides, taxi drivers and or-

dinary citizens. For lower-middle classes in India, English can mean a ticket to a prized call-center job. "With call centers, no longer is speaking English one of the important skills to get a good job," says Raghu Prakash, who runs an English-language school in Jaipur. "It is *the* skill." At the new Toyota and Peugeot plant in the Czech Republic, English is the working language of the Japanese, French and Czech staff. Says Jitka Prikrylova, director of a Prague English-language school: "The world has opened up for us, and English is its language."

Governments, even linguistically protectionist ones, are starting to agree. Last year Malaysia decided to start teaching school-level math and science in English. In France, home of the Academie Francaise, whose members are given swords and charged with defending the **sanctity** of the French language, a commission recommended last fall that basic English be treated like basic math: as part of the mandatory core curriculum beginning in primary school. As it turns out, the minister of Education didn't agree. No matter; French schoolchildren are ahead of their government: 96 percent of them are already studying the language as an **elective** in school.

Technology also plays a huge role in English's global triumph. Eighty percent of the electronically stored information in the world is in English; 66 percent of the world's scientists read in it, according to the British Council. "It's very important to learn English because [computer] books are only in English," says Umberto Duirte, an Uruguayan IT student learning English in London. New technologies are helping people pick up the language, too: Chinese and Japanese students can get English-usage tips on their mobile phones. English-language teachers point to the rise of Microsoft English, where computer users are drafting letters advised by the Windows spell check and pop-up style guides. In the temple town of Varanasi, India, Sanjukta Chaterjee says she's astonished by the way her 7-year-old son learns the language, through CDs and video. "Our teachers were strict that we should practice, and speak the language till we were near-perfect," she says. "Now there's an additional technological finesse to learning English."

Schools are becoming more and more creative. Last August, South Korea set up its first English immersion camp. The Gyeonggi English Village, built on a small island in the Yellow Sea and subsidized by the provincial government, comes complete with a Hollywood-style fake bank and airport, where students must conduct all transactions in English. "Through the camp, we want to train capable global citizens, who can help Korea win international competition in this age of globalization," says Sohn Hak Kyu, governor of Gyeonggi province, who started the program. In one class, eighth grader Chun Ho Sung, wearing a long black wig and posing as British heartthrob Orlando Bloom, sweats under the lights of a mock television studio as he prepares to be interviewed. "Do you think you are handsome?" asks the anchorwoman. Shyly, in **broken English**, Chun responds: "Yes, I do. I am very handsome." The audience of other students **collapses in giggles**.

While courses like Gyeonggi's sound simple, English and its teaching are **inexorably** becoming more complex. Ilan Stavans, an Amherst College professor, recently finished a translation of Cervantes's "Don Quixote" into Spanglish, the English-Spanish hybrid spoken in the United States and Mexico. Writing in the journal English Today last spring, Hu Xiaoqiong argued for reorientating China's English curriculum toward China English, incorporating Chinese phrases like "pay New Year calls," a Spring Festival tradition, and "no face," to be ashamed – as Standard English. In countries like Germany, where most kids begin English as early as the second or third grade, the market for English studies is already shrinking. German language schools no longer target English beginners but those pursuing more-expert niches: business English, phone manners or English for presentations. Beginning-English classes are filled with immigrants from places like Turkey and Russia, eager to **catch up with** the natives. As with migrants the world over, they're finding that their newfound land is an English-speaking one.

[From *Newsweek* March 07, 2005. © 2005. The Newsweek/Daily Beast Company LLC. All rights reserved. #2; bold face added.]

Vocabulary

Look up the following words and expressions in a monolingual English dictionary: conjure images, dank rooms, rickety chairs, congested suburb, storefront shops, ragged, cryptic, laced with, indigenous, unprecedented, shrinking minority, emulate, erode, don, execs, jabber, hawk instant access to, buoyant, sanctity, elective, collapse in giggles, inexorably, and catch up with.

Definitions

1. Find definitions for the following terms and expressions: Mandarin, 'Hungry kya?', Apartheid, Afrikaans, Xhosa, Anglophones, Brighton English, Boston English, patois, and broken English.
2. In the text, the author talks about "a German Eurocrat hammering out laws in Brussels". Who does the word 'Eurocrat' refer to? Which pattern of word formation is this new coinage built on?

COMPREHENSION

1. What is implied by the article's title?
2. Look at the first paragraph of the text. Describe in your own words what the Cambridge School of Languages in New Delhi looks like.
3. Describe the ways in which non-native speakers of English transform this language.
4. According to Jennifer Jenkins, "owning English is very big business". Explain how this is the case. Give examples from the text.
5. Describe the factors contributing to the importance of English. Give examples from the text.

Flags

ANALYSIS

1. Read the text one more time. What is the main message of the text?
2. How many parts can you identify in its structure?
3. Assign a number of key words to each part that you identified.
4. Analyse how the author develops her argument to support the idea of English becoming a truly global language.

WORD ANALYSIS

1. Take a look at line 47. How do you understand the expression "the turbine engine of globalization"?
2. In your own words, try to explain the meaning of "common linguistic denominator" in line 147.

DISCUSSION

1. Why, do you think, are there so many countries willing to promote the idea of a global language?
2. Do you think that English is predestined to play the role of a global language in the future? Explain.
3. Do you think some other language might become an international lingua franca? Explain.
4. Jennifer Jenkins suggests that it is not necessary for non-native speakers of English to learn how to pronounce the difficult *th*-sound. Do you agree? Explain.

PROJECT I

1. Try to identify all countries in which English has the status of an official or co-official language.
2. Assign the countries you found to the inner circle and the outer circle, as defined by Braj Kachru's concentric circles model.

PROJECT II

1. Investigate the major grammatical properties of English (word order, tenses, aspects, morphology, phoneme inventory, ...).
2. Compare English to your mother tongue.
3. Do you think that the grammar of English makes this language particularly suitable as a global language?

 READING COMPREHENSION

The changing role of English in Europe

by Jennifer Jenkins

Despite the linguistic richness of the European Union (EU), and the eleven languages given official status (Danish, Dutch, English, Finnish, French, German, Greek, Italian, Portuguese, Spanish and Swedish), three languages dominate – English, French and German. Europe has become, in Graddol's (1997: 14) words, 'a single multilingual area, rather like India, where languages are hierarchically related in status. As in India, there may be many who are monolingual in a regional language, but those who speak one of the "big" languages will have better access to material success.' By the end of the twentieth century, however, a single one of the three 'big' languages, English, had become the 'biggest', the *de facto* European ***lingua franca***. And for the time being at least, it seems, those who speak English will have the best access to such material success, hence, in part, the current popularity of learning English among Europe's young that Cheshire (2002) documents.

Some scholars, most vociferously Phillipson (1992, 2003), but including Cheshire herself, believe it is critical for all Europeans to learn each other's languages rather than for everyone to learn English. Nevertheless, Cheshire (2002) notes that European English appears to be developing the scope to 'express "emotional" aspects of young people's social identities' by means of phenomena like code switching and code mixing (e.g. the use of half-German half-English hybrid compounds such as *Telefon junkie* and *Drogenfreak* in German youth magazines).

House (2001), whose position is for the most part diametrically opposed to that of the 'Phillipson camp', finds the EU's language policy hypocritical and ineffective. Rather than having several working languages and making heavy use of a translation machinery, she argues, the EU should opt officially for English as its *lingua franca* or, as she puts it, the 'language of communication'. On the other hand, House does not appear to consider the possibility that English can express the 'social identities' of its European non-native speakers. Instead, she believes that individual speakers' mother tongues will remain their 'language for identification' (House 2001: 2–3).

The positioning of English (or **Euro-English** as it is increasingly being labelled) as Europe's primary *lingua franca* is so recent that it is too soon to be able to say with any certainty whether it

65 will remain so, how it will develop, and whether it will expand to become fully capable of expressing social identity as well as performing a more transactional role in politics, business and the like.
70 The linguistic outcome of European political and economic developments is predicted by some scholars to be a nativised hybrid variety of English, in effect, a European English which contains
75 a number of grammatical, lexical, phonological and discoursal features found in individual mainland European languages along with some items common to many of these languages but not to
80 standard British (or American) English.

Berns (1995: 6–7), for example, characterises the nativisation process that English in Europe is undergoing as follows: 'In the course of using English
85 to carry out its three roles [native, foreign and international language], Europeans make adaptations and introduce innovations that effectively **de-Americanize** and **de-Anglicize** English.' She
90 talks specifically of a 'European English-using speech community' who use English for intra-European communication, and for whom

the label *European English* identifies those uses of English that are not Brit- 95 ish (and not American or Canadian or Australian or any other native variety) but are distinctly European and distinguish European English speakers from speakers of other [English] varieties. 100

In her view, it is possible that British English will eventually be considered merely as one of a number of European varieties of English alongside **nativised** 105 **varieties** such as French English, Dutch English, Danish English and the like.

European speakers are, nevertheless, as Berns (1995: 10) concludes, 'in the midst of an exciting, challenging, and 110 creative social and linguistic phase of their history' in which 'they have the potential to have significant influence on the spread of English'. The situation is, as she puts it, one of 'sociolinguistic his- 115 tory-in-the-making' and one which will therefore need to be reviewed regularly as empirical evidence becomes increasingly available.

[Jennifer Jenkins 2003: 42–43. #3; bold face added]

Explanations

lingua franca: a means of international communication; **Euro-English**: the English spoken in Europe; **de-Americanize**: to lessen the influence of the traditions and culture of the United States on something; **de-Anglicize**: to lessen the influence of the traditions and culture of Great Britain on something; **nativised varieties**: distinct forms of English that originated in the countries in which English is not spoken as a native language. These varieties have developed specific linguistic features of their own.

COMPREHENSION

What role does the English language play in Europe?

ANALYSIS

1. Why has the English language achieved such enormous pre-dominance in the countries of Western Europe? Start with the arguments given in the text and add others you consider to be relevant.
2. Analyse the positions that are proposed by the scholars Phillipson and House. Which of the two positions do you consider more convincing and why?

COMMENT WRITING

Comment on the pros and cons of English spreading around the globe and penetrating into different spheres of social life in countries where it is not spoken as a native language.

PROJECT

In this project, we propose a debate on World Englishes: *Who is the native speaker of English?*

1. On the following page, read the stories about different people learning English in different contexts.
2. Who, in your opinion, is *a* or *the* native speaker of English? Explain your choice.

Santvana was born in Mumbai. Her parents moved to London when she was twelve years old. Since her father is a businessman, Santvana visited a private school for girls, where she did her A-Levels. She is now studying biology at the University of Cambridge.

Jenny was born in Baltimore, MD (USA). Being rather well-off, her parents were able to send her to a prestigious high school, after which she studied journalism at Yale University. Jenny is currently looking for a job and applying to various English-speaking newspapers and magazines all over the world.

Sebastian started learning English at the age of seven when he went to primary school. Because his parents wanted him to have a very good command of English, they hired an English tutor when the boy was ten. Sebastian is now fifteen. He enjoys reading English novels and watching American films in English. He has already been to England, Scotland, and New Zealand. Next year, he is going to participate in a student exchange programme and spend one year in the United States.

Bidisha was born in Kolkata, West Bengal. Her father was a Bengali, whereas her mother came from New Delhi. Her father started teaching her English when she was six. He would explain to her the meanings of different English words in Bengali. When Bidisha became older, her parents sent her to a convent, a private school for girls, where classes were taught in English. Bidisha studied Languages and Linguistics at Jawaharlal Nehru University in New Delhi. She is now married and works as a translator for a company in New Delhi. Bidisha has a three-year-old son. Because her husband comes from Gujarat, they speak English in their family.

Drawings of students

LISTENING COMPREHENSION

Learn English by learning other people's stories
Listen to the sound files you can find at the links listed below. You will hear different people telling stories about their lives. Some of them are native and some of them are non-native speakers of English. Moreover, they come from different regions in the world.

- » http://web.ku.edu/~idea/europe/england/england42.mp3
- » http://web.ku.edu/~idea/australiaoceania/australia/australia16.mp3
- » http://web.ku.edu/~idea/europe/italy/italy4.mp3

1. Listen to the sound files and retell each of the stories in your own words!
2. Which story do you find most fascinating? Explain.
3. Listen to the speaker's language one more time. Decide what helps you to indentify whether a given speaker is a native speaker of the language or not. Explain.

MINI PROJECT

English has spread all over the world. The influence, however, has been mutual. Many words have recently come into English from other languages. Here are some examples:

Language	Word	Meaning	Example
Italian	spaghetti	a type of pasta	spaghetti served with meat
French	café au lait	a type of coffee	café au lait to go
German	pretzel	a bread roll	a Bavarian pretzel
Russian	sputnik	satellite	launch a sputnik

Think of words that have come into English from your native language.

SELF-STUDY I

Write an essay about why it may or may not be important to learn English. Give at least three arguments. In addition, describe the role that English plays as a global language today.

The following statements about English may help you to get started:

1. English exerts influence on different cultures and different languages all over the world.
2. English mixes with other languages (for example Chinese, Japanese, Hindi, etc.) and thus develops into new forms.
3. English is destroying other peoples' cultures and languages.
4. English is the medium of Internet communication.
5. English is the language of youth culture.
6. English is taught as a foreign language in schools much more often than other languages such as French, Spanish, Italian, etc.
7. English is important because it will help you to get a well-paid job.
8. English is the language of the global media and pop culture.
9. English not only shapes but is also shaped by other cultures and languages.
10. The languages of the major trade blocs (such as Arabic, Malay, Chinese, Russian, Spanish, and German) are likely to replace English as means of international (business) communication in the future.

SELF-STUDY II

Take a look at the mind map given below. Expand the list of the Englishes belonging to the inner, outer, and expanding circles. Don't forget to explain your choice.

McArthur's model of Englishes

Tom McArthur is the author of a much discussed model of World Englishes published in the July issue of *English Today* in 1987. In his model, he proposes that Englishes should be organised into three different circles. At the very centre of the model there is World Standard English, which is an idealised variety of written English. The second circle of the model is allotted to those regional varieties of English that have developed or have started to develop their own standards. The third circle of the model is occupied by those forms of English that are not codified in grammatical and lexicographic descriptions. In other words, these Englishes are not standardised. You can find an adaptation of McArthur's model in the table below.

1. Learn more about McArthur's model by reading the article 'The English languages?' published in *English Today* (1987:3, 9–13).
2. Do you think the notion of World Standard English as elaborated on by McArthur (1987) is a useful term? Explain!
3. Discuss advantages and disadvantages of the model proposed by McArthur in pairs.
4. Write down all of your pros and cons and write an essay in which you argue for or against the model of World Englishes suggested by McArthur.

	Standard(ising) Englishes	Non-standard varieties
World Standard English	British and Irish	English English, Scottish English, …
	American	Northern, Midland, Southern, …
	Canadian	Quebec, Newfoundland, Athabascan, …
	Caribbean	Jamaican, Barbadian, Trinidadian, …
	African	Nigerian, Ghanaian, South African, …
	South Asian	Indian, Pakistani, …
	East Asian	Hong Kong, Singapore, …
	Australian, New Zealand	Australian, Aboriginal, New Zealand, …

Sources

TEXTS

[1]   Crystal, David. 2003. *English as a Global Language.* Cambridge: Cambridge University Press, 59–60. © David Crystal, 1997, 2003, published by Cambridge University Press, reproduced with permission.

[2]   Power, Carla. 2005. "Not the Queen's English". *Newsweek*, March 07, 2005, 63–67. © 2005 The Newsweek/Daily Beast Company LLC. All rights reserved. Used by permission and protected by the Copyright Laws of the United States. The printing, copying, redistribution, or retransmission of the Material without express written permission is prohibited.

[3]   Jenkins, Jennifer. 2003. *World Englishes: A Resource Book for Students.* New York: Routledge, 42–43. © 2003 Reproduced by permission of Taylor & Francis Books UK.

PICTURES AND FIGURES

Map of World Englishes: © Isabel Peters. Hamburg, 2011.

Circles of English: Crystal, David. 2003. *English as a Global Language.* Cambridge: Cambridge University Press, 61. © David Crystal, 1997, 2003, published by Cambridge University Press, reproduced with permission.

Summer school: © Isabel Peters. Hamburg, 2011.

Multilingual society: Linguistic Diversity Management in Urban Areas (LiMA), University of Hamburg. Hamburg, 2011.

Flags: © Isabel Peters. Hamburg, 2011.

Drawings of students: © Isabel Peters. Hamburg, 2012.

REFERENCES AND FURTHER READING

Crystal, David. 2003. *English as a Global Language.* Cambridge: Cambridge University Press.

McArthur, Tom. 1987. The English languages? *English Today* 3:3, 9–13.

Mesthrie, Rajend. 2006. World Englishes and the multilingual history of English. *World Englishes* 25:3/4, 381–390.

Mesthrie, Rajend and Rakesh M. Bhatt. 2008. *World Englishes. The Study of New Linguistic Varieties (Key Topics in Sociolinguistics).* Cambridge: Cambridge University Press, 3–6.

[i]   The International Corpus of English. Singaporean Component. Spoken Texts. S1A-004.

[ii] Lewis, M. Paul (ed.). 2009. *Ethnologue: Languages of the World*. Dallas, Tex.: SIL International. Online version: http://www.ethnologue.com/.

[iii] Flood, Alison. 2009. "Vikram Seth writes Suitable Boy sequel". *The Gurdian Online*, July 03, 2009. <http://www.guardian.co.uk/books/2009/jul/03/vikram-seth-suitable-boy-sequel>, September 01, 2011.

Inner circle

Chapter 2

Irish English

Introduction

Irish English, also known as Hiberno-English, is one of the so-called Celtic Englishes, i.e. varieties of English spoken in the regions originally inhabited by the Celtic population. These areas include Ireland, Scotland, the Isle of Man, and Cornwall.

The variety of Irish English is the result of contact between English and Irish Gaelic, the history of which can be traced back to the 12th century, when the country was invaded by a joint force comprising Anglo-Normans, English, Welsh, and some Flemish (Hickey 2007: 30). English did not really gain ground at that time, though. Rather, the colonisers became proficient in two languages gradually shifting to Irish (Mesthrie and Bhatt 2008: 14). English, however, continued to be spoken in the area around Dublin and its hinterland up until the 16th century. Vernaculars of English spoken in these parts of Ireland may even today still bear traces of the language associated with the first English settlement (Hickey 2007: 432).

It was not until the beginning of the 17th century that English steadily began to gain ground throughout Ireland. The 19th century was marked by an increasing shift towards English and a concomitant decline of Irish. Three events in particular account for these processes: The emancipation of the Catholic community, the Great Famine of the late 1840s, and the emigration to the New World. The first event led to the establishment of an educational system in which instruction took place in English. The Great Famine decimated the Irish-speaking population, which died from starvation, and caused massive poverty in Ireland. Those who could afford to left Ireland for North America and Australia.

English thus was adopted as a second language by large parts of the population. Many people did not learn English at school but acquired it spontaneously from native speakers or more proficient peers. The immediate repercussion of this sociolinguistic situation was that the English of these speakers retained many grammatical, lexical, and phonological features associated with the direct influence of the Celtic mother tongue.

This chapter introduces some of these features in the Reading Comprehension activities *The Great Famine*, *A letter from home*, and *Janey Mac!*. The editorial *Irish English* from *Spotlight Magazine* introduces you to the differences between standard English and Irish English. *Finnegan's Wake*, a traditional Irish song, broadens your knowledge of Irish English and Irish culture as does *A quick guide to Ireland* at the outset of the chapter.

A quick guide to Ireland

Shamrock

What languages do people speak?

According to the Irish constitution, Irish is the first and English only the second official language of the country.

However, the everyday language of most people is actually English, and Irish is spoken by only a small proportion of the population as a first language. Nevertheless, it is a compulsory school subject and some proficiency of it is a require-ment for some posts in the public service.

Within Ireland, we can further distinguish two important Hiberno-English dialect boundaries: There is a marked north-south divide resulting from the influence of Scottish settlers arriving in Northern Ireland mainly in the 17th century. Within the South, an east-west division can be observed, as English gained ground much quicker in the East of Ireland, and Irish remained more stable in the West.

Flag of Ireland

What kind of country is Ireland?

Shortly after World War I, the southern part of Ireland gained independence from the United Kingdom. Ireland has changed enormously since it joined the European Economic Community in 1973. From a rather less developed European coun-try with a largely agricultural society, Ireland evolved into a modern, high-tech economy with a rather high standard of living.

What are *shamrocks* and *leprechauns*?

They are both symbols traditionally associ-ated with Ireland. The shamrock is a small green plant that has three leaves. Shamrocks with four leaves are normally extremely rare and thus considered to be a symbol of luck.

A leprechaun is a small male creature with magical powers believed to inhabit the lonely parts of Ireland. Leprechauns usually take the form of old men who engage in shoe-making and playing tricks.

Leprechaun

Map of Ireland

ULSTER (Ireland)
ULSTER (Northern Ireland)
Belfast
CONNACHT
ULSTER (Ireland)
Roscommon
Tuam
Galway
LEINSTER
Dublin
Kildare
MUNSTER
Wexford
Dingle
Cork

What about Irish culture?

Although Ireland is quite small, it has produced many world-famous authors such as George Bernard Shaw, William Butler Yeats, Samuel Beckett, and Seamus Heaney, all of whom won the Nobel Prize for Literature.

Apart from literature, the Irish tradition of folk music and folk dance is known worldwide.

Furthermore, Ireland is also the home of many internationally successful pop and rock bands and singers such as U2, Enya, Bob Geldof, The Cranberries, and Rory Gallagher, many of whom incorporate elements of traditional Irish music and culture into their work.

William Butler Yeats

What was the *Great Famine*?

The *Great Famine* (1845–1849), also called the *Irish Potato Famine*, was a time of hunger, misery, and mass emigration originally caused by a potato disease, and which ultimately had dramatic effects on the population and demographic development of Ireland. During this time, approximately one million people died from hunger and diseases and between one and two million people emigrated from Ireland. Although the underlying potato disease affected the whole of Europe, the consequences in Ireland were much worse due to the political, social, and economic circumstances.

What is the *Water of Life*?

It is an Irish specialty and is commonly known as *whiskey*. The word *Whiskey* derives from the Irish Gaelic phrase *uisce beatha* which means 'water of life'.

Whiskey is just one example of the group of English words which are of Irish or Gaelic origin. Others include such well-known terms as *slogan*, *bog*, *clan*, and *Tory*.

The Great Famine

Whiskey bottle

[Based on #i – #vii]

INTRODUCTORY EXERCISE FOR *A LETTER FROM HOME*

The Great Famine

Put the verbs in brackets into the correct tense.

Although, Ireland _____(rule) by England for several centuries, it was only in 1801 that it officially became a part of the United Kingdom. In the following decades, however, the British rulers _____(have to) realise that governing Ireland was extremely difficult. Enquiries of the British government _____ (reveal) that Ireland _____(be) in danger of starvation, and that despite the extremely poor standard of living and the fact that three-quarters of the Irish work-force _____(be) unemployed, its population _____(be) rapidly increasing.

The census of 1841 _____(count) more than eight million people in Ireland of whom the majority depended directly on agriculture for their living. However, many farms were so small that the only crop that _____(can, grow) to sustain a family on these tiny parcels of land was the potato.

The result was a major catastrophe between 1845 and 1849, when one po-tato crop after the other failed due to a plant disease, called potato blight. Many farmers _____(can) now neither feed their families nor pay the rent to their landlord, who, in turn, _____(drive) them off their farms. Furthermore, as the potato constituted the main or even the sole food for a substantial part of the Irish population, hunger and disease were the inevitable consequence.

Today, it is estimated that about one million people _____(die) in Ire-land between 1846 and 1851. In addition, between one and two million people _____(emigrate) from Ireland to other countries during this period, particu-larly to Great Britain and the United States. The areas that _____(suffer) the most from the Great Famine _____(be) the South and the West of the island, which by that time were the areas in which the native Irish Gaelic language was still the dominant one. As a result, the Great Famine, together with the British policy that clearly favoured and enforced the use of the English lan-guage, was also responsible for the massive shift from Irish Gaelic to English that _____(take) place in the 19th century. This, in turn, _____(make) English the clearly dominant language in Ireland.

Apart from this language shift, there are other effects of the Great Famine that can still be felt today: The population of Ireland _____(never, return) to the pre-famine population level of over eight million people and emigration _____(be) a mass phenomenon in Irish culture and society ever since. Within the last thirty years, thousands of people _____(leave) the Republic of Ireland. However, since the 1990s the number of Irish emigrants _____ (constantly, decrease) and Ireland has even become a land of immigration due to its enormous economic growth and increasing standard of living.

[Based on Cecil Woodham-Smith 1991: 15–53, #i and #iii]

 READING COMPREHENSION

A letter from home

As you certainly know, instances of non-standard grammar occur quite often in spoken language, though they rarely do so in written language. Some 160 years ago, however, when schooling was not as good as it is today, written language – especially letters – frequently resembled the way people actually spoke.

The following text is an authentic letter from an Irish woman to her relatives, who emigrated from Ireland to the United States. The letter not only allows for interesting insights into the personal life of the woman but also illustrates some of the most striking aspects of Irish English grammar in a written form, most of which can only be heard today in informal conversations.

Emigrants leave Ireland

Before reading the text, discuss the following questions:

1. In which kinds of texts or situations do you use words, phrases, and grammatical constructions that you would not use in an academic essay, for example?
2. Why do you use these "non-standard" words, phrases or grammatical constructions?

Mt Mellick September 22nd 1847

My dearly beloved brother and sister,

you cannot but be greatly surprised I did not answer your letter of the 12 of June last but the reason was at that time I thought I would be going so soon myself that I would not have time to write and that I would be with you as soon as the letter myself. the day before I got your letter which was the 30th of June, I met with a great deal of trouble from William's bad treatment to me. He turned out very disagreeable to me by reason of him drinking, he has my heart broke. I could not describe all I went through since you all went. My heart was overjoyed the day I got the letter, when I read it he said he would not go at all. I then put it off till the next month which was august as he gave in to go at that time [...]. We sold the remaining things we had to go and I was ready up to the very day. the morning we were to go he got up early and went off to Mr Oconners funeral to Dublin. he told me he was going to measure some of his customers for some clothes and that he could not go to America till next month that would be September but he was only making a fool of me all the time. I think I thought to go myself but he would not give me my bed nor bed clothes and I would not please them to leave it behind me. [...]. He has agreed to go now in either at the 2 last months which is January and February. I don't like to go in these months as they are so very hard but the terror of the sea is no trouble to me by reason of me having such a longing desire to be with you all once more, as I hope *my days will be more happy then than they have been. I did not hear from my uncle Billy this 2 months. I am just after writing it to him 2 days ago but got no answer yet. I think the reason he did not write was he thought I was gone to America as I told him I was going. the fever raged dreadfully in Ireland this summer, we hear dreadful accounts of fever in the vessels going over to America. [...]. I am only sketching everything to you now as I am in a hurry writing this, afraid William would see what I have in it. it is quite late in the night that I took the opportunity of writing this. I would have wrote before now but my mind was so disturbed that I did not know whether I would go or not at the time. Nothing in the world would please the old pair but me going by myself and if he does not go in the time I mentioned I will go myself. I hope you got the 2 letters I sent you in April and may. [...]*

My dear brother and sister Jane, I send my love to you, [...] hoping [...] I shall in very short have the happiness of seeing you and spending the last of my days with you, nothing breaks my heart rightly but the thought of being so long separated from you [...]. don't pretend when you are answering this any thing about William's bad conduct [...].dont neglect answering this as soon as you get it as I will depend on you to write. [...].

dear brother I remain your ever affectionate and loving sister Hannah Lynch

[Hannah Curtis Lynch to her brother, John Curtis, and sister (name unknown), September 22, 1847. Curtis family papers [MSS072], folder 11. The Historical Society of Pennsylvania. #1; punctuation added]

GRAMMAR EXERCISES

1. As you might have already recognised while reading, there are some tense
    forms in this letter which you would not expect in a British or American English
    letter. Even today, these remain characteristic of Hiberno-English. Translate
    the constructions from the letter listed in the table below into standard Eng-
    lish and name the standard English tense forms that are substituted by the
    non-standard construction. Describe in your own words what makes the Irish
    construction different from the British or American one.

Example	British English translation	Tense substituted	Describe in your own words what is different
… he has my heart broke.			
I could not describe all I went through since you all went.			
I did not hear from my uncle Billy this 2 months.			
I am just after writing it to him 2 days ago …	a)		
	b)		
… but got no answer yet.			
… he thought I was gone to America.			
I would have wrote before now but my mind was so disturbed …			

2. Take a look at the table on the previous page: Which standard English tense is most often substituted by non-standard Hiberno-English forms? Which of these constructions are, in your opinion, the most difficult to understand? Give arguments for your opinion.

3. As we have just seen, the grammar of Irish English differs from that of British or American English. Discuss one of the following questions:

   a. Can the use of non-standard language encourage social prejudice? Discuss potential answers to this question. (Write 200–300 words!)

   b. Discuss how differences in speaking Irish English may have influenced the way other people thought about the Irish and their English, especially when they emigrated to England, Scotland, or the United States! (Write 200–300 words! You may refer to the newspaper ad on the right.)

New York Times

W. COLE, No. 8 Ann-st.

GROCERY CART AND HARNESS FOR SA—In good order, and one chestnut horse, 8 years old excellent saddle horse; can be ridden by a lady. Also, young man wanted, from 16 to 13 years of age, able to wi No Irish need apply. CLUFF & TUNIS, No. 270 w: ington-st., corner of Myrtle-av., Brooklyn.

BILLIARD TABLE FOR SALE—Of Leona manufacture; been used about nine months. Also, tures of a Bar-room. Inquire on the premises. No.

ROLE-PLAYING GAME

Work with a partner: Imagine that you are William and Hannah and you have been arguinging over and over again whether it is better to emigrate to the United States or to stay in Ireland. Come up with at least six arguments for each side and prepare yourself and your arguments in a way that you can defend your point of view in a discussion.

COMMENTS AND CREATIVE WRITING

1. Imagine you are Hannah's brother in America, and you have just received her letter. Write a dialogue in which you and your sister Jane discuss Hannah's situation, what she should do, and what you could do to help her. (Write a minimum of 200–300 words!)

2. Again, imagine you are Hannah's brother. Write a reply to Hannah's letter in which you try to be supportive of her and avoid mentioning what Hannah said about William's bad behaviour. (Write a minimum of 200–300 words!)

3. Discuss circumstances under which you might consider emigrating to another country. Which country would you go to? (Write a minimum of 200–300 words!)

EXERCISE: IRISH ENGLISH DOMINO

Find the matching counterpart to each of the Irish English constructions.

↓

He has my heart broke.	I have not heard from my uncle Billy for 2 months.	I could not describe all I went through since you all had gone.	I wrote it to him but had not got an answer yet.
I could not describe all I went through since you all went.	He thought I gone to America.	I will not hear from my uncle Billy for 2 months.	I would wrote before now but my mind was so disturbed.
I did not hear from my uncle Billy for 2 months.	I have just written it to him.	I would write before now but my mind was so disturbed.	I could not describe all I went through since you all will go.
I am just after writing it to him 2 days ago.	I wrote it to him but have got no answer yet.	He broke my heart.	He thought I had gone to America.
I wrote it to him but got no answer yet.	I do not hear from my uncle Billy for 2 months.	I could not describe all I have gone through since you all went.	I was just writing it to him.
He thought I was gone to America.	I just wrote it to him.	He has broken my heart.	He thought I was being gone to America.
I would have wrote before now but my mind was so disturbed.	He has my heart broken.	I wrote it to him but will not get an answer yet.	I would have written before now but my mind was so disturbed.

READING COMPREHENSION

The following text is taken from the *The Irish Independent*, one of the most important daily newspapers in the country. The author of the comment, Kim Bielenberg, discusses changes in the English spoken in Ireland.

Map of Ireland

JANEY MAC!

IRISH-ENGLISH IS BANJAXED,

SO IT IS...

Dort-speak is killing off our distinctive accents and expressions, a UCD professor said this week. Kim Bielenberg reports.

[…] Yer man, Professor Terry Dolan, the leading authority on **Hiberno-English** in Ireland, is after saying that our traditional Irish way of talking English is
5 banjaxed.

Fewer shoppers go to "get messages" (groceries); we may no longer "make a hames" of a job (make a mess); and the population is no longer going
10 out to get "scuttered" (drunk).

The Professor of English at **UCD** is "**vexed**". He says our distinctive way of talking English, which is heavily influenced by Irish and includes **archaic**
15 English terms, is fast being replaced by a **dumbed-down**, **homogenised**, middle class accent.

Like **Estuary English**, the Beckhamesque **déclassé** way of talking that
20 spread all over Southern England, Dort-speak is now threatening to infect the language in every corner of the country.

"I was in a cafe in Roscommon and I heard young women talking like they were in Dublin 4," says Professor 25
Dolan, who compiles the Dictionary of Hiberno-English. "It is mostly women who are spreading it, because they think it is smarter."

Encouraged by soap operas, Ameri- 30
can TV, text speak, the internet and the intonation favoured by some **OAR-T-E** presenters – not to mention fictional couple **Dan 'n' Becs** – a vast **segment** of the population has started to speak 35
like a Yummy Drummy (an Ugg-booted **airhead** who hangs around the **South County** paradise, the Dundrum Shopping Centre).

Professor Dolan says the growing accent is one part Irish, one part unsuccessful imitation of a **posh** English **Sloane Ranger** accent, and one part American.

Growing up in Ireland, it is easy to **take** the distinctive Irish way of talking **for granted**. In other countries, English speakers do not tend to refer to soft drinks as "minerals"; they do not **refer to** a loaf of bread as a "sliced pan"; and they certainly do not put "delph" in their cupboards.

And of course, generous free-spending types are not "flaithiulach" with their cheque books.

Even though English has been the dominant language here for centuries, until recently many people have **clung on to** the grammar of the Irish language.

Expressions such as "I'm after eating my dinner" and "I do be here every day" are taken directly from Irish.

In common with America and other former British **outposts**, Ireland is affected by a linguistic phenomenon known as "colonial **lag**". Ways of talking that disappeared in England centuries ago have survived here. At least, until now.

Truant children no longer "mitch" off school in England, but the Shakespearean word continues to be used here. "Tis" is still used for "It is" and "ye" is still common in the countryside for "You". But these **idiosyncrasies** are now being **ironed out**.

Professor Dolan says that in recent years we have started to adopt a flatter, less colourful language.

Hiberno-English is suffering a similar fate to the Irish language, which declined rapidly in the 19th century.

"People stopped speaking Irish, because speaking English was seen as the way to **get ahead**," he says. "The same is now happening with Hiberno-English. People are taking on the Dublin 4 accent rather than their local accent, because it is seen as the way to get ahead. Our Irish way of speaking is considered backward. That is why so many people now talk about pawking their caw."

The term Dort-speak was actually first **coined** by Kevin Myers in the mid-1990s. He described it as a middle-class Irish accent "overlaid by an Anglo-American **argot**", peppered with words like "kyool", "loike", and "know what I mean".

Having originated in South County Dublin, Dort-speak has spread like an out-of-control Winter vomiting bug.

The effects of Dortification can be heard most strongly in counties in Leinster close to Dublin. Local accents have been **swept away** by suburban invaders. The Kildare accent, **typified** by Christy Moore, is just one of the accents that is in danger of becoming extinct.

Craic, a word apparently used by every visiting English **hack** to describe our supposed sense of fun, is regarded by some as the **quintessential** Hiberno-Irish word. But Professor Dolan regards it as an **abomination**.

"English people think it is Irish, but is actually an old English word and there is no reason why it should be spelt in Irish."

120 Fortunately, Dortification has not yet taken over every pocket of the country.

While the Irish use of language may be becoming more uniform as a result of the rise of television and other modern 125 communications, local words and ways of speaking have survived and even thrived in some areas of the country. And some new expressions have been added.

130 Dubs hail a "Joe Maxi" (taxi) in **Dublin**, Cork people still go for a "bazzer" (haircut), and "sucking diesel" is a popular term for making progress in the countryside. In **Cavan** they still have a 135 "Bachelor's Button", a nail used to hold together articles of clothing in place of a button.

Nowhere is the language more colourful than Tuam, Co **Galway**, a town remarkable for its distinctive vocabu- 140 lary. You can still hear people referring to a woman as a "tome feek". In Tuamspeak, a house is a "cane", splendid is "peach", and local people have been known to call a church a "pineapple". 145

Sure, why do they call a church a pineapple, at all? As they used to say in Wexford, "Don't ax me why."

Kim Bielenberg
[From *The Irish Independent* February 9, 2008. #2; bold face added.]

Vocabulary

1. Look up the following words and expressions in a monolingual English dictionary: vexed, archaic, dumbed-down, homogenised, déclassé, segment, airhead, posh, take sth for granted, refer to, cling on to sth, outpost, lag, truant, iron out, get ahead, coin, argot, sweep away, typify, hack, quintessential, and abomination.

2. The text features some references to Irish culture and the Irish way of life. Find out what the following words and expressions mean: OAR-T-E, Dan 'n' Becs, and Sloane Ranger.

Definitions

1. Give definitions of the following linguistic terms: Hiberno-English, Estuary English, and idiosyncrasy.

2. In the text, we find the names of some geographical locations. Find out more about the following places (consult a dictionary or web sources, if necessary): UCD, South County, Dublin, Cavan, and Galway.

EXERCISES

1. There are several words, phrases, and sentences in the text in which the author of this article tries to imitate both the pronunciation of "Dort-speak" and of traditional Irish English. Try to find these instances and translate them into their standard English spellings.
2. Summarise all major characteristics of the Irish English vocabulary as described in the text.
3. According to the text, which grammatical expressions are directly taken from Irish? Try to interpret and translate them with a partner. Can you find more of these constructions in the text? If so, translate them as well.

Find the equivalents in the following table and fill in the blanks.

Hiberno-English	British English
	I have just eaten my dinner.
craic	
	woman
	it is
ye	
cane	
	loaf of bread
delph	
	broken, ruined
messages	
scuttered	
	an expression of surprise
	generous
Joe Maxi	

	haircut
mitch	
I do be here every day.	
	your
minerals	
	make a mess

COMMENTS AND CREATIVE WRITING

According to the text, Hiberno-English and "Dort-speak" are heavily influenced by the Internet, TV, and the media in general. Write an essay in which you discuss the influence of the Internet and the media on local dialects and language in general. You may refer to this text but your essay should go beyond it.

Write a comment:
1. "Don't give up your local or social accent! It is part of your identity!" Discuss this thesis. (Write a minimum of 200–300 words!)
2. "Giving up your local or social accent is a way to get ahead!" Discuss this thesis. (Write a minimum of 200–300 words!)

ROLE-PLAYING GAME: PROFESSOR MEETS STUDENT

Imagine that you are an Irish student spending your free time with your friends in a café in Dublin. Suddenly, you are approached by a professor of Irish English who wishes to discuss the way you speak and the peculiarities of Hiberno-English with you.

Write a dialogue in which you critically discuss with the professor the advantages and disadvantages of traditional Hiberno-English compared to your modern "Dort-speak".

Work in groups of four.

REPETITION EXERCISE: IRISH ENGLISH DOMINO

Take a look at the dominos given below. Try to arrange and number them in a way so that the corresponding Irish English and British English constructions lie next to each other and write the matching pairs down in your exercise book.

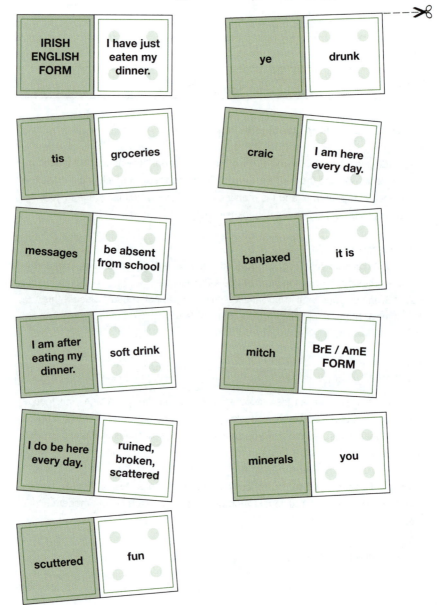

REPETITION EXERCISE: IRISH ENGLISH TABOO

Explain what the following terms and phrases mean in your own words. You are not allowed to use the terms and phrases themselves.

archaic	segment	lag	homogenise
posh	take sth for granted	quintessential	cling on to
vexed	to coin	refer to	iron out
abomination	typify	idiosyncrasy	argot

 READING COMPREHENSION

Editorial

The following article is taken from *Spotlight Magazine*, an English language maga-zine. The author gives a brief account of the historical development and his impres-sions of the English language in Ireland.

Summary: It sounds a lot like stand-ard English, but if you listen carefully in Ireland, you'll hear something quite different.

In that great song of **exile**, "Galway Bay", we learn that the women in the West of Ireland "speak a language that the strangers do not know". So which
5 language would that be, then? Perhaps it's this: *"Na cuir isteach ar dhaoine eile agus fón póca in úsáid agat."* Or maybe it's this: "Yer wan got plastered last night and ended up in a feckin' deadly mill."
10   The first example above is Gaelic and means "be considerate of others when us-ing your mobile phone", while the sec-ond sentence is the kind of English that makes perfect sense to people in Ireland,
15 but almost nowhere else. It means: "That woman got very drunk last night and was involved in an amazing fight."
    Many people believe that the Irish speak standard English, but a recent visit
20 to Ireland proved to me that in spite of the best efforts of the school system, they still don't. A small minority speak Gaelic but almost everyone else speaks something linguists call Hiberno-English.
25 A quick history lesson is perhaps needed

here. In 1649, Oliver Cromwell, Lord Protector of England, led a successful military campaign to establish control over Ireland, and by the end of the 1650s, the English of Cromwell's soldiers was 30 the language of power. To survive, the Irish had to learn it, and to run the country and do business with the natives, the Cromwellians had to learn some Gaelic. Hiberno-English, then, is the resulting 35 **fusion** of the two languages.

Discípline and discipline
One of the problems that the Irish faced 350 years ago was that they had no 40 schools. So they had to learn their Eng-lish from self-taught teachers, who **relied on** what they knew about Latin and Greek to understand English grammar and syn-tax, and who guessed the pronunciation 45 of difficult words. The mistakes made then were passed on to the next genera-tions and have now become part of Eng-lish as it is spoken in Ireland.
    As a result, one very noticeable fea- 50 ture of Hiberno-English is the tendency to stress a different syllable from the one stressed in standard English. Irish people say discípline and architécture, where the English say díscipline and árchitecture. 55

Then there's **malapropism**, the use of a word in a meaning that it does not have in standard English. Recently, a government minister in Dáil Eireann, the Irish parlia-
60 ment, asked what could be "**deducted**" from a statement made by the opposition, when he clearly meant "**deduced**". [...]

Like Gaelic, Hiberno-English is considered too **unsophisticated** for social,
65 political and economic use by Ireland's elites and that's why the school system is determined to replace it with standard English. This is "arseways" (dreadfully mistaken) in my opinion, as Hiberno-English, with a vocabulary and structure 70 based on the best of Gaelic and English, is ideally suited to be the national language of Ireland.

Eamonn Fitzgerald
[From *Spotlight Magazine* June 16, 2004. © 2004. #3; bold face added.]

Vocabulary

1. Look up the following words in a monolingual English dictionary: exile, fusion, rely on, malapropism, deduct, deduce, and unsophisticated.
2. Explain in your own words the difference between the verbs 'deduct' and 'deduce'.

TEXT EXERCISE

1. Summarise all major factors mentioned in the text that led to the differences between Hiberno-English and standard English.
2. Assess how some of the special features of Hiberno-English, such as the specific pronunciation of difficult words and malapropisms, might have influenced the way people from Great Britain and the United States thought and spoke about the Irish. (Write a minimum of 200 words!)

COMMENT: LETTER TO THE EDITOR

1. Write a letter to the author of this article explaining why you fully agree with his opinion that the replacement of Hiberno-English is "arseways". Give arguments and examples in favour of maintaining the particularities of Hiberno-English also highlighting the aspects of personal and cultural identity often associated with a certain dialect. (Write a minimum of 200–300 words!)
2. Write a letter to the author of this article explaining why you completely disagree with his opinion that the replacement of Hiberno-English is "arseways". Give arguments and examples in favour of the replacement of Hiberno-English by standard English. (Write a minimum of 200–300 words!)

 READING AND LISTENING COMPREHENSION

Finnegan's Wake

Finnegan's Wake is one of the most famous Irish folk songs. Its setting is a wake, a traditional Irish ceremony where relatives and family mourn the loss of a departed friend or relative, the body of whom is still present in the house until the funeral begins. Listen to this song on the Internet where you can find many versions of it.

Tune

Tim Finnegan lived in Walkin Street
A gentleman Irish, mighty odd;
He'd a beautiful brogue so rich and sweet
And to rise in the world he carried a **hod**.
Now Tim had a sort o' the **tipplin'** way
With a love of the liquor poor Tim was born
And to help him on with his work each day
He'd a drop of the craythur ev'ry morn.

Chorus
Whack fol the dah now dance to your partner
Welt the flure, your **trotters** shake;
Wasn't it the truth I told you
Lots of fun at Finnegan's wake!

One mornin' Tim was rather full
His head felt heavy which made him shake,
He fell from the ladder and broke his skull
And they carried him home his **corpse** to wake.
They **wrapped** him up in a nice clean sheet
And laid him out across the bed,
With a **gallon** of whiskey at his feet
And a **barrel** of porter at his head.

His friends assembled at the wake
And Mrs. Finnegan called for lunch,

First they brought in tea and cake
Then pipes, tobacco and whiskey punch.
Biddy O'Brien began to cry
"Such a nice clean corpse, did you ever see?"
"Arrah, Tim, mavourneen, why did you die?"
"Ah, shut your gob" said Paddy McGee!

Then Maggy O'Connor took up the job
"O Biddy," says she, "You're wrong, I'm sure":
Biddy gave her a belt in the gob
And left her **sprawlin'** on the floor.
And then the war did soon engage
'Twas woman to woman and man to man,
Shillelagh law was all the rage
And the **row** and the **ruction** soon began.

Then Mickey Maloney ducked his head
When a **flagon** of whiskey flew at him,
It missed, and fallin' on the bed
The liquor **scattered** over Tim.
Tim revives! See how he rises!
Timothy rising from the bed
Sayin': "**Whirl** your liquor around like blazes!
Thanam o'n Dhoul! D'ye think I'm dead?"

[*Finnegan's Wake*. #4; bold face added]

Vocabulary

1. Look up the following words and expressions in a monolingual English dictionary: hod, tipple, welt the flure, trotter, corpse, wrap, and sprawl.
2. The words 'barrel' and 'flagon' both refer to specific types of containers. Find the definitions of these words in a monolingual English dictionary and explain in your own words the differences between the two.
3. The words 'row' and 'ruction' both describe specific types of disagreements. Look up these words in a monolingual English dictionary and explain in your own words the differences between the two.
4. The word 'gallon' is a unit of measurments for liquids. It refers to slightly different volumes of liquids in the UK and in the US when measured in litres. Find out more about this difference!
5. The verbs 'scatter' and 'whirl' describe different types of movement. Look up these words in a monolingual English dictionary and describe in your own words what kinds of movement these verbs refer to.
6. In the lyrics of the song, we find the expression *Whack fol the dah*. Try to find out more about this expression and its overall contribution to the poem. You may consult a dictionary or web sources, if necessary.

EXERCISES

1. Take a look at the memory cards given on the next page. When you have found the matching pairs, write them down in your exercise book.
2. Can you find any other words or constructions in the song lyrics which had already been identified as being typical of Irish English earlier in this chapter?

QUESTIONS

1. Even today, this song is one of the most widely performed Irish folk songs, both in Ireland and abroad. Analyse what makes this song particularly Irish, the picture of the Irish and Irishness drawn in the song. Try to assess what makes this song so popular.
2. This song also inspired James Joyce, who wrote a novel called *Finnegans Wake* based on this song. Discuss why this song inspired James Joyce to write a book dealing with the circle of life. What role do both *whiskey* and *wake* play in this context?

REPETITION EXERCISE: IRISH ENGLISH MEMORY

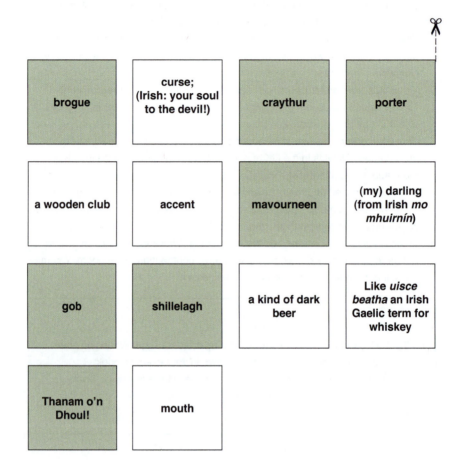

brogue	curse; (Irish: your soul to the devil!)	craythur	porter
a wooden club	accent	mavourneen	(my) darling (from Irish *mo mhuirnín*)
gob	shillelagh	a kind of dark beer	Like *uisce beatha* an Irish Gaelic term for whiskey
Thanam o'n Dhoul!	mouth		

Sources

TEXTS

[1]   Hannah Curtis Lynch to her brother, John Curtis, and sister [name unknown], September 22, 1847. Curtis family papers [MSS072], folder 11. The Historical Society of Pennsylvania. Transcribed with the permission of the Historical Society of Pennsylvania/ Philadelphia.

[2]   Bielenberg, Kim. 2008. "JANEY MAC! IRISH-ENGLISH IS BANJAXED, SO IT IS …". *The Irish Independent* [Dublin], February 09, 2008. <http://www.independent.ie/opinion/ analysis/janey-mac-irishenglish-is-banjaxed-so-it-is-1285816.html>, February 19, 2008. Reproduced with permission of Newspaper Licensing Ireland Limited.

[3]   Fitzgerald, Eamonn. 2004. "Editorial: Irish English". *Spotlight-Online* [Planegg/Germany], June 16, 2004. <http://www.spotlight-online.de/CoCoCMS/generator/viewDocument. php?doc=13437>, February 19, 2008. © Spotlight 2/2008, www.spotlight-online.de, reproduced with permission.

[4]   "Finnegan's Wake". <http://en.wikisource.org/wiki/Finnegan%27s_Wake> (Public Domain), August 31, 2011.

PICTURES AND FIGURES

Shamrock: <http://commons.wikimedia.org/wiki/File:Irish_clover.jpg> (GNU Free Documentation License), April 20, 2011.

Leprechaun: <http://commons.wikimedia.org/wiki/File:Rainbow_Leprechaun.png> (Creative Commons Attribution-ShareAlike 3.0), April 20, 2011.

Flag of Ireland: © Isabel Peters. Hamburg, 2011.

Map of Ireland: © Isabel Peters. Hamburg, 2011.

William Butler Yeats: <http://commons.wikimedia.org/wiki/File:William_Butler_Yeats_1.jpg> (Public Domain), April 20, 2011.

Whiskey bottle: © Isabel Peters. Hamburg, 2011.

The Great Famine: <http://en.wikipedia.org/wiki/File:Skibbereen_1847_by_James_Mahony. JPG> (Public Domain), April 20, 2011.

Emigrants leave Ireland: <http://en.wikipedia.org/wiki/File:Emigrants_Leave_Ireland_by_Henry_ Doyle_1868.jpg> (Public Domain), April 20, 2011.

New York Times: <http://en.wikipedia.org/wiki/File:NINA-nyt.JPG> (Public Domain), April 20, 2011.

Map of Ireland: © Isabel Peters. Hamburg, 2011.

Tune: © Isabel Peters. Hamburg, 2011.

REFERENCES AND FURTHER READING

Filppula, Markku. 2008. Irish English: morphology and syntax. In: Kortmann, Bernd and Clive Upton (eds.), *Varieties of English,* Vol. 1. *The British Isles.* Berlin/New York: Mouton de Gruyter, 328–359.

Görlach, Manfred. 1997. Celtic Englishes? In: Tristram, Hildegard (ed.), *The Celtic Englishes.* Heidelberg: Winter, 27–54.

Hickey, Raymond. 2007. *Irish English. History and Present-Day Forms.* Cambridge: Cambridge University Press.

Hickey, Raymond. 2008. Irish English: phonology. In: Kortmann, Bernd and Clive Upton (eds.), *Varieties of English*, Vol. 1. *The British Isles.* Berlin/New York: Mouton de Gruyter, 7–104.

McCafferty, Kevin. 2007. Northern Irish English. In: Britain, David (ed.), *Language in the British Isles.* Cambridge: Cambridge University Press, 123–134.

Mesthrie, Rajend and Rakesh M. Bhatt. 2008. *World Englishes. The Study of New Linguistic Varieties (Key Topics in Sociolinguistics).* Cambridge: Cambridge University Press, 12–17.

Woodham-Smith, Cecil. 1991. *The Great Hunger.* London: Penguin.

[i]   "Ireland." Encyclopædia Britannica. Encyclopædia Britannica Online Academic Edition. Encyclopædia Britannica, 2011. <http://www.britannica.com/EBchecked/topic/293754/Ireland>, August 29, 2011.

[ii]   "Celtic languages." Encyclopædia Britannica. Encyclopædia Britannica Online Academic Edition. Encyclopædia Britannica, 2011. <http://www.britannica.com/EBchecked/topic/101778/Celtic-languages>, August 29, 2011.

[iii]   "Irish Potato Famine." Encyclopædia Britannica. Encyclopædia Britannica Online Academic Edition. Encyclopædia Britannica, 2011. <http://www.britannica.com/EBchecked/topic/294137/Irish-Potato-Famine>, August 29, 2011.

[iv]   "English language." Encyclopædia Britannica. Encyclopædia Britannica Online Academic Edition. Encyclopædia Britannica, 2011. <http://www.britannica.com/EBchecked/topic/188048/English-language>, August 29, 2011.

[v]   "Leprechaun." Encyclopædia Britannica. Encyclopædia Britannica Online Academic Edition. Encyclopædia Britannica, 2011. <http://www.britannica.com/EBchecked/topic/336866/leprechaun>, August 29, 2011.

[vi]   "Ireland country profile." The BBC, 2009. <http://news.bbc.co.uk/2/hi/europe/country_profiles/1038581.stm#leaders,%20>, April 23, 2009.

[vii]   "Ireland." The World Factbook. Central Intelligence Agency, 2011. <https://www.cia.gov/library/publications/the-world-factbook/geos/ei.html>, August 29, 2011.

Inner circle

Chapter 3

Scottish English

Introduction

Scottish English is another Celtic variety of English. To understand what the term 'Scottish English' refers to, we need to take a closer look at the history of languages in Scotland.

To start with, Scottish Gaelic is a Celtic language that was the dominant language spoken in Scotland before the English-speaking population arrived. Its importance, however, started to decline from the 11th century onwards (cf. Melchers and Shaw 2003: 61) as Anglo-Norman influence began to assert itself.

The eastern and southern parts of Scotland were home to a variety of English commonly referred to as 'Scots' in the relevant literature. Scots is a form of English related to varieties of Northern Old English, which are believed to have been mutually intelligible (Romaine 1982: 57). As a medieval variety, Scots thrived in the 15th century. It was during this period that it became a language of administration and government, boasting an extensive and diverse national literature and a set of distinct grammatical, lexical, and phonological features. Scots established itself as a distinct form of English used in virtually all social domains.

When King James VI of Scotland inherited the English throne in 1603, Scots began to be heavily influenced from the English spoken in England, specifically London (see Romaine 1982 for further details). The process of unification slowly but surely led to Scots losing many of its original features so that the present-day variety of English spoken in Scotland (Scottish English) can be described as one that largely conforms to the British standard, even though it inherited a strong accent and a few grammatical and lexical features from Scots. The Scottish people are immensely proud of their identity and their Scottish roots, which are typically manifested through language. Movie stars such as Gerard Butler and James McAvoy consciously adhere to their native vernaculars while giving interviews or otherwise presenting themselves in public.

This chapter gives you a chance to learn more about the pronunciation, vocabulary, and grammar of Scots and Scottish English in the Viewing and Reading Comprehension (*The Acid House*) and in the Reading Comprehension (*The Sivven Sons o Knock Castle*). Scottish English pronunciation, vocabulary, and grammar are treated in the Listening Comprehension (*John and the Orkney Islands*) and in the Reading Comprehension (*Trainspotting*). The text *Accents and Dialects of Scotland* from the British Library deepens your knowledge of the English in Scotland. *A quick guide to Scotland* and the song *Auld Lang Syne* enrich your understanding of Scottish traditions and culture.

A quick guide to Scotland

Kilt

What kind of country is Scotland?

• • • • • •

Scotland has been part of the United Kingdom since it officially joined it in 1707. Before that, it was an independent state. Since 1999, when legislative powers were given back to a reconstituted Scottish Parliament, it has enjoyed a high degree of self-government.

With regard to its geography, three regions can be distinguished: the Highlands and Islands, a densely populated Central Belt (Lowlands), including the two biggest cities Edinburgh and Glasgow, and finally the Southern Uplands on the border to England.

As in Ireland, a small proportion of the population still speaks a Celtic language, although Scottish Gaelic is mainly restricted to the Highlands and the Western Scottish Isles and is spoken only by about one per cent of the Scottish population, i.e. roughly 60,000 people.

What do Scotsmen wear under their kilts?

Well, that actually depends on the individual wearer. In some contexts, however, especially in the Scottish regiments of the British army, underwear is actually prohibited according to the regiments' military dress code. Tradition has it anyway that a "true Scotsman" should wear nothing under his kilt. However, many people today consider this custom as "childish" and "unhygienic".

• • • • • • • • • • • • • •

Are there any differences between Scotland and England?

Of course there are: Apart from the different forms of English, there are many other interesting differences between Scotland and England. For example, some Scottish banks still print their own banknotes, which are valid in Scotland and Northern Ireland but do not have to be accepted in England. Many differences result from the fact that Scotland is semi-autonomous. Thus, the Scottish parliament may decide on issues concerning education, justice, economic development, the environment, and justice, to mention just a few. The linguistic diversity of present-day Scotland is acknowledged by the fact that Scottish Gaelic, English, and Scots are recognised as official working languages of the Scottish Parliament.

Gentlemen Only, Ladies Forbidden?

Although you often hear this phrase when you ask for the meaning of one of those sports most readily associated with Scotland, this is of course only a joke. The origin of the word *golf* has not been fully clarified but it may derive from the medieval Dutch word *kolf* or *kolve* which means 'club'. It is believed that the word somehow entered the Scots language and was then passed on to English.

However, *golf* is not the only word that has entered the English language from or via Scots. Other well-known examples include *glamour*, *pony*, *tweed*, *scone*, *lassie*, *laddie*, and *wee*.

Golf ball _____

What's the *Saltire*?

The *Saltire* or *St. Andrew's Cross* is the old national flag of Scotland. According to legend, it goes back to the eighth or ninth century. However, we only know with certainty that it has been used since the 13th century. After the union of Scotland and England in 1707, Scotland's white cross on a blue background merged with England's red cross on a white background to form the *Union Jack*.

Flag of Scotland

What do Dr Jekyll, Sherlock Holmes, and Harry Potter all have in common?

They have Scottish parents, as all of them were created by Scottish authors, namely by Robert Louis Stevenson, Arthur Conan Doyle, and J.K. Rowling.

To be sure, the list of famous Scottish authors is much longer, including writers that mainly wrote or still write in Scots or Scottish English, such as Robert Burns and Irvine Welsh. You will get to know them in this chapter.

[Based on #i – #ix]

EXERCISES

1. Form groups (of two to four) and assign a few boxes to each member of the group. Report the content of your boxes to your fellow group members.
2. Discuss the content of the boxes in your groups: What did you already know and what is new to you? Can you add something? Have you ever been to Scotland? Have you ever met Scottish people? Do you know any famous Scottish people? Do you know anything else that is often considered to be typical of Scotland? Do you know any famous Scottish artists, etc.?
3. Record the most important facts from the boxes and from your discussion in a mind map.

VIEWING AND READING COMPREHENSION

The Acid House: The Granton Star Cause

The following dialogue is taken from the screen adaptation of the short story *The Granton Star Cause* by Irvine Welsh, which is part of the film *The Acid House*. The film is based on a collection of short stories with the same title.

In his works, Irvine Welsh often uses his Scottish dialect. Furthermore, he also uses words which are typically used in Scotland and are less likely to occur in British or American (standard) English.

This story is about Robert (Boab) Coyle, a young guy from Edinburgh who has been going through a rough time recently. Within the last 36 hours, he was kicked out of the Granton Star football team by his friends, thrown out of his home by his parents, left by his girlfriend Evelyn, arrested and beaten up by the police, and, finally, he got fired by his boss Rafferty. Now, he is sitting in a pub pitying himself when suddenly a stranger approaches him and introduces himself as "God". The film is available on DVD.

Fly

God:	Yuv fucked this one up, ya daft cunt!
Boab:	Eh? What?
God:	You. Boab Coyle. Nae hoose,
5	nae joab, nae burd, nae mates, polis record, sair ribs, aw in the space ay a few ooirs. Nice one!
Boab:	How the fuck dae you ken my business? Eh? Whit the fuck's it
10	goat tae dae with you? Eh?
God:	It's ma fucking business tae know. Ah'm God.
Boab:	Way tae fuck ya auld radge!
God:	Fuckin hell. Another wise cunt
15	… Robert Anthony Coyle, born on Friday the 23rd of July to

Robert McNamara Coyle and Doreen Sharp. Younger brother of Cathleen Siobhain Shaw, who is married to James Allan Shaw. 20 They live at 21 Parkglen Cresent in Gilmerton and they have a kid, whae is also called James. You have a **crescent**-shaped birth-mark on your inner **thigh**. Until 25 recently, you were working in furniture removals, lived at hame, hud a bird called Evelyn, whom you couldn't sexually satisfy, and played football for Granton Star, 30 like you made love, employing lit-tle effort and even less skill.

Boab: If you're God, what ur ye daein sitting here, wastin time oan the likes of me? Eh?

God: Good question, Boab. Good question.

Boab: Ah mean, thir's bairns starvin, likesay, oan telly n that. If ye wir that good, ye could sort aw that oot, instead ay sitting here **bev-vyin** wi the likes ay me. Eh?

God: Hud oan a minute, pal. Lit's git one thing straight. Every fuckin time ah come doon here, some **wide-o** pills ays up aboot what ah should n shouldnae be fuckin daein. Either that or ah huv tae enter intae some philosophical discourse wi some wee **under-graduate** twat aboot the nature ay masel, the extent ay ma **om-nipotence** n aw that shite. Ah'm gittin a wee bit fed up wi aw this self-justification; it's no for yous cunts tae criticise me. I gied yous the place. Ah made yous cunts in ma ain image. Yous git oan wi it; yous fuckin well sort it oot. [God lights a cigarette] And that cunt Nietzsche wis wide ay the mark whin he sais that ah wis deid. Ah'm no deid; ah jist dinnae gie a fuck.

Boab: You're a fuckin toss. See, if ah hud your fuckin powers …

God: If you hud ma powers ye'd dae what ye dae right now: sweet fuck all. Look, you've goat the power tae cut doon oan the **pints** ay **lager**, right?

Boab: Aye, bit …

God: Nae buts aboot it. You've goat the power tae git fit and make a mair positive **contribution** tae the Granton Star **cause**. You hud the power tae pey mair attention tae that wee burd ay yours. She

Boab and God. © 1998 Film4.

wis tidy. Ye could've done a loat
80   better there, Boab.

Boab: Mibbe ah could, n mibbe ah
couldnae. Whit the fuck's it goat
tae dae with you? Eh?

God: Ye hud the power tae git oot fae
85   under yir ma n dad's feet, so's
they could get a decent cowp in
peace. Bit naw. No selfish cunt
Coyle. Jist sits thair watchin
Coronation Street n **Brookside**
90   while they perr cunts ur **gaun up**
the waws wi frustration.

Boab: S'nane ay your business.

God: Everything's ma business. That
cunt Rafferty, ye didnae even
95   tell the cunt tae stick his fuckin
joab up his erse.

Boab: So what! So fuckin what! Eh?

God: So ye hud they powers, ye jist
couldnae be bothered usin thum.
100   That's why you interest me
Boab. You're jist like me. A lazy,
apathetic, **slovenly** cunt. Now
ah hate bein like this, but bein
immortal, ah cannae punish ma-
105   sel. Ah kin punish you though,
mate. And that's jist whit ah intend tae dae.

Boab: But ah …

God: Shut it cunt! Ah've fuckin hud
110   it up tae ma eyebaws wi aw this
repentance shite. **Vengeance** is
mine, n ah intend tae take it, oan
ma ain lazy n selfish nature, oan
the species that ah created, oan
115   thir representative. That's you.

Boab: Ye jist look like ah always imagined …

God: That's cause ye've nae imagina-
tion, ya daft cunt. Ye see me n
hear me as ye imagine me. And 120
you're fuckin **claimed**, **radge**!

[From the script of *The Acid House*. ©
1998 Film4. #1; bold face added.]

Irvine Welsh

INFO

Irvine Welsh (*1958 in Edinburgh) is
a Scottish author. He mainly writes
in his Scottish dialect and often de-
picts the life of the lower classes
in Edinburgh in his work. His most
famous piece of work probably is
his novel *Trainspotting,* a very successful screen adaptation of which
was released in 1996. [Based on #x
– #xi]

Vocabulary

1. Look up the following words and expressions in a monolingual English dictionary: crescent, thigh, bevvy, undergraduate, omnipotence, pint, lager, contribution, cause, go up the wall (gaun up the waws), apathetic, slovenly, repentance, vengeance, and be claimed.
2. The text features a variety of offensive words and expressions. Find these in the text and consult a monolingual dictionary to find out what these words and expressions mean.
3. The text features some references to British culture and the British way of life. Find out what the following expressions refer to: Coronation Street and Brookside.

Definitions

Give definitions of the following words and expressions stemming from Scottish English: wide-o and radge.

PRE-WATCHING ACTIVITIES

1. As you can see in the film script, the spellings of many words have been changed in order to illustrate how they are pronounced by speakers of Scottish English. In addition, there are also some words and expressions in the text that are characteristic of Scottish English and that you would not expect to find in a standard English text. Work with a partner and try to find them.
2. Can you find any differences in grammar between Scottish English and standard English?
3. Take a look at the words for which the spelling has been changed. Can you determine any specific rules for Scottish pronunciation based on the spelling of these words?

It might be helpful for you to go through the text sentence by sentence and read each sentence aloud to your partner.

WHILE-WATCHING ACTIVITIES

1. While watching the video two or three times, follow along in the text and check to see if your Scottish pronunciation rules are correct.
2. Can you find any additional Scottish pronunciation rules? Give examples.

POST-WATCHING ACTIVITIES

1. In the table given below, summarise all of the differences in vocabulary, grammar, and pronunciation that you have found in the film.
2. Discuss which of the differences are, in your opinion, the most difficult ones for learners of English. Give examples and reasons for your opinion. (Write a minimum of 200–300 words!)

Pronunciation	Grammar	Vocabulary

HOMEWORK

1. How might the story go on? Continue the dialogue. (Write a minimum of 200–300 words!)
2. Imagine you are an exchange student in Edinburgh. After your first week in Scotland, you write an e-mail to your friends or family in which you describe your first impressions of the town and of the English that people speak there. Explain why it is sometimes difficult for you to understand the people you meet. (Write a minimum of 200–300 words!)
3. At the end of the dialogue, God says to Boab: "Ye see me n hear me as ye imagine me." Thus, God speaks in the way that Boab has always imagined him doing so, i.e. in his Scottish dialect and also using plenty of swear words. Now imagine that another person such as the Prime Minister or the Queen of England were in Boab's position. Rewrite the first 66 lines of the dialogue in a very polite and formal language style. You may use a dictionary.

REPETITION EXERCISE: ACID HOUSE MEMORY

Take a look at the memory cards given below. Work with a partner and try to find the matching pairs. Write down the correct pairs.

ken	know	nae	radge
you (pl.)	not	bird / lassie	give
auld	yous	child	yes
likesay	you (sg.)	aye	wee
girl(friend)	gie	crazy person	ye
little	you know	old	bairn

LISTENING COMPREHENSION

As you already know, there are important and occasionally enormous differences between what is known as standard British English and the varieties of
English spoken in Scotland. Thus, Scottish English can initially be very hard to
understand before one becomes familiar with its peculiarities.

    You also learnt that you can find a
continuum of varieties in Scotland ranging from Scots to standard Scottish English. The subsequent exercise will introduce you to a form of English spoken in
Scotland that is quite different from that
portrayed in *The Acid House*.

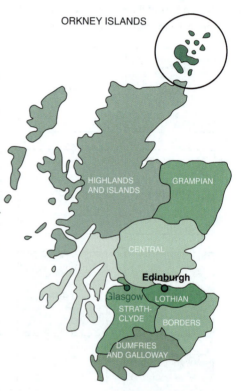

ORKNEY ISLANDS

HIGHLANDS AND ISLANDS

GRAMPIAN

CENTRAL

Edinburgh

Glasgow   LOTHIAN

STRATH-CLYDE

BORDERS

DUMFRIES AND GALLOWAY

Map of Scotland

John and the Orkney Islands

You will be introduced to John, a resident of the Orkney Islands and a real speaker
of Scottish English. As you can see from the map above, the Orkneys are a group
of Islands in the very North of Scotland. John talks about his life on the Orkneys, the
Orkney Islands in general, and his dialect. You will probably have to listen very carefully in order to understand fully what John says. [*John* is a fictitious name.]

The following text is the transcript of John's speech. While you listen to the recording again, try to complete the while-listening activities given below.

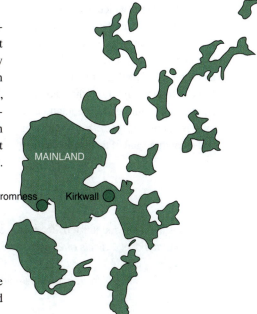

"I was born and brought up in the Orkney Islands here, just off the north coast o' Scotland, and eh, some, almost fifty years ago, I suppose. And I was born
5   into a, into a farming family and eh, I, get off to college to Aberdeen and I studied agriculture and I was lucky enough to come back and get a job here in what is now the local, the local college then.
10 And, eh, I work for, for Orkney College and, eh, we've sort o' moved, we've, we've diversified out of just agriculture. We're now into computing and tourism. It's quite a big college
15 now, I've been working for them for about 22 years. And, eh, ya ken, we're now a, just a big further education and

MAINLAND

Stromness   Kirkwall

Map of Orkney

higher education college, in Orkney. But apart fae that, I still, well, still live on a 20 farm and still sort o' farm part time [...]. Orkney's just a, it's a collection of about 70 islands and about 16 or 17 of them are inhabited, but most of the folk live on what we call the mainland. You ken, 25 when we, when folk, when folk in Orkney speak about the mainland we talk, we mean the mainland of Orkney and not the mainland of Scotland. We would tend to look upon and term the mainland 30 of Scotland, or anything in that kinda general direction is just termed as, as south. Orkney's still ... there, you ken, agriculture still plays a big ... a very important part in our economy but, eh, 35 so does the oil ... we've an oil terminal on the islands which takes in a lot o' money, to that. And they also, like, like a ... tourism and, eh, surely manufacture and there are a couple of distilleries 40 and a brewery. And ... it's quite a busy place, Orkney, and [...] the economy is, eh, really quite good. Populations in total is about 20,000 ... between seven and eight thousand of that be in the main

town of Kirkwall and there's another 45 sort of smaller town called Stromness which has a couple of thousand folk and the rest of the population is sort of spread through the ... the, eh, ... country areas then and, and the smaller islands. 50

I, I, I suppose me dialect would, would be ... I would like to call it ... to say it was average, but, eh, I suppose the younger generation would likely say that I was, I spoke maybe a slightly broader, 55 eh, form of dialect than, than, than most of the younger, the younger population would do nowadays. Ehm, as, as compared with the, with the, ehm, dialect of a hundred year ago, ehm, I would, mine 60 would not be that desperately different I suppose other than there would been at that time a sort of universal use o' the, o' "thee" and "thou" instead o', instead o' "you", then, you ken, in dialect ... [...] 65 there is that ... eh, but, eh, I say a hundred year ago it would have been sort of universal."

[From *The International Dialects of English Archive*. #2.]

Listen to the sound file of John's speech. It can be accessed at the *International Dialects of English Archive* (IDEA):

»   http://web.ku.edu/~idea/europe/scotland/scotland2.mp3

WHILE-LISTENING ACTIVITY

Try to identify all differences between John's pronunciation and the pronunciation of standard British English and note them either in the text or in your exercise book. Your underlined words might be useful.

POST-LISTENING ACTIVITIES

1. Form groups: Now compare the notes you made while listening to the text and try to determine rules for the sounds and contexts in which Scottish English differs from (standard) British English. Try to give examples!
2. Discuss in your group why Scottish English might be hard to understand, especially for learners of English. Which aspects might be most difficult to understand? Consider all of the aspects you have seen in this exercise in which Scottish English differs from (standard) British English and write your results in the form of a short comment in your exercise book. (Write a minimum of 200–300 words!)

 HOMEWORK

1. As you have just heard, John works at Orkney College. Do you think he would speak differently if he worked for a college in England or on the Scottish mainland? Do you think it is good for a teacher to maintain his or her dialect as part of his or her identity, or do you think that teachers should try to give up their local dialects or accents? Write a short essay answering these questions. (Write a minimum of 200–300 words!)
2. Imagine that you have just returned from a student exchange to Scotland. Back home, you have to tell your fellow students and your teacher, who have no idea about Scotland or Scottish English, about your experiences. Write a short dialogue in which you explain the most important aspects of Scotland and Scottish English to your teacher and your fellow students. (Write a minimum of 200–300 words!)

 READING COMPREHENSION

Accents and dialects of Scotland

The following text from the British Library describes not only some of the most important characteristics of the English language in Scotland, but also illustrates how it can be difficult to differentiate between a language in its own right and mere varieties of languages.

The **linguistic** landscape of Scotland is considerably more complex than it is in most of England and Wales, with a broad **range** of dialects and older lan-
5 guage forms **contributing** to a rich and **varied** national voice. [...]

English in Scotland

The type of English spoken in Scotland
10 is more difficult to define than elsewhere in the UK. From the time of the Union of Parliaments in 1707, the official written language of Scotland became **aligned with** that of England. As such, Standard
15 English has been used as the language of religion, education and government and so it became the socially **prestigious** form **adopted** by the **aspiring** middle classes. Unlike in England, however,
20 Standard English continued to be spoken with a variety of local accents.

RP – the regionally non-specific accent of the upper middle classes in England – has a **negligible** presence in Scot-
25 land (unlike Wales, for example, where it **retains** a certain degree of prestige in some areas). This means that even the most socially prestigious forms of English spoken in Scotland contain elements that are characteristically Scottish. The
30 variety of speech we might recognise as educated Scottish English contains the occasional word – *outwith* for 'outside' – or grammatical structure – *I've not heard* for 'I haven't heard' – that is
35 **distinctively** Scottish.

Above all, though, Scottish English is recognisable by its pronunciation: speakers do not make the same distinctions in **vowel** length made by speakers
40 with other English accents and the vast majority of speakers in Scotland are *rhotic* – that is, they pronounce the <r> sound after a vowel in words like *farm*, *first* and *better*.
45

Scots dialect

Alongside Standard Scottish English, the local **vernacular** language, Scots, a dialect **descended from** Old English
50 and closely related to **Northumbrian dialects** has **maintained** a strong presence, especially in rural communities. There has been **heated debate** among linguists for many years as to whether
55 Scots **constitutes** a dialect or a distinct

language in its own right. It has recently been officially classified as a 'traditional language' by the Scottish Executive and
60 recognised by the European **Charter** for Regional or Minority Languages, but even in Scotland experts remain divided over the **issue**. Whatever its status – language or dialect – large numbers of
65 speakers would certainly claim to speak Scots, not English. Indeed Scots boasts a literary tradition dating back long before **Robert Burns** in the eighteenth century and still **thriving** today, as dem-
70 onstrated by contemporary authors such as **Irvine Welsh**.

Blurred boundaries

In practice, the distinction
75 between those who speak Scots and those who speak Standard Scottish English is rather **blurred**. In some cases we might instantly be
80 able to categorise an individual according to which variety he or she speaks, but more often than not, perhaps particularly in urban areas, speakers tend to **drift**
85 between the two alternatives depending on context. In other words, they might speak a version of Standard English with a local accent, but frequently use features that we **asso-**
90 **ciate with** Scots, such as saying *wee* for

'little', or using grammatical constructions like *does nae* for 'doesn't' or simply **sprinkling their speech with isolated** archaic pronunciations such as rhyming *house* with *goose* or *head* with *heed*.

[From *The British Library*. #3; bold face added.]

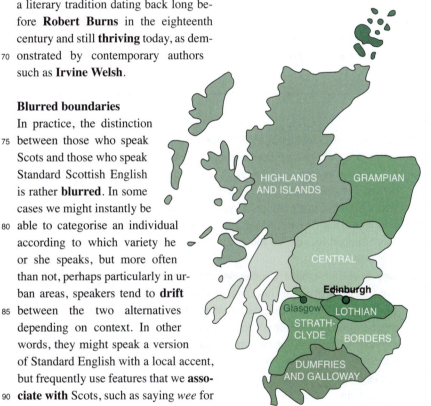

Map of Scotland

Vocabulary

1. Look up the following words and expressions in a monolingual English diction-
    ary: range, contribute, varied, aligned with, prestigious, adopt, aspiring, negli-
    gible, retain, distinctively, descend from, maintain, heated debate, constitute,
    charter, issue, thrive, blurred, drift, associate with, sprinkle sb's speech with, and
    isolated.
2. The text features references to Robert Burns and Irvine Welsh. Find out more
    about these authors.
3. The text features a reference to Northumbrian dialects. What part of England
    does the name Northumbria refer to?

Definitions

Find definitions of the following linguistic terms. You may use a dictionary or web
sources, if necessary: linguistic, RP, vowel, and vernacular.

EXERCISES

1. Summarise the reasons given in the text as to how "the linguistic landscape"
    in Scotland differs from that in most other regions of Great Britain.
2. As has been mentioned in the text, it is quite difficult to distinguish clearly
    between what is called "Scots" and "Standard Scottish English". Try to as-
    sess to which of these categories you would assign the speakers whom you
    have met in this chapter. Would you perhaps place them in a different cate-
    gory? Support your choice with arguments and examples. (Write a minimum
    of 200–300 words!)
3. Why do you think that it is sometimes difficult to say whether a variety is
    "only" a dialect of a given language or whether it can be considered to be
    a language of its own? Discuss possible answers to this question. (Write a
    minimum of 200–300 words!) You may refer to the text or come up with your
    own examples. Think, for instance, of the differences between High German
    and Swiss German, Mandarin and Cantonese, German and Dutch, Swedish
    and Norwegian, Russian and Ukranian, Serbian and Croatian, and so on
    and so forth.

REPETITION EXERCISE: SCOTTISH ENGLISH TABOO

In your own words, explain what the following terms and phrases mean. You are not allowed to use the terms and phrases themselves.

archaic	Received Pronunciation	vernacular language	rural area
aspiring	Scots	wee	blurred boundary
linguistic	vowel	dialect	urban area
-nae	Scottish English	landscape	Northumbria

READING AND LISTENING COMPREHENSION

Auld Lang Syne

Auld Lang Syne was originally a Scottish poem written by the famous Scottish author Robert Burns in 1788. It is sung in many English-speaking countries to celebrate the start of the New Year at midnight on New Year's Day. Although you probably all know it and many of you might have already sung it, maybe some of you do not know that this song was written in Scots. Some of you might also not be aware of what this song is actually about. Take a close look at the text and the exercises given below. [Based on #xii]

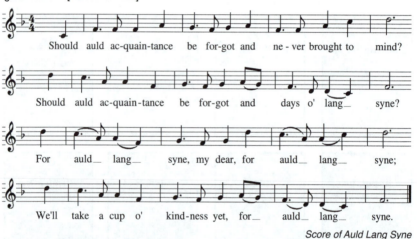

Should auld ac-quain-tance be for-got and ne - ver brought to mind?

Should auld ac-quain-tance be for-got and days o' lang__ syne?

For auld__ lang__ syne, my dear, for auld__ lang__ syne;

We'll take a cup o' kind-ness yet, for__ auld__ lang__ syne.

Score of Auld Lang Syne

Robert Burns

INFO

Robert Burns (1759–1796) is often considered to be the national poet of Scotland. He is most famous for his satires, poems, and songs, many of which he wrote in Scots. However, much of his writing is also in English, or a rather Scots-flavoured dialect which is more easily accessible for an audience outside of Scotland. [Based on #xiii]

Should auld **acquaintance** be forgot,
and never brought to mind?
Should auld acquaintance be forgot,
and auld lang syne?

CHORUS:
For auld lang syne, my dear,
for auld lang syne,
we'll tak a **cup o' kindness** yet,
for auld lang syne.

And surely ye'll be your pint-stoup!
and surely I'll be mine!
And we'll tak a cup o' kindness yet,
for auld lang syne.

CHORUS

We twa hae run about the braes,
and pou'd the gowans fine;
But we've wander'd mony a **weary fit**,
sin' auld lang syne.

CHORUS

We twa hae paidl'd in the burn,
frae morning sun till **dine**;
But seas between us braid hae **roar**'d
sin' auld lang syne.

CHORUS

And there's a hand my **trusty** fiere!
and gies a hand o' thine!
And we'll tak a right **gude-willie** waught,
for auld lang syne.

CHORUS

[Robert Burns 1788. #4; bold face added]

 EXERCISE: Listen to *Auld Lang Syne* on the Internet!

Vocabulary
1. Look up the following words and expressions in a monolingual English diction-ary: acquaintance, cup of kindness, weary fit, dine, roar, and trusty.
2. The last but one line of the song features the Scottish word 'gude-willie'. Try to find the appropriate standard English equivalent and explain what it means. You may consult a dictionary, if necessary.

EXERCISE: MEMORY

1. Take a look at the memory cards given below. Try to find out which cards belong together with the help of the song lyrics and a partner. When you have found the matching pairs, write the correct answers down in your exercise book.
2. Try to translate the song lyrics into standard English with a partner.
3. Try to explain what this song is about and comment on why you think it is sung especially on New Year's Eve.

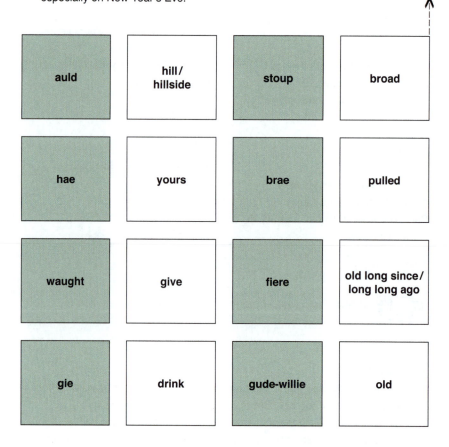

auld	**hill/ hillside**	**stoup**	**broad**
hae	**yours**	**brae**	**pulled**
waught	**give**	**fiere**	**old long since/ long long ago**
gie	**drink**	**gude-willie**	**old**

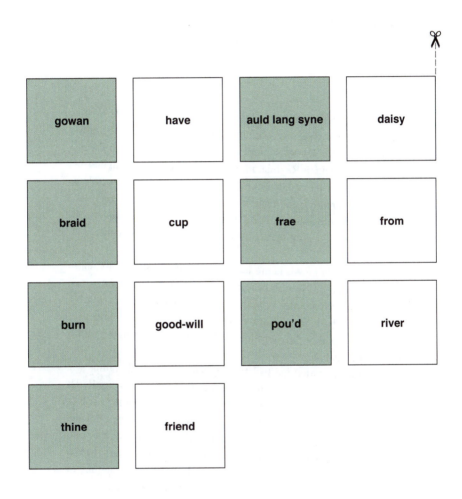

gowan	have	auld lang syne	daisy
braid	cup	frae	from
burn	good-will	pou'd	river
thine	friend		

 READING COMPREHENSION

Trainspotting

… first published in 1993, is the first novel written by the Scottish author Irvine Welsh. It is set in Edinburgh and deals with the lives and problems of a group of heroin users and their friends.

> [...] 'Mother Superior' wis Johnny Swan; also kent as the White Swan, a dealer whae wis based in **Tollcross** and covered the **Sight-hill** and **Wester Hailes schemes**. Ah preferred tae **score** fi Swanney or his **sidekick** Raymie, rather than Seeker n the **Muirhoose-**
> 5 **Leith mob**, if ah could. Better **gear**, usually. Johnny Swan hud once been a really good mate ay mines, back in the auld days. We played fitba thegither fir Porty Thistle. Now he wis a dealer. Ah remember um saying tae us once: Nae friends in this game. Jist associates.
> 10   Ah thought he wis being **harsh**, **flippant** and show-oafy, until ah got sae far in. Now ah ken precisely what the cunt meant.
>   Johnny wis a junky as well as a dealer. Ye hud tae go a wee bit further up the ladder before ye found a dealer whae didnae use. We called Johnny 'Mother Superior' because ay the length ay time
> 15 he'd hud his habit.
>   Ah soon started tae feel fucking shan n aw. Bad cramps wir beginning tae hit us as we mounted the stairs tea Johnny's **gaff**. Ah wis dripping like a **saturated** sponge, every step bringing another **gush** fae ma pores. Sick Boy wis probably even worse, but the
> 20 cunt was beginning no tae exist fir us. Ah wis only aware ay him **slouching** tae a halt oan the **banister** in front ay us, because he wis blocking ma route tae Johnny's and the **skag**. He wis struggling fir breath, haudin grimly oantay the railing, looking as if he wis gaunnae **spew** intae the **stairwell**. [...]

[From *Trainspotting* by Irvine Welsh, published by Vintage Books. #5; bold face added.]

Vocabulary

1. Look up the following words and expressions in a monolingual English dictionary: scheme, score, sidekick, mob, gear, harsh, flippant, gaff, saturated, gush, slouch, banister, skag, spew, and stairwell.
2. The text features a reference to 'Mother Superior'. Find out whom this expression refers to.
3. In the text, you also find the names of some geographical locations. Find out what the following geographical locations refer to: Tollcross, Sighthill, Wester Hailes, and Muirhoose-Leith.

EXERCISES

1. Work with a partner or in small groups and try to identify all English words for which the spelling has been adjusted to the Scottish English pronunciation and try to give their standard English equivalents. It might be helpful to go through the text sentence by sentence and read each sentence aloud to your partner(s).
2. Apart from the English words that have been adapted to fit the Scottish English pronunciation, there are some words in the text that occur specifically in Scottish English and do not normally occur in standard British English. Try to identify these Scottish English words.
3. Can you find any differences in grammar between the language used in this text and what you would expect to find in a standard British English text?
4. Take another look at the Scottish English "translations" of the English words in EXERCISE 1. Can you recognise a certain system used to change these words?
5. Now, try to translate the text passage into standard English.

 HOMEWORK

1. Find out what *Trainspotting* originally meant and what kinds of activities this word is often associated with. Discuss why this title may have been chosen for a novel about drug users. (Write a minimum of 200–300 words!)
2. Many of Irvine Welsh's stories are set in and around Edinburgh. Discuss the advantages and disadvantages of writing novels and stories in a certain dialect and give reasons and examples for your opinion. (Write a minimum of 200–300 words!)

 READING COMPREHENSION

The Sivven Sons o Knock Castle

A Scottish Folk Tale by Les Wheeler

As we have discussed before, it is sometimes difficult to distinguish between what is called standard Scottish English on the one hand and Scots on the other. The following text is written in Scots rather than in standard Scottish English. Are you still able to understand it and answer the questions given below?

Noo, its bin said by fowk that ocht tae ken better, that the Gordons hid the knack o killin an o bein killt. But they've **aye** bin a gran clan for haein bairns sae
5 ye can kill as mony as ye like an there'll aye be plenty left! Weel, whither that's true or no there wis nae excuse for the wye Forbes o Strathgirnoc treated the Gordon **loons** o Castle Knock. This wis
10 the wye o't.

Ae day Gordon o Knock gave his loons a shout an said they'd need tae be getting some peats intae the store sae if the winter turnt bad they'd hae plenty
15 for the castle fires. Sae the loons said they wid gyan aff an cut some peats an stack them tae dry afore liftin an storin. Sae the loons set aff wi thir flauchterspads on thir shooders. [A flauchter-spad
20 is a spad used for cuttin peats.] Noo, the loons made the mistake o castin for thir peats on land that belanged tae Forbes o Strathgirnoc.

Forbes hid bin wytin for a lang time tae get revenge on the Gordons. Ye see, 25 at the Battle o the Crabstanes in 1591 Forbes o Strathgirnoc hid bin captured by Henry Gordon o Knock, the brither o the Laird wi sivven sons. Fan Knock's sivven sons hid set tae wirk they'd bin 30 spied by een o Forbes's tenant **chiels** an he wis quick tae tell his maister. Forbes gaithered a **puckle** men, aa airmed tae the teeth, an set aff tae deal wi the sons o Knock. 35

The loons could see they hid nae chunce agin this **kirn** o Forbeses an laid doon thir spads tae see fit wis adee. Forbes wisna for spikkin. He pullt oot his sword an wi his ain haun hackit aff 40 the heid o every een o the sivven loons. **Syne**, tae mak things even worse, een by een he stuck the heids on the cross-heid o **ilka** loon's flauchter-spad. Syne the spads wi the heids on tap wir stuck in a 45 line on the hill that faced Knock Castle. It wis this **affa sicht** that wis seen by een o the servants o Knock an wint rinnin tae tell his laird.

50 The Laird wis at the tap o the stairs **abeen** his ha fin he heard the full horror o fit hid taen place. The shock wis **ower muckle** for the aul man an he collapsed wi the agony o it an fell heid first
55 ower the bannisters an wis killt in the ha o his ain hoose. Can onybody doot that Forbes hid killt him jist as surely as he'd killt his loons?

Forbes hid tae be dealt wi an the
60 King decided that the Knock lands wid gyan tae Gordon o Abergeldie an **forbye** that Abergeldie wis tae get Forbes o Strathgirnoc's land an castle as weel. Abergeldie set aff tae get justice for the Gordons an it didna tak him lang tae 65 capture Forbes an he hung him in his ain hoose tae avenge the murder of the Laird o Knock an his sivven sons. If ye tak the road fae Ballater tae Abergeldie ye can still see Castle Knock an the place far 70 these terrible things happent.

[From *Ephinstone Kist – Stories for Bairns*. #6; bold face added.]

Explanations

aye: (Scots) always, still; **loon:** (Northeast Scots) boy, lad; **chiel:** (Scots) young man; **puckle:** imprecise amount, a few; **kirn:** a group of foot soldiers; **syne:** (Scots and North England) since, (here) afterwards; **ilka:** (Scots) each, every; **affa:** awful; **sicht:** (Scots) sight; **abeen:** above; **ower muckle:** (Scots) too much; **forbye:** (Scots) in addition, also.

COMPREHENSION AND ANALYSIS

1. Try to summarise the story in your own words.
2. There are several words in this text that you have seen before in this unit. What are they? Do they have the same meaning or are they used differently here? What do they mean?

COMPOSITION

1. When you compare this text to the texts / transcripts you have discussed before, why do you think that this text was written in Scots rather than standard Scottish English? In a short essay, describe why the text is more difficult to understand than others and give reasons and examples. (Write a minimum of 200–300 words!)
2. Try to translate the first 49 lines of this text into standard English.

Sources

TEXTS

[1]   Welsh, Irvine. 1998. *The Acid House* (Screenplay). Taken from the script courtesy of
       Film4. © 1998 Film4.

[2]   "Scotland Two". The International Dialects of English Archive. <http://web.ku.edu/~idea/
       europe/scotland/scotland2.htm>, June 28, 2009. Transcribed and reprinted by special
       permission from the *International Dialects of English Archive*.

[3]   "Accents and dialects of Scotland". The British Library. <http://www.bl.uk/learning/langlit/
       sounds/find-out-more/scotland/>, June 16, 2009. © The British Library Board, reproduced
       with permission.

[4]   Burns, Robert. 1788. "Auld Lang Syne". <http://en.wikisource.org/wiki/Auld_Lang_Syne>
       (Public Domain), September 06, 2011.

[5]   Welsh, Irvine. 1993. *Trainspotting*. Vintage Books, 6–7. Reprinted by permission of The
       Random House Group Ltd.

[6]   Wheeler, Les. The sivven sons o knock castle. In: Wheeler, Les and Sheena Blackhall
       (eds.), *Elphinstone Kist – Stories for Bairns*. Abeerdeen: University of Aberdeen. <http://
       www.abdn.ac.uk/kist/search/display.php/The+Sivven+Sons+o+Knock+Castle+%28A+Sco
       ttish+Folk+Tale%29%0A?lwe102.dat>, January 04, 2012. Reproduced with permission of
       Elphinstone Kist, Elphinstone Institute, University of Aberdeen.

PICTURES AND FIGURES

Kilt: <http://commons.wikimedia.org/wiki/File:Black_watch_kilt.JPG> (Public Domain), April 17,
       2009.

Flag of Scotland: © Isabel Peters. Hamburg, 2011.

Golf ball: © Isabel Peters. Hamburg, 2011.

Fly: <http://de.wikipedia.org/w/index.php?title=Datei:Fly_close.jpg&filetimesta
       mp=20080604225650> (Public Domain), January 18, 2012.

Boab and God: *The Acid House*. 2007. Director: Paul Mc Guigan. Performers: Ewan Bremner,
       Kevin McKidd, Stephen McCole, and Jemma Redgrave. DVD Senator. Screenshot
       courtesy of Film4. © 1998 Film4.

Irvine Welsh: <http://en.wikipedia.org/wiki/File:Irvine_Welsh_by_Kubik.JPG> (Creative
       Commons Attribution-ShareAlike 3.0), picture taken by Mariusz Kubik, April 17, 2009.

Map of Scotland: © Isabel Peters. Hamburg, 2011.

Map of Orkney: © Isabel Peters. Hamburg, 2011.

Map of Scotland: © Isabel Peters. Hamburg, 2011.

Score of Auld Lang Syne: Koellner, Richard (ed.). 2012. *Auld Lang Syne* (in F-major). <http://
www.notenseiten.de/lieder/pdf/AuldLangSyne-G1B.pdf> (Public Domain), January 17,
2012.

Robert Burns: <http://en.wikipedia.org/wiki/File:Robert_burns.jpg> (Public Domain), April 17,
2009.

REFERENCES AND FURTHER READING

Johnston, Paul A. 2007. Scottish English and Scots. In: Britain, David (ed.), *Language in
the British Isles*. Cambridge: Cambridge University Press, 105–121.

Miller, Jim. 2008. Scottish English: morphology and syntax. In: Kortmann, Bernd and Clive
Upton (eds.), *Varieties of English*, Vol. 1. *The British Isles*. Berlin/New York: Mouton
de Gruyter, 299–327.

Stuart-Smith, Jane. 2008. Scottish English: phonology. In: Kortmann, Bernd and Clive
Upton (eds.), *Varieties of English*, Vol. 1. *The British Isles*. Berlin/New York: Mouton
de Gruyter, 48–70.

Melchers, Gunnel and Philip Shaw. 2003. *World Englishes (The English Language Series)*.
London: Arnold (Hodder Headline Group), 60–71.

Romaine, Suzanne. 1982. The English language in Scotland. In: Bailey, Richard W. and
Manfred Görlach (eds.), *English as a World Language*. Ann Arbor, MI: University of
Michigan Press, 56–83.

[i]   "Scotland." Encyclopædia Britannica. Encyclopædia Britannica Online Academic
Edition. Encyclopædia Britannica, 2011. <http://www.britannica.com/EBchecked/
topic/529440/Scotland>, September 05, 2011.

[ii]   "Scots Gaelic language." Encyclopædia Britannica. Encyclopædia Britannica Online
Academic Edition. Encyclopædia Britannica, 2011. <http://www.britannica.com/
EBchecked/topic/529692/Scots-Gaelic-language>, September 05, 2011.

[iii] "Scots language." Encyclopædia Britannica. Encyclopædia Britannica Online
Academic Edition. Encyclopædia Britannica, 2011. <http://www.britannica.com/
EBchecked/topic/529546/Scots-language>, September 05, 2011.

[iv]   "Golf." Encyclopædia Britannica. Encyclopædia Britannica Online Academic
Edition. Encyclopædia Britannica, 2011. <http://www.britannica.com/EBchecked/
topic/238012/golf>, September 05, 2011.

[v]   "Accents and dialects of Scotland." The British Library. The British Library Board,
2009. <http://www.bl.uk/learning/langlit/sounds/find-out-more/scotland/>, June 16,
2009.

[vi]   "Scotland, flag of." Encyclopædia Britannica. Encyclopædia Britannica Online

Academic Edition. Encyclopædia Britannica, 2011. <http://www.britannica.com/ EBchecked/topic/1355495/Scotland-flag-of>, September 05, 2011.

[vii]   "Scots tradition hit by cover-up ruling." *The Times Online* [Wapping], August 02, 2004. <http://www.timesonline.co.uk/tol/news/uk/article464594.ece>, September 01, 2011.

[viii]   "Draught guidance: a kilt need underwear." *The Telegraph Online* [London], October 22, 2011. <http://www.telegraph.co.uk/news/uknews/scotland/8149592/Draught-guidance-a-kilt-need-underwear.html>, September 01, 2011.

[ix]   "The SPCB Language Policy." The Scottish Parliamentary Corporate Body (SPCB). <http://www.scottish.parliament.uk/PublicInformationdocuments/lang-pol.pdf>, January 18, 2012.

[x]   "Irvine Welsh." Deutsche Nationalbibliothek. <https://portal.dnb.de/opac.htm;jsessio nid=1A8D2FAAF044D7ADDB92762C62E0E8A6.prod-worker5?method=moveDown &currentResultId=Woe%3D115629394%26any&categoryId=persons>, January 18, 2012.

[xi]   "Irvine Welsh." BBC – Writing Scotland. <http://www.bbc.co.uk/scotland/arts/ writingscotland/writers/irvine_welsh/works.shtml>, January 18, 2012.

[xii]   "Robert Burns." BBC. <http://www.bbc.co.uk/arts/robertburns/works/auld_lang_ syne/>, January 18, 2012.

[xiii]   "Robert Burns." Encyclopædia Britannica. Encyclopædia Britannica Online Academic Edition. Encyclopædia Britannica, 2011. <http://www.britannica.com/EBchecked/ topic/85716/Robert-Burns>, September 06, 2011.

Inner circle

Chapter 4

British and American English

Introduction

The varieties of British English and American English are important as they typically perform the function of target varieties for non-native speakers learning English in a classroom setting. However, the labels of British English and American English fail to account for the enormous linguistic heterogeneity encountered both in Britain and in the United States.

In England, dialects spoken in the North are quite distinct from those spoken in the South. The most diverse and sociolinguistically complex area in England is London. London features three major sociolects that reflect societal differentiation: Cockney English spoken by the working class, Received Pronunciation (RP) spoken by the upper class, and Estuary English representing middle class speech (cf. Mesthrie and Bhatt 2008: 4). Being promoted through many celebrities, Estuary English has found increasing acceptance as a credible dialect associated with a strong sense of identity.

In the United States, the major dialectal boundary line also separates the South from the North. In addition, we find African American Vernacular English (AAVE), a major ethnic variety. It is not completely clear whether AAVE is related to white vernaculars, particularly those spoken in the South, having retained many historical features non-

existent in contemporary white dialects, as argued by William Labov (1998: 149), or whether it can be traced back to a Creole that preceded its emergence – a hypothesis advocated by John R. Rickford (1998: 189–191).

Other types of Englishes can be encountered in the United States, too. Chicano English is a so-called 'immigrant English' spoken by the Mexican population. It is essentially a second-language variety exhibiting a number of distinct features, on the one hand, and a high degree of assimilation with American English on the other (cf. Mesthrie and Bhatt 2008: 5–6). Valley Girl Talk ('Valleytalk') is a sociolect originally associated with the speech of middle and upper-middle class young females from the San Fernando Valley in Los Angeles.

This chapter begins with exercises to increase your awareness of the differences in vocabulary between British and American English. The ensuing texts by David Crystal and Zoltán Kövecses look at the history of American English and the languages that influenced it. This chapter also contains Reading Comprehensions on Northern English dialects, American slang and African American English. There is also an exercise dealing with regional diversity in England and in the United States. Two Self-Studies and a concluding exercise complete the chapter.

INTRODUCTORY EXERCISE

Read the dialogues below. Are the speakers British or American? Explain your choice.

A: "Hey, you guys! I haven't seen you in quite a while. How are you?"
B: "Oh, we are fine. Trying to get everything ready for that summer camping trip."

A: "How's school going?"
B: "Oh, just fine. It starts Monday. I finally got the grant to go to graduate school."

A: "How do you like those chips?"
B: "You mean French fries? Oh, they are delicious. Should we get some candy on the way home?"
A: "Yes, some sweets would be nice."

A: "Gosh, it's cold in here. Would you mind closing the window?"
B: "Shall I make you a cup of tea? There is a pot under the tea cosy right there on the table."

A: "Hey, Susan! I have gotten your e-mail. Is everything all right?"
B: "Yes, Steve. Everything is fine. Thanks for checking in. I got stuck in the elevator on my way to the office today. My brother was kicked out of high school for smoking pot, so that he's not gonna get to go to college. But other than that, things are rocking in here."

A: "What is your main subject at school?"
B: "Chemistry. But I am also thinking of taking physics at least over the summer."

A: "What do you think of Mike?"
B: "A really nice bloke."
A: "Shall I invite him to the party Ema is throwing tonight?"
B: "That's a bloody good idea!"

Vocabulary

Read the following British and American English words and put them in the two columns below: mobile phone, closet, lift, dustbin, cell phone, zip code, high school, French fries, main subject, line, trousers, candy, drugstore, university, chips, secondary school, wardrobe, queue, major, luggage, postcode, college, sweets, chemist, pants, elevator, underground, trash can, baggage, and subway.

British English	American English

 READING COMPREHENSION

British English vs. American English: How it all began …

British English and American English are fairly different in terms of grammar, vocabulary, and pronunciation. In order to understand the origin of these differences, we have to look at the historical development of American English. In the following text, David Crystal, one of the most renowned experts in the field of World Englishes, explains how English expanded throughout the territory now known as the United States of America.

America

The first **expedition** from England to the New World was **commissioned by** Walter Raleigh in 1584, and **proved to be**
5 **a failure**. A group of explorers landed near Roanoke Island, in what is now North Carolina, and established a small settlement. Conflict with the native people followed, and it proved necessary
10 for a ship to return to England for help and supplies. By the time these arrived, in 1590, none of the original group of settlers could be found. The mystery of their disappearance has never been
15 solved.

The first **permanent** English **settlement** dates from 1607, when an expedition arrived in Chesapeake Bay. The colonists called their settlement Jamestown
20 (after James I) and the area Virginia (after the 'Virgin Queen', Elizabeth). Further settlements quickly followed along the coast, and also on the nearby islands, such as Bermuda. Then in November
25 1620, the first group of Puritans, thirty-five members of the **English Separatist Church**, arrived on the *Mayflower* in the company of sixty-seven other settlers. Prevented by storms from reaching Virginia, they landed at Cape Cod Bay, and 30 established a settlement at what is now Plymouth, Massachusetts.

The group was extremely mixed, ranging in age from young children to people in their 50s, and with diverse 35 regional, social, and occupational backgrounds. What the 'Pilgrim Fathers' (as they were later called) had in common was their search for a land where they could find a new religious kingdom, free 40 from **persecution** and '**purified**' from the church practices they had experienced in England. It was a successful settlement, and by 1640 about 25,000 immigrants had come to the area. 45

The two settlements – one in Virginia, to the south, the other to the north, in present-day New England – had different linguistic backgrounds. Although the southern colony brought settlers 50

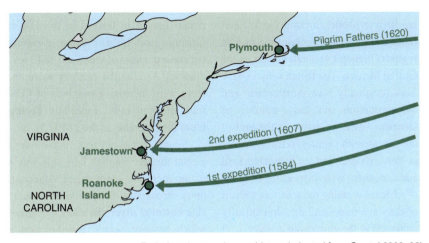

Early American settlement history (adapted from Crystal 2003: 32)

from several parts of England, many of them came from England's 'West Country' – such counties as Somerset and Gloucestershire – and brought with
55 them its characteristic accent, with its 'Zummerzet' voicing of *s* sounds, and the *r* strongly pronounced after vowels. Echoes of this accent can still be heard in the speech of communities living in
60 some of the isolated valleys and islands in the area, such as Tanger Island in Chesapeake Bay. These 'Tidewater' accents, as they are called, have changed somewhat over the past 300 years, but
65 not as rapidly (because of the relative isolation of the speakers) as elsewhere in the country. [...]

During the seventeenth century, new shiploads of immigrants brought an increasing variety of linguistic back- 70 grounds into the country. [...]

Then, in the eighteenth century, there was a vast wave of immigration from northern Ireland. [...] Many [Irish] stayed along the coast, especially in the 75 area of Philadelphia, but most moved inland through the mountains in search of land. [...]

It was not only England which influenced the directions that the English 80 language was to take in America, and later in the USA. The Spanish had occupied large parts of the west and southwest. The French were present in the

Vocabulary

1. Look up the following words and expressions in a monolingual English dictionary: expedition, commissioned by, prove to be a failure, permanent settlement, persecution, purify, hinterland, flee from, cultural diversification, and glue.
2. Find out more about the following terms: English Separatist Church and pogroms.
3. Paraphrase the following expression: "as the century wore on".

85 northern territories, around the St Lawrence River, and throughout the middle regions (French Louisiana) as far as the Gulf of Mexico. The Dutch were in New York (originally New Amsterdam) and
90 the surrounding area. Large numbers of Germans began to arrive at the end of the seventeenth century, settling mainly in Pennsylvania and its **hinterland**. In addition, there were increasing numbers
95 of Africans entering the south, as a result of the slave trade, and this dramatically increased in the eighteenth century. [...]

The nineteenth century saw a massive increase in American immigration,
100 as people fled the results of revolution, poverty, and famine in Europe. Large numbers of Irish came following the potato famine in Ireland in the 1840s. Germans and Italians came, escaping the consequences of the failed 1848 rev-
105 olutions. And, **as the century wore on**, there were increasing numbers of Central European Jews, especially **fleeing from** the **pogroms** of the 1880s. [...]

Some commentators have sug-
110 gested that the English language was a major factor in maintaining American unity throughout this period of remarkable **cultural diversification** – a 'glue'
115 which brought people together and a medium which gave them common access to opportunity. [...]

[David Crystal 2003: 31–36. #1; bold face added]

COMPREHENSION

1. Summarise the history of major European settlements in America before the 17th century.
2. Describe the major waves of immigration to the United States in the 17th, 18th, and 19th century.

DISCUSSION AND ANALYSIS

1. Why do you think English acquired such amazing significance in the United States?
2. Do you think it is necessary for a country to have a national language? Why or why not?
3. Why, do you think, have British English and American English drifted apart?

CREATIVE WRITING

Imagine that you are a designer and part of an international film crew shooting a movie that takes place in London and Las Vegas. You meet different British and American actors, with whom you soon become friends. In your own words, describe the major differences in the language that these actors use. Pay attention to the way they sound. Comment on the words and grammatical structures that they use.

READING COMPREHENSION

The influence of languages of the colonial period

The first languages with which the English-speaking settlers came into contact in the 17th and 18th centuries include the various native American languages, as well as Spanish, French, Dutch, and German. The following text explains the effects the German language had on American English.

There is one important difference between the early German settlers and the other settlers […]. While the Spanish, Dutch, and French were rival colonists to the British settlers, the Germans were the first non-colonizing immigrants, who were rather fleeing from religious **persecution** at home. The German settlers began to arrive on the new continent in 1683, their main **destination** being Pennsylvania. […] The German settlers maintained many of their language habits, which gave rise to what is called *Pennsylvania Dutch*. This was of course a **misnomer** based on the German word for German, which is *Deutsch* (McCrum, *et al.*, 1986: 125).

Several "German cities" in the United States accommodate the seven million Germans. They include Cincinnati, Milwaukee, and St. Louis. Many German words have been taken over by American English, several of them being in daily use, such as […] *delicatessen*, *ecology*, […] *kindergarten* […]. Most of the German words that have been borrowed have to do with food and drink. These are words such as […] *hamburger*, *frankfurter*, *noodle*, *pretzel*, *sauerkraut* […] and *lager*. The word *hot dog* is an American coinage that came about as a result of a change in American attitude toward the Germans in the wake of the First World War. The brief **rash** of anti-German feeling at this time made many change their names, and the wave of "Americanizing" German words produced *hot dog* in place of *frankfurter*. The Germans were respected for the quality of their education, and American English borrowed several German words from this domain, such as *festschrift*, *semester*, and *seminar*. […]

[Zoltán Kövecses 2000: 33–34. #2; bold face added]

Vocabulary

Look up the following words and expressions in a monolingual English dictionary: persecution, destination, misnomer, and rash.

PROJECT

Try to determine what words came into American English from other European languages. Use the Internet as your resource.

SELF-STUDY I

Draw a mind map depicting the differences in spelling, vocabulary, and grammar between standard British English (BrE) and American English (AmE). If necessary, consult the following websites:

» http://esl.about.com/library/vocabulary/blbritam.htm
» http://en.wikipedia.org/wiki/American_and_British_English_differences
» http://www.englisch-hilfen.de/words/be-ae.htm

The mind map below should help you to come up with your own ideas.

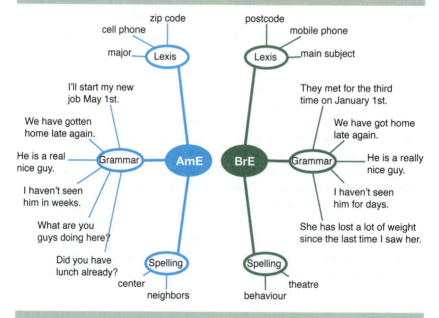

SELF-STUDY II (ADVANCED)

It is a well-known fact that many American English words have found their way into the British vocabulary as a result of globalisation. For instance, although originating in the United States, the word *movie* is now widely used by many British people. Similarly, the American English lexeme *hash browns* is now a part of the British English vocabulary. What other American words can you think of that have penetrated into the British lexicon? Why do you think some words are more susceptible to borrowing than others?

 READING COMPREHENSION

Northern English dialects

A majority of English people take pride and interest in the language of the area where they grew up. There are only few people who speak English with an accent that does not give away their origin. The vast majority of the English people speak their language in a manner that associates them with a particular area. Read the text below about English dialects spoken in the North of England in order to learn more about some of their most prominent characteristics.

Traditional Northern English dialects cover the areas of Northumberland, Cumbria and Durham, the Lake District, and northern Lancashire stretching into northern and eastern Yorkshire (Trudgill 1999: 39–40). Like other vernaculars, Northern English dialects exhibit a bundle of distinct features in the domains of phonology, morphosyntax, and lexis. Whereas some of these features are idiosyncratic in character and are representative of only these dialects, others are more general in nature, being attested in other forms of English as well. In what follows, we look at the most **essential properties** of Northern English dialects.

Perhaps, one of the easiest ways to spot various dialects is to watch out for the differences in pronunciation. This is why most of the traditional descriptions of English dialects are based on phonological rather than morphosyntactic or lexical distinctions (see Beal 2010: 10–12 for a brief overview).

Two features in pronunciation are likely to give away speakers of Northern English dialects. This is particularly true of elderly speakers in rural areas. Firstly, words ending in -*ight* are realised with a long vowel /iː/ so that *night*, *light* become 'neet', 'leet' (cf. Trudgill 1999: 33). Secondly, *long* is pronounced as 'lang' /læŋ/ here, which provides a striking contrast to all other English vernaculars (cf. Trudgill 1999: 33).

Among the grammatical features characterising Northern English dialects, particularly those spoken in Yorkshire and Lancashire, the **reduction** of definite articles is perhaps the most important one as it represents a **diagnostic** of these English vernaculars. Thus, the definite article *the* is frequently shortened to *t'* or is simply dropped (see also Beal 2004: 120).

Another interesting feature is the usage of *was/were*-forms. In contrast to standard English, the form *were* tends to be used with all subjects, both singular and plural, in the traditional dialects of Lancashire and Yorkshire (see Beal 2004: 122). A recent study of York English pointed to a link between the *was*-forms and positive clauses on the one hand, and the *were*-forms and negative clauses on the other (Tagliamonte 1998, cited in Beal 2004: 122).

Northern English dialects also **attest** the so-called "Northern Subject Rule", as in *They break into houses and steals* (Pietsch 2005: 144). In its most general reading the rule predicts that "concord verbs take the *-s*-form with all subjects, except with the personal pronouns *I*, *we*, *you* and *they* when they are directly **adjacent to** the verb" (Pietsch 2005: 128). The following examples demonstrate how the idealised version of this rule operates in the data:

1. *These people smiles.*
2. *These people often smiles.*
3. *They smile.*
4. *They often smiles.*

Going back to the Middle English period, the pattern has been described as one of the most important features of Northern English dialects although it is not unique to these dialects, having been attested for Scots and Irish English, especially the varieties spoken in Ulster (see Pietsch 2005: 126). Variations of this **intriguing** dialectal feature have also been documented in other parts of the English-speaking world (see, for instance, Tagliamonte 2012: 207–216 for an overview).

There are some lexical peculiarities setting Northern English dialects apart from other vernaculars spoken in England. These comprise Scandinavian, French, Dutch, Celtic as well as Romani influence (cf. Beal 2010: 54–62). *Beck*, for example, is a word of Scandinavian origin found in northern English vernaculars. It competes with the Old English lexemes *burn* and *brook*, both of which mean *stream* in standard English. Whereas the use of *burn* is restricted to the area of Northumberland, *brook* covers larger parts of southeastern, southwestern, and central England (see Beal 2010: 54–56). Traces of French influence on Northern English dialects are revealed by dialectal words such as *howlet* meaning 'owl', *poke* meaning 'sack', and *rammel* meaning 'rubbish' (cf. Beal 2010: 58). Beal also reports the Dutch word *ploat* meaning 'to pluck (a fowl)' as being **localised**

Dialect Areas of England. Adapted from Trudgill, Peter. 1990. The Dialects of England. Oxford: Basil Blackwell, 63. © John Wiley & Sons Ltd.

in its use to Northumberland, Durham, North Yorkshire as well as eastern parts of Cumberland and Westmoreland (Beal 2010: 58–59), all of which belong to the northern dialectal area. There is at least one word of Celtic origin reported for the North of England, the adjective *car-handed* for 'left-handed' being a case in point. The **etymology** of *car* can be traced back to Gaelic *cearr*. It is perhaps not surprising, then, that this compound is used in northern Northumberland (see also Beal 2010: 60). The vernacular vocabulary of Northern English dialects appears to have been enriched by words of Romani origin. In his contribution on the website 'BBC Voices' Yaron Matras suggests that speakers of the Northumbrian dialect borrowed some Romani words (*gaji* for 'woman' and *chavvy* for 'boy', to mention just a few) into their everyday speech as there used to be Romani settlements in this area.

[Written by Julia Davydova based on #i – #vi.]

COMPREHENSION

1. In sum, what are the most prominent characteristics of the dialects spoken in the North of England?
2. Explain in your own words what the Northern Subject Rule is.

Vocabulary

Look up the following words and expressions in a monolingual English dictionary: essential properties, reduction, diagnostic, attest, adjacent to, intriguing, localised, and etymology.

ANALYSIS

Describe in your own words in what ways Northern English dialects are different from standard English.

COMMENT WRITING

They say that the way we speak is an important part of who we are. Is it true or not? Given at least three arguments in favour of your point of view and explain your choice.

SELF-STUDY (ADVANCED)

In his monograph *The Dialects of England*, Peter Trudgill distinguishes between traditional and modern dialects of England. Read this book and explain the differences between the two types of dialects. Then summarise their major characteristics.

BRITISH ENGLISH AND AMERICAN ENGLISH: REGIONAL DIVERSITY

Dialects in England
[Based on #vii – #viii]

Although a small country, England boasts a number of highly diverse dialects. The major dialect boundary runs through the Midland area, dividing 'Southerners' from 'Northerners'. The following boxes highlight the most important characteristics of the Englishes spoken in different parts of England. Read the info-boxes below and sum-marise the major dialectal differences in England. Take notes, if necessary. Work in pairs.

Dialects of the North

Dialects spoken in the North of England exhibit distinct features of their own. Some diphthongs are realised differently than in Received Pronunciation (RP). For instance, the word *made* is pronounced as 'mehd' (/meːd/). The vowels in *cut*, *bus*, and *but* are also pronounced differently: They are realised with the back closed vowel /ʊ/, as in RP *good*. In Lancashire, the *r*-sound has been retained in words like *arm*, which con-stitutes a striking contrast to Received Pronunciation.

Dialects of the South

Dialects spoken in the South of England are more similar to Received Pronunciation, at least in some ways. For example, the words *cut* and *bus* as well as *gate* and *made* are pronounced as required in Received Pronun-ciation in the Upper and Central Southwest, South Midlands, and East Anglia.

Speakers of Bristol English attach the *l*-sound to words such as *area* and *idea* so that there is no difference in pronunciation be-tween words like *area* and *areal* or *idea* and *ideal*. Trudgill (1999: 76) believes that this may be a result of the linguistic process of hy-percorrection.

British Creole

In the last century, Britain offered shelter to many immigrants from the Caribbean who spoke Creole languages, mainly Jamaican Creole. These varieties came into contact with urban vernaculars, thus giving rise to British Creole.

The Home Counties

London has been highly influential in determining the most recent emerging characteristics of the English in the Southeast, some parts of East Anglia, most of the Eastern Southwest and most of the Central East. These newly emerged areas are collectively labelled as the Home Counties. Some distinctive features of Home County English are the pronunciation of *by* as /bɒɪ/ (Trudgill 1999: 79) and that of *made* as /maɪd/ (Trudgill 1999: 62, 79). In addition to that, words like *mother* or *thing* are typically pronounced as 'muvver' and 'fing'. Technically speaking, interdental fricative sounds are replaced with labio-dental fricatives. These features are also strongly associated with Cockney speech.

Within the Home County zone, Londoners are still fairly easy to identify as the *l*-sound in words such as *hill* or *milk* has become vocalised (i.e. pronounced as a vowel) in their speech. Trudgill (1999: 79) believes that some features of London speech, including the vocalisation of /l/, will influence other dialects in the near future.

Estuary English

The term 'Estuary English' is actually a misnomer, as it is not used to refer to English dialects spoken in the estuary of the Thames, but rather to a sociolect associated with the middle class. Its major characteristics result from socially mobile speakers retaining some features of their regional accent.

Estuary English has incorporated some important dialectal features from Southeast England. For instance, *made* is pronounced as /maɪd/. Words such as *milk* exhibit variable pronunciation: /mɪʊk/ and /mɪʊɫk/. The words *bet* and *what* are realised with a final glottal stop: /bɛʔ/ and /wɒʔ/ (Trudgill 1999: 80–81).

Dialects of England: Some lexical and grammatical features

Many non-standard vernaculars spoken in England today use the pronouns *them* or *they* meaning 'those', e.g. *them cold rice rolls*, *they books on the shelf*.

Non-standard speech also features negation patterns quite different from those found in standard English. For instance, speakers of non-standard dialects can use forms such as *I ain't coming* meaning 'I am not coming' or *You ain't done it* meaning 'You haven't done it' in their speech. It is also possible to use *never* to negate a single past situation or occasion, e.g. *I never done it*.

Differences in vocabulary include *child* vs. *bairn*, *to play* vs. *to lake*, *hungry* vs. *leer(y)* vs. *thirl* vs. *clamned*.

Dialects in the United States
[Based on #ix – #xi]

People living in different parts of the United States tend to speak differently. The info-boxes below describe the most important differences between major American dialects. Read the info-boxes and summarise the major characteristics of each dialectal zone of the United States. Take notes, if necessary. Work in pairs.

The northern dialect region

In the North, we can differentiate between the state of New York, New England and the inland Northwest as distinct dialect areas.

In the northern dialects, the *r*-sound is pronounced after the vowel in words like *car*. New York and eastern New England are exceptions to this rule. Furthermore, there is no difference in the pronunciation of the words *matter* and *madder* in the northern dialects. Both words can be pronounced with the so-called 'flap' *d*-sound. This feature is variable, however; it is not categorical and is attested in other dialects of American English as well.

In contrast to other American dialects, the vowels in words like *cot* and *caught* are pronounced differently. There are also cities with distinct and famous dialects within the northern dialect area. These include New York City and Boston speech.

The southern dialect region

This dialectal region encompasses Virginia, the Carolinas, and the Gulf states, including larger parts of Texas.

Americans coming from these areas do not pronounce the grapheme <r> in words like *car*.

In these dialects, some vowels are joined or merged into one. For example, the words *cents* and *since* are pronounced /sɪns/. The speakers from these regions also tend to pronounce the words *tone* and *torn*, *bone* and *born* as /ton/ and /bon/.

The word *hide* is pronounced as /had/. Similarly, the words *time*, *mile*, and *private* may be pronounced with an /aː/.

Americans call this type of accent the "Southern drawl".

The western dialect region

The largest area geographically, the western dialect region comprises the territory west of the Mississippi River, reaching out to the Pacific Ocean.

The settling of this area is associated with the California gold rush in the mid-19th century. The settlers arrived from all over the United States, which created an enormous pool of demographic and linguistic variation.

The dialects of this region, which covers most of the Pacific coast, are rhotic, i.e. we find the *r*-sound at the end of *car*. Similar to the Midland dialect, the pairs *tot-taught*, *cot-caught* are pronounced identically.

New York English

The English spoken in New York City (NYC) has been recognised as a distinct US dialect. Some of the most prominent features of New York speech include the non-realisation of the postvocalic *r*-sound (non-rhoticity) and the preservation of the *cot-caught* distinction. The latter feature implies that words like *caught* are pronounced with the low back vowel /ɔ/, whereas words like *copy* are realised with /ɑ/.

Appalachian English

Appalachia is a region that lies between New York in the North and Mississippi in the South, encompassing fragments of more than 13 states. But it is the state of West Virginia that can be considered to be the heart of the Appalachian region and the Appalachian English dialect.

Some traditional features of this dialect such as preverbal *done*, e.g. *I done cooked breakfast*, and *a*-prefixing, e.g. *We a-worked*, are slowly but surely disappearing from Appalachian English grammar. These structures are highly stigmatised and are not used by the youth.

The midwestern dialect region

The Midwest region begins in Philadelphia, reaching out westward into Ohio, Indiana, and Illinois and southwest through Kentucky and Tennessee into Missouri and Arkansas.

In the Midwest region, the *r*-sound in the word *car* is heard very clearly. Here, the vowels in *cot-caught* and *tot-taught* are merged so that the pronunciation of these words is identical.

 READING COMPREHENSION

American slang

Representing a very informal (or **casual**) style of speech, American slang manifests an important part of American language and culture. Like any type of language, American slang is a **work in progress**. Different people at various times have been involved in its formation.

The history of American slang can be traced back to the 17th and 18th centuries, although it was not until after the middle of the 19th century that it began to thrive (cf. Kövecses 2000: 118). The discovery of gold in California (also known as the Golden State) attracted many fortune seekers, whose creativity and adventurous spirit gave rise to some famous slang phrases such as *lucky strike* (cf. Kövecses 2000: 122). Other important creators of American slang were cowboys. Because they had close contacts with non-native speakers exhibiting some limited knowledge of English, cowboys developed a very simple language that included phrases such as *long time no see* and *no can do* (cf. Kövecses 2000: 122).

Similar to slangs in other languages, the criminal vocabulary became an inherent part of American slang. Criminal jargon entered American English and began to **prosper** early in the 20th century (cf. Kövecses 2000: 120). The city of Chicago was particularly influential in this process. The word *godfather* used

by the gangsters to refer to the head of a Mafia clan became extremely popular worldwide as a result of the enormous success of Francis Ford Coppola's films bearing the same title. Several other criminal words were adopted into everyday speech. For example, the expression *hot seat* originally meaning "electric chair" is now employed to describe a difficult situation (cf. Kövecses 2000: 120).

Other sources for American slang are speech styles of ethnic groups. *Soul brother*, *soul music*, *soul language*, and *soul shake* are African American words that have gained currency well beyond the Black American **community** (cf. Kövecses 2000: 122–123). Lexical items like *schmaltz*, *schmuck*, *shlep*, and *mensch* originate in **Yiddish** (see also Kövecses 2000: 123–124 for further examples). For instance, the word *schmuck* refers to a silly person and is very similar in meaning to *jerk*. The German language also exerted an influence on the formation of American slang and American vocabulary in general. The *Oxford English Dictionary* lists *Schadenfreude*, *Zeitgeist*, *spiel*, and *angst* as lexical items with German roots, thereby showing just how important the German language was for American English.

Young people's speech is yet another important source for American slang. Probably the most famous teen-

ager slang is known as 'Valleytalk' in the United States. Valleytalk is a slang originally spoken by teenage girls from the middle class families in the San Fer-
75 nando valley in California (cf. Kövecses 2000: 125). It has now spread throughout California and many other parts of the United States. Thus, many young people are very likely to use the word
80 *awesome* to describe things that they are very much into or the words *totally* or *to the max* meaning 'completely' (cf. Kövecses 2000: 125). The word *like*, as in *She is like sitting there all the time*, is also among their favourite expressions. 85

[Written by Julia Davydova based on Zoltán Kövecses 2000: 117–125.]

Vocabulary

Look up the following words and expressions in a monolingual English dictionary: casual, work in progress, prosper, community, and awesome.

Explanations

Yiddish: a Germanic language originating in the Jewish communities of Central and Eastern Europe that is heavily influenced by Hebrew and some Slavic languages.

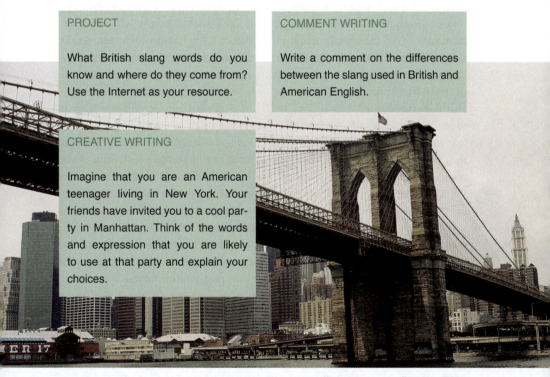

PROJECT

What British slang words do you know and where do they come from? Use the Internet as your resource.

COMMENT WRITING

Write a comment on the differences between the slang used in British and American English.

CREATIVE WRITING

Imagine that you are an American teenager living in New York. Your friends have invited you to a cool party in Manhattan. Think of the words and expression that you are likely to use at that party and explain your choices.

Brooklyn Bridge

 READING COMPREHENSION

African American English

African American English (AAE), also known as 'Ebonics', is an ethnic dialect spoken by the Black population in the United States. For a long time, AAE was considered to be a type of speech inferior to mainstream American English because it does not follow its rules and is thus not "correct". Many statements made about this dialect in the press have frequently been based on a lack of knowledge of language and dialects. The following statement written by the Working Group on African American English at the University of Massachusetts explains how language prejudice may arise and how we can increase language diversity within individuals.

Reducing Language Prejudice

People without linguistic training are seldom aware that they have language prejudices. They commonly make as-
5 sumptions about the inferiority of some dialects, like AAE, and the superiority of others, like British English. They may also draw unfounded connections between "correctness" of standard gram-
10 mar and logic of thought. When they do this, they ignore decades of linguistic research which show us that "standard" English became the standard for historical and political reasons, not because it
15 was better at communicating. That is, the group who speak a particular dialect have achieved power over groups who speak other dialects. It is the *speakers* who have power; the status of the dialect
20 merely reflects the social and economic status of the group using it. People trained in linguistics, unlike lay people, generally consider that all dialects and modes of speech are equal. They are all adequate to communicate any message, 25 at least among people who share the dialect. Even linguists, who are usually non-judgemental though, recognize that some contexts favor the use of a particular variety over another. 30

African-American children learn to speak as well as any children, but *from a model that differs from SAE* [Standard American English] in systematic ways. In order to become competent speakers 35 of AAE, they must internalize very subtle aspects of the language system, with complicated rules governing whether sentences are grammatical or not. The dialect that they are learning serves the 40 same purposes of normal communication, as well as solidarity and in-group communication as other major varieties, like Scottish English or the dialect of southern white speakers. Just as Scottish 45 is most useful within Scotland, AAE is less useful outside the AAE community.

The need for bi-dialectalism

Few people would deny that in 20th century America Standard English is the most useful dialect in the widest number of contexts. It is the language of literacy and power and economic opportunity. Like most African American spokespeople and parents, we feel children should be encouraged to learn SAE, but we favor having children ADD SAE to their repertoire of language competence, not subtract AAE. Like most people who learn a second language or dialect after a "critical age" (generally 5–8 years), AAE speakers of SAE will rarely eliminate all traces of their native dialect while speaking SAE. Therefore, at the same time as we encourage as much bi-dialectalism as possible, we recognize that language prejudice is not diminishing, so every child should also learn to be aware of and minimize his or her own negative judgements of other people based on dialect.

We agree with the educators and language teachers who say that instilling shame about the native dialect is a poor way to teach SAE. After all, no one is asked to disparage English in order to learn French. Likewise, there should be no need to eradicate the child's native dialect in order to add a new dialect. The true debate in Ebonics is, or should be, how best to achieve bi-dialectalism among African American children, in the inspiring tradition of the many African-Americans who have achieved success in America through that path. In John Rickford, a scholar at Stanford's, words, "The student who is led to greater competence in English by systematic contrast with Ebonics can switch between the vernacular and the standard as the situation merits, and as Maya Angelou (see her poem, "The Thirteens") and Martin Luther King and Malcolm X undoubtedly did too, drawing on the power of each in its relevant domain."

[The Working Group on AAE at the University of Massachusetts. #3]

COMPREHENSION

1. Describe how non-professionals think about language and dialects, according to the authors of this statement.
2. Describe how dialects of a particular language should be learnt, in the authors' opinion.

DISCUSSION

1. African American English is also known as 'Black English'. Do you think this is a politically correct term? Explain.
2. Discuss whether it is important for a person to be politically correct towards other people. Give your arguments.
3. How is political correctness looked at in your country? Is it viewed in positive or negative light? Explain.

Taking a final look at
British and American English

Read the short dialogues below and try to figure out what people are talking about.
Pay attention to the words in *italics*.

1. Anna: "Who is that guy standing next to Mark?"
Susanne: "I don't really know him. He doesn't come here very often.
But Mark says he is a real *schmuck*."

What is Mark saying about the guy?
- □   *He is a foolish person.*
- □   *He is always late.*
- □   *He doesn't like girls.*
- □   *He doesn't come from the US.*

2. Anna: "Do you know where exactly Long Beach is?"
Mark: "Oh no, sorry. I have never been to the *Golden State*."

Which US state are Anna and Mark referring to?
- □   *Illinois*
- □   *New York*
- □   *California*
- □   *Texas*

3. Anna: "*Long time no see*. How have you been?"
Susanne: "Fabulous!"

What idea is Anna trying to convey with her opening line?
- □   *That it's been a long time.*
- □   *That she and her friend have not seen each other
  in a really long time.*
- □   *That they are old friends.*
- □   *That time passes quickly.*

4. Chris: "Would you care for some ice cream?"
Steven: "That's a *bloody* good idea!"

What does Steven think about the idea of eating some ice cream?
- ☐ *He thinks it's a very good idea.*
- ☐ *He does not really know what to say.*
- ☐ *He does not like the idea of eating some ice cream.*
- ☐ *He has already had some ice cream.*

5. Mark: "Where did I put my *pants*?"
Peter: "I haven't the slightest idea."

What is Mark looking for?
- ☐ *his glasses*
- ☐ *his piece of clothing*
- ☐ *his underwear*
- ☐ *his plants*

REVISION EXERCISE

Translate the following American English sentences into British English.

1. *Did you have lunch already?*
2. *What are you guys doing here?*
3. *I've gotten your e-mail but haven't had time to answer it.*
4. *She is real nice. I am gonna ask her out on Friday.*
5. *He is a real nice guy.*
6. *I'll start school Monday the 5th.*
7. *The subway system in Hamburg is excellent.*
8. *I was trying to get in touch with you but your line at work was busy. Get a cell phone.*
9. *I will go to the supermarket to get some French fries.*
10. *Jim wanted to study chemistry after finishing high school.*
11. *Every family has a skeleton in their closet.*
12. *I got stuck in the elevator on my way to the office today.*

Sources

TEXTS

[1]   Crystal, David. 2003. *English as a Global Language*. Cambridge: Cambridge University Press, 31–36. © David Crystal, 1997, 2003, published by Cambridge University Press, reproduced with permission.

[2]   Kövecses, Zoltán. 2000. *American English: An Introduction*. Peterborough, Ontario: Broadview Press, 33–34. Copyright © 2000 by Zoltán Kövecses. Reprinted by permission of Broadview Press.

[3]   "UMASS NIH AAE Working Group Position Statement on Ebonics (also known as African American English)." The Working Group on AAE at the University of Massachusetts. <http://www.umass.edu/aae/position_statement_.htm>, December 31, 2011, reproduced with permission.

PICTURES AND FIGURES

Early American settlement history: © Isabel Peters. Hamburg, 2012. Adapted from Crystal 2003: 32.

Dialect Areas of England: Adapted from Trudgill, Peter. 1990. *The Dialects of England*. Oxford: Basil Blackwell, 63. © John Wiley & Sons Ltd. 1990, reproduced with permission.

Brooklyn Bridge: © Isabel Peters. Hamburg, 2011.

REFERENCES AND FURTHER READING

Beal, Joan. 2004. English dialects in the north of England: morphology and syntax. In: Kortmann, Bernd, Kate Burridge, Rajend Mesthrie, Edgar W. Schneider, and Clive Upton (eds.), *A Handbook of Varieties of English*, Vol. 2. *Morphology and Syntax*. Berlin/New York: Mouton de Gruyter, 114–141.

Labov, William. 1998. Co-existent systems in African-American vernacular English. In: Mufwene, Salikoko S., John R. Rickford, Guy Bailey, and John Baugh (eds.), *African-American English. Structure, History, and Use*. London/New York: Routledge, 110–153.

Hazen, Kirk, Paige Butcher, and Ashley King. 2010. Unvernacular Appalachia: an empirical perspective on West Virginia dialect variation. *English Today* 26:4, 13–22.

Kövecses, Zoltán. 2000. *American English: An Introduction*. Peterborough, Ontario: Broadview Press.

Mesthrie, Rajend and Rakesh M. Bhatt. 2008. *World Englishes. The Study of New Linguistic Varieties (Key Topics in Sociolinguistics)*. Cambridge: Cambridge University Press.

Rickford, John R. 1998. The creole origins of African-American vernacular English: evidence from copula absence. In: Mufwene, Salikoko S., John R. Rickford, Guy

Bailey, and John Baugh (eds.), *African-American English. Structure, History, and Use.* London/New York: Routledge, 154–200.

Sebba, Mark. 2004. British Creole: morphology and syntax. In: Bernd Kortmann, Kate Burridge, Rajend Mesthrie, Edgar W. Schneider, and Clive Upton (eds.), *A Handbook of Varieties of English*, Vol. 2. *Morphology and Syntax.* Berlin/New York: Mouton de Gruyter, 196–208.

Trudgill, Peter. 1999. *The Dialects of England.* Oxford/Malden: Blackwell.

Wong, Amy Wing-Mei. 2010. New York City English and second generation Chinese Americans. *English Today* 26:3, 3–11.

[i]   Beal, Joan. 2004. English dialects in the north of England: morphology and syntax. In: Kortmann, Bernd, Kate Burridge, Rajend Mesthrie, Edgar W. Schneider, and Clive Upton (eds.), *A Handbook of Varieties of English*, Vol. 2. *Morphology and Syntax.* Berlin/New York: Mouton de Gruyter, 120, 122.

[ii]   Beal, Joan. 2010. *An Introduction to Regional Englishes.* Edinburgh: Edinburgh University Press, 10–12, 54–62.

[iii]   Pietsch, Lukas. 2005. "Some do and some doesn't": verbal concord variation in the north of the British Isles. In: Kortmann, Bernd, Tanja Herrmann, Lukas Pietsch, and Susanne Wagner. *A Comparative Grammar of British English Dialects. Agreement, Gender, Relative Clauses (Topics in English Linguistics).* Berlin/New York: Mouton de Gruyter, 126, 128, 144.

[iv]   Tagliamonte, Sali A. 2012. *Variationist Sociolinguistics. Change, Observation, Interpretation.* Malden/Oxford: Wiley-Blackwell, 207–216.

[v]   Trudgill, Peter. 1999. *The Dialects of England.* Oxford/Malden: Blackwell, 33, 39–40.

[vi]   Matras, Yaron. "The history of Romani". BBC Voices. <http://www.bbc.co.uk/voices/multilingual/romani_history.shtml#A>, January 27, 2012.

[vii]   Trudgill, Peter. 1999. *The Dialects of England.* Oxford/Malden: Blackwell, 62–64, 68, 70, 76, 79, 80–83, 85, 104–105, 120.

[viii] Sebba, Mark. 2004. British Creole: morphology and syntax. In: Kortmann, Bernd, Kate Burridge, Rajend Mesthrie, Edgar W. Schneider, and Clive Upton (eds.), *A Handbook of Varieties of English*, Vol. 2. *Morphology and Syntax.* Berlin/New York: Mouton de Gruyter, 196.

[ix]   Kövecses, Zoltán. 2000. *American English: An Introduction.* Peterborough, Ontario: Broadview Press, 64–71.

[x]   Wong, Amy Wing-Mei. 2010. New York City English and second generation Chinese Americans. *English Today* 26:3, 5–6.

[xi]   Hazen, Kirk, Paige Butcher, and Ashley King. 2010. Unvernacular Appalachia: an empirical perspective on West Virginia dialect variation. *English Today* 26:4, 13, 16–18.

Inner circle

Chapter 5

Australian English

Introduction

The history of Australian English goes back to the year of 1788, when the first penal colony was established by the British Empire in what is now known as New South Wales. Free, non-convict populations began to arrive in the mid-19th century. As time went by, British settlements expanded to encompass southeastern, northern, and western Australia (Schneider 2007: 118). One of the major consequences of this expansion was the slow but steady decimation of the Aboriginal population through the introduction of alcohol, eviction from their fertile lands, and violence escalating into manslaughter (Schneider 2007: 119). Many Aboriginals were forced to shift to English as their first and only language with the result of many indigenous languages being lost or endangered.

There is little regional variation in Australian English, even though early signs of such developments can be discerned (Trudgill 1986; Schneider 2007). This is remarkable, as Australia is a continent thirty-five times larger than Britain. Even though some Australians perceive clear differences in the use of certain words or lexemes between different regions in Australia, these differences do not result in distinct dialects (Burridge and Kortmann 2004: 548).

There are, however, clearly perceivable accents of Australian English. Spoken by the upper class, Cultivated Australian is very close to Received Pronunciation. General Australian is associated most closely with the middle class population, whereas Broad Australian is linked to the lower socioeconomic strata and speakers from rural areas. The term *wogspeak* refers to ethnolects spoken by the white population from Southern Europe.

Australian Vernacular English is an informal, non-standard type of speech, usually spoken by the working class and those living in the country (Pawley 2004: 611). This form of English, however, is endangered as more and more speakers strive to speak General Australian.

Australian English is perhaps best known for its distinctive pronunciation and vocabulary. The Reading Comprehensions *Coping with Aussie English* and *Learning to speak Aussie English* contain useful information on Australian English words and expressions, followed by exercises on Australianisms. The song *Waltzing Matilda* features some words which are no longer in use, yet unveil important facets of Australian culture. Andrew Denton's interview with Steve Irwin reveals what typical Australian English sounds like. *A quick guide to Australia* provides essential facts about the country and its people, whereas the text *Australian English* offers an academic summary of the topic. The chapter concludes with a mind map.

A quick guide to Australia   [Based on #1, #2, #5 and #i – #xi]

Ayers Rock

What languages do people speak?

Well, as you might have already guessed, English is the national language of Australia. The English spoken in Australia is clearly one of the most prominent native varieties of English marked by differences in pronunciation and vocabulary. Though, of course, influenced by both British and American English, its grammar and spelling are based on British English. The influence of American English is difficult to ascertain, even though many lay people think that this is a problem.

In 2006, English was spoken as a first language by approximately 80 per cent of the population. Although there used to be between 200 and 300 Australian Aboriginal languages when the first European settlers arrived, many of them have not survived and an Aboriginal language is spoken as a first language only by about 50,000 people, amounting to 0.25 per cent of the population. This means that today more Australians speak Chinese as a first language (2.1 per cent) than a native Australian language.   ● ● ● ● ● ● ● ● ● ●

Aborigines 1

What about the native Australians?

Aborigines 2

Indigenous Australians are often called Aboriginal people. However, they often prefer to be called *Koori*, a native Australian word meaning 'person'.

Remarkable about the native inhabitants of Australia is the sharp contrast between the simple hunter and gatherer lifestyle that they retained for a long time and the tremendous intricacies of their cultural, religious, and social practices. Only very few words of the native Australian languages have made it into Australian English. Not surprisingly, mainly names for places, flora, and fauna (for example, *dingo*) were adopted.

What are wombats and platypuses?

They are only two examples of the huge variety of animals that are unique to Australia. Wombats are rather small animals resembling small bears that carry their young in a pouch on the front of the mother's body.

Platypuses are even more special: Though they are mammals and have a tail like a beaver, they lay eggs and have a flat beak like a duck.

Wombat

• • • • • • • • •

What do *Oz*, *Strine*, *sheila*, and *pollie* mean?

One of the most famous characteristics of Australian English is its use of so-called 'Australianisms', i.e. words and phrases that are only used in Australia or have a special meaning there. A very famous example is the use of the term *sheila* for 'girl'.

Another striking characteristic of Australian English is its tendency to shorten words to one or two syllables: Thus, 'Australia' may be shortened to *Oz* or *Straya*, 'Australian' to *Aussie* or *Ozzie*, 'politician' to *pollie*, and 'afternoon' to *arvo*.

Kangaroo road sign

Map of Australia

EXERCISES

Form groups and assign two of the above boxes to each group member. Describe the content of your boxes to your fellow group members.

1. Discuss the content of the boxes in your groups: What did you already know and what was new? Can you add something? Have you ever been to Australia? Have you ever met anyone from Australia? Have you ever thought of going to Australia one day? What do you think is fascinating about Australia? What places would you like to visit in Australia and what things would you like to see? Can you think of any other words that might be of Aboriginal origin?
2. Record the most important facts from the boxes and your discussion in a mind map.

 READING COMPREHENSION

Coping with Aussie English

by David Cervi and Ruth Wajnryb

Some features of Australian English that may confuse the unwary foreigner.

SOON after arriving to live in Australia, David Cervi was invited to an informal party and was asked to bring a plate.

'Of course,' he replied. 'Is there
5 anything else you're short of – glasses, knives and forks, for example?'

'No', replied his host, 'I've got plenty of dishes. Just bring some food for everyone to share.'

10   David immediately realised that, although as a native speaker he had understood the words, he had misunderstood their meaning. If he had been asked to bring a bottle, he would have
15 immediately understood that this meant a full bottle, most likely of alcohol. But the request to bring a plate was, for him, an unfamiliar way of expressing a familiar **concept**: a party where each
20 guest brings a dish of food for everyone to share – what in North America, for example, is often called a 'pot luck' supper. **Superficially** familiar language had been **transplanted** into a context in
25 which the words were used in an unfamiliar way.

The interaction, though it was **ostensibly monolingual**, bore some resemblance to interactions between native
30 and non-native speakers of a language, where a non-native speaker's lesser degree of **idiomatic** familiarity with a language, as **opposed to** lexical knowledge of it, is the cause of many misunderstandings. […]   35

A laid-back lingo

Perhaps the most **striking feature** of Australian English is its relaxed **informality**. This seems to **reflect** the coun- 40 try's relaxed lifestyle and its people's informal, relatively **egalitarian** relationships. For example, the well-known Australian use of *mate* ('How're you going, mate?') as a form of address 45 between friends is merely a way for a speaker to **put** their listener **at ease**; it **indicates** none of the **disrespect** towards the listener that the word *mate* frequently signals in Britain.   50

Australians often show this informality in speech by using shortened forms of words and names. For example, names of things which are thought to be small or pleasant, friendly or amusing 55 often take a *-y* or *-ie* ending: *mozzie* for mosquito, *footie* for football, even *pollie* for politician, and of course *Aussies* for Australians. Sometimes, words are shortened by using an *-o* ending: *arvo* 60

for afternoon, *lingo* for language and *smoko* for a smoking break. Often, such words ending in *-o* may be disrespectful, for example, *garbo* for garbage collec-
65 tor, *reffo* for a refugee, *weirdo* for an odd or strange person, *blotto* for drunk and *nasho* for **compulsory** national military service.

Another feature of the Australian
70 **vernacular** is the liberal use of vulgar or **profane** language, often with little or no offensive or obscene meaning. In most cases, this appears not to be **gratuitous** profanity, but rather to reflect the lack of
75 **gentility**, the **rugged** character and the low level of education of the early white settlers (**convicts**, **stockmen** and the like) who **contributed to** the shaping of Australian English. It may also be re-
80 garded in part as a reflection of the laid-back and mildly **larrikin** or **subversive** character of the nation. Thus, **expletive epithets** such as 'bloody', 'damn' and even some taboo words, such as 'fuck-
85 ing', have become greatly **devalued in meaning** and are now much less shocking than, for example, in British English. Similarly, the expression 'you bastard', used in non-angry or **jocular** contexts,
90 has even acquired overtones of mateship (affection) and **compassion** (as in 'you poor bastard').

What's in an accent?

95 Visitors to Australia have sometimes complained that Australian English is harder to understand than British or North American varieties of English. Some students are **reluctant** to study English in Australia because they think
100 that they will **acquire** an unusual accent and learn non-standard words and expressions.

Certainly, there *is* an Australian accent. In fact, it has three varieties: *Cul-*
105 *tivated Australian*, *General Australian*, and *Broad Australian*. *Cultivated Australian*, which is not very different from the BBC or Queen's English spoken in southern Britain, is spoken regularly by
110 only a small minority of people. *General Australian*, the variety spoken by over half the population, is a still careful but much more relaxed kind of speech. *Broad Australian* (nicknamed *Strine*), is
115 the most heavily accented variety. Broad Australian, the variety most people immediately recognise as Australian English, is not dissimilar to the Cockney dialect spoken in some parts of Lon-
120 don; this is because many of the earliest white settlers in Australia were convicts and their **jailers**, and came from south-eastern England.

By contrast, however, with Britain
125 or North America, where both the meaning and the pronunciation of words **vary** greatly according to region, the Australian accent in its three varieties is neither region-specific nor class-specific.
130 Whereas in America and especially in Britain, a person's regional origin and educational and/or social status are often easily **detected** by listening to their speech, in Australia, it is almost impos-
135 sible to **generalise about** a person's background in this way: the local *pollie* may sound the same as the local *garbo*.

Aboriginal influence

140 There are many words **embedded in**
Australian English that **derive from**
non-English sources, most notably from
the languages of the **indigenous** people,
the Aborigines. Place names and names
145 of native plants and animals often derive from local languages. Thus, among
names for animals, we have: *kangaroo*,
koala, *wombat*, *brumby* (a wild horse),
galah (a small, pink and grey cockatoo),
150 *barramundi* (a lungfish) and *bunyip* (a
fabulous amphibious monster). Many
of the words that have an Aboriginal
source are quite removed from their par-
ent word, having been taken up origi-
155 nally by white settlers who had not mas-
tered the sounds of the local tongue and
then passed down, quite haphazardly,
until a standard spelling was (often quite
fortuitously) decided upon.
160   What indeed is surprising is that the
Aboriginal influence on the Australian
dialect has been so limited. The reasons
are **two-fold**. Firstly, the white settlers
were simply not interested in the local
165 languages, feeling that their own technological **superiority** meant they had
little to learn from the local language or
culture. Secondly, the **marked** regional
variation of Aboriginal languages meant
170 that taking on any one language would
result in little widespread application
or currency. As a result, there are very
few **etymological** examples in Austral-

ian English that **relate to** or derive from
Aboriginal culture and lifestyle.   175

Some sticky situations

Of course, some Australians' speech
may at times be difficult for unaccus-
tomed listeners to understand, whether 180
they are native or non-native speakers
of English. For example, the sound /ei/
(as in 'pay') can sound rather like /ai/
(as in 'pie'). There is the well known an-
ecdote, most likely **apocryphal**, about 185
an Australian soldier in Vietnam at the
end of the war: when he said that he was
'going home today', his interlocutor understood him to say that he was 'going
home to die'. [...]   190
   Not only pronunciation, but also
choice of words can occasionally cause
confusion. A female linguist friend of
the authors, when living in England,
went into a **stationer's shop** to ask for 195
some *Durex*. In Australia, *Durex* is a
brand name for a make of sticky tape,
and is often used (like *Sellotape* in the
UK) as a **generic name** for the prod-
uct. In Britain, however, *Durex* tape is 200
unknown, and the name *Durex* **signifies**
only the well-known brand of condoms.
The shopkeeper's surprise and the customer's **embarrassment** on discovering
her mistake are not hard to imagine.   205

[David A. Cervi and Ruth Wajnryb
1992. #1; bold face added]

Vocabulary

1. Look up the following words and expressions in a monolingual English diction-ary: cope, unwary, superficially, transplant, ostensibly, opposed to, laid-back, striking, informality, egalitarian, put sb at ease, disrespect, compulsory, profane, gratuitous, gentility, rugged, convict, stockman, larrikin, subversive, expletive, epithet, devalued in meaning, jocular, compassion, reluctant, jailer, embedded in, two-fold, superiority, apocryphal, stationer's shop, generic name, and embar-assment.
2. The following verbs can be used to talk about language. Look them up in a dic-tionary and construct a sentence with each verb: reflect, indicate, contribute to, acquire, vary, detect, generalise about, derive from, and relate to.
3. When talking about language, you may also find the following words helpful. Find out what these words mean: concept, monolingual, idiomatic, feature, ver-nacular, indigenous, marked, etymological, and signify.

COMPREHENSION

1. Identify all reasons given in the text why Australian English is referred to as "a laid-back lingo" and give examples.
2. What is so special about the Australian accent compared to other varieties?
3. Summarise the most important aspects of the Australian English vocabulary as given in the text.

ANALYSIS

1. Which of the unique aspects of Australian English might be most difficult for people who are not used to or familiar with this variety? (Write a minimum of 200–300 words!)
2. "The local *pollie* may sound the same as the local *garbo*." As-sess the extent to which Australian history and the homeland of its early settlers have influenced the way English is spoken there. (Write a minimum of 200–300 words!)

COMPOSITION

1. "Australian English is a very democratic variety of English as it does not pay as much attention to politeness, formality, and social or regional background as other varieties do." Critically discuss this thesis in a comment. (Write a minimum of 200–300 words!)
2. Imagine that you are an Australian student who is on an exchange programme to London. After your first week in school and in your host family, you have discovered that many people have trouble understanding you or seem confused by what you say. Write an e-mail to your friends or family in Australia in which you describe your situation and the problems other people have in understanding you. (Write a minimum of 200–300 words!)

ROLE-PLAYING GAME

Talk show: Australians versus language teachers
1. Form groups of three to four students.
2. Imagine that you are guests on an Australian talk show with the topic "Australian English – progressive, liberal lingo or rude, gruesome gobbledygook?" Now work with your partners and make up a dialogue between an Australian politician, who defends Australian English as part of the nation's identity that also abolishes class barriers, an Australian English teacher, who thinks that the particularities of Australian English should be done away with, as they are not only hard to understand but may also offend other people, and, of course, the host of the show, who tries to mediate between the two positions. Write a minimum of 300 words! Each of the people involved should speak at least six times. The words and phrases in the box below might help you.

relaxed	not offensive	unusual accent
informal	lack of gentility	not class-specific
egalitarian	laid-back	not region-specific
disrespect	subversive	social status
shortened forms	less shocking	affection
liberal	compassion	[...]
vulgar	hard to understand	
obscene	reluctant	

Are you still "Coping with Aussie English"?

Fill in the blanks in the following table and give the appropriate equivalent.

Australian English	British English
larrikin	
	compulsory national military service
	Australian animal with a strong tail and back legs that moves by jumping; the female carries its young in a pocket of skin on the front of its body
	afternoon
footie	
weirdo	
	politician
	mosquito
	Australian
reffo	
	language
brumby	

 READING COMPREHENSION

April 5th 2009 · The Sunday Times

Learning to speak Aussie-English

by Kathy Foley

Before coming to Australia, I had a few worries. Sunburn was a potential concern, as was the fact I had no idea how to tell the deadly poisonous spi-
5 ders from the regular, fly-eating, web-weaving sort. Not once did it occur to me, however, I might have problems understanding the locals or **deciphering** the newspapers. As a veteran Home and
10 Away watcher (1989-1991), I was confident I would be able to comprehend Australians and, indeed, communicate with them.

After all, they speak English, **albeit**
15 with slightly **mangled** vowels, and they use the same words we do, apart from the occasional **"Fair dinkum!"** and **"You flamin' galah!"**. Don't they?

No, actually. They have an entire vo-
20 cabulary unto themselves. Like America and England, Ireland and Australia are nations divided by a common language. I first noticed this when it came to drinking, which says a lot about my **priorities**
25 upon arriving.

In the pub, Aussies don't drink pints. They drink little glasses of beer called, variously, **schooners**, **middies** and **pots**. At home, they drink **tinnies** and **stub-
bies** (small bottles of beer, which are 30 kept cool with **insulated** stubby-hold-ers) or **goon** (wine in a box).

They buy their take-out alcohol in bottle shops and sometimes bring it to the beach in **Eskies** (coolers). By the 35 way, Australia has drive-through bottle shops, which could be a **recession-proof** idea for someone. The drive-through **off-licence** must surely be up there with the **funeral home** in terms of **viability** 40 during a **downturn**.

Strine or Strayan – the language spoken in this great land of Straya – is not limited to **booze**. I've found myself perplexed by the language barrier in all 45 sorts of situations.

In a department store, I hunted in vain for the bedlinen section, where I wanted to buy a **duvet**. Eventually, a shop assistant told me to head for the 50 Manchester department and ask for a doona. Key to becoming a fluent Strine speaker is the awareness that Aussies can't be bothered sounding out words of more than two syllables. Relations are rellos and ambulance drivers are ambos. Both referees and refugees are reffos, which may lead to some confusion at footy matches. Those often take place in the arvo. Petrol stations are servos, an uncoordinated person is unco and binmen are garbos.

While these abbreviations are slang, they are used regularly in newspapers and magazines, as are all sorts of other words peculiar to Australia. I've learnt, for example, that diggers are soldiers, ockers are **louts** and bogans are, well, **skangers**. In an article about the nude photos of politician Pauline Hanson, the word r**ting was used, replete with asterisks. It dawned on me the missing letters were oo and I made a mental note not to tell anyone I was rooting for the Sydney Swans in footy games. Instead, I'll barrack for them because that's what people do here.

Some Australian words and expressions are only useful in this country. If you bumped into someone on Grafton Street and told them you were **mad as a cut snake**, they would just look at you like you **had a kangaroo loose in the top paddock**. But there are a few words of Strine I think would be **apposite** in Ireland these days.

Rort: To **misappropriate** public money or resources, to fiddle the system (usually used of politicians). Yup, they've been rorting us for years and now we have a word for it.

Wowser: An annoyingly **pious** person with strong moral views. You know that **insufferable**, holier-than-thou colleague who is forever **pontificating** about how all the **feckless** Celtic tiger-era **spendthrifts** deserve their **ignominious downfall**? Total wowser.

Retrenched: **Laid off**. The problem with "laid off" is that it doesn't **convey** the **stomach-churning** horror of losing your job. Being retrenched suggests a struggle to stay alive in a swampy **trench**, with bullets whizzing overhead. Much more appropriate.

Bludger: Chronically unemployed person on social welfare by choice. Irish bludgers are currently **aghast** at the numbers of retrenched people joining the queues and causing delays at the dole office.

Battler: Someone who struggles by on very little, but never gives up. Calling someone a battler is the great Aussie compliment and should probably become the great Irish compliment over the next few months and years. […]

Have the shits: **Be in a foul temper**. I learnt this one when an Aussie friend announced grumpily he had the shits and then looked puzzled when I offered him Imodium. If you don't have the shits by now about the spectacular mismanagement of Ireland Inc, there's no saving you. And that's fair dinkum.

[From *The Sunday Times* (Dublin) April 05, 2009. © *The Sunday Times* / NI Syndication. #2; bold face added.]

Vocabulary

1. Look up the following words and expressions in a monolingual English dictionary: decipher, albeit, mangled, fair dinkum, flamin' galah, priority, schooner,
   insulated, recession-proof, off-licence, funeral home, viability, downturn, booze,
   duvet, lout, skanger, apposite, misappropriate, pious, insufferable, pontificate,
   feckless, spendthrift, ignominious, downfall, laid off, convey, stomach-churning,
   trench, aghast, and be in a foul temper.
2. Here is a list of Australian English words and expressions. Look them up in a
   dictionary and explain in your own words what they mean: middy, pot, tinny,
   stubby, goon, esky, Strine, mad as a cut snake, and have a kangaroo loose in
   the top paddock.

COMPREHENSION

1. Summarise the most important differences between Australian
   English and standard English as given in the text. Give examples.
2. "Aussies can't be bothered sounding out words of more than two
   syllables." Explain the result of this tendency and list all examples
   given in the text.

ANALYSIS

1. Take a look at lines 78–84: Examine the choice of
   words in this section and discuss the effect the author
   wishes to achieve.
2. Analyse the general style of this article and assess the
   extent to which it demonstrates important characteristics of Australian English.

ROLE-PLAYING GAME: "CLASH OF CULTURES"

Irish meets Aussie: Work with a partner!
Bearing in mind that the article above was published in an Irish newspaper and written by an Irish author, think of a situation of your choice
and make up a dialogue in which you illustrate the difficulties an Irish
person might have in understanding an Aussie and vice versa. The
words and phrases given in the text may help you with this task. You
may also refer to what you have learnt about Irish English. (Write a
minimum of 200–300 words!)

COMPOSITION

1. "Like America and England, Ireland and Australia are nations divided by a
   common language." Explain what is meant by this statement and discuss the
   extent to which you agree with it. (Write a minimum of 200–300 words!)
2. Discuss answers to the following question in a comment: In what way can
   the author's point of view be seen as typically Irish, and to what extent do her
   statements concerning the difficulty of understanding Australian English apply to both other native speakers of English and learners of English? (Write a
   minimum of 200–300 words!)

LEARNING TO SPEAK AUSSIE-ENGLISH
REPETITION EXERCISE: AUSTRALIANISMS MEMORY

Take a look at the memory cards given below. Work with a partner and try to find the matching pairs. Write down the correct pairs.

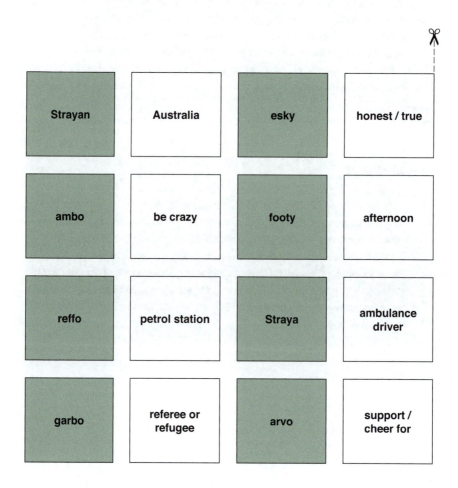

Strayan	Australia	esky	honest / true
ambo	be crazy	footy	afternoon
reffo	petrol station	Straya	ambulance driver
garbo	referee or refugee	arvo	support / cheer for

fair dinkum	very angry	have a kangaroo loose in the top paddock	binman
Strine	cool box	barrack	football
servo	relation	mad as a cut Snake	Australian English
rello	Australian		

LEARNING TO SPEAK AUSSIE-ENGLISH
REPETITION EXERCISE: VOCABULARY MEMORY

Take a look at the memory cards given below. Work with a partner and try to find the matching pairs. Write down the correct pairs.

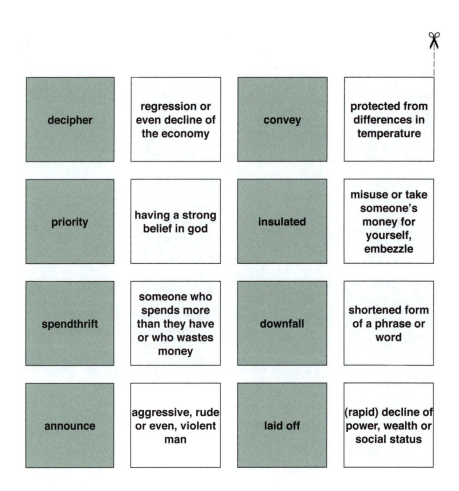

downturn	something more important compared to other things	misappropriate	find out the meaning of sth difficult or a code
fluent	losing one's job, getting fired	abbreviation	difficult to tolerate or bear, very annoying
insufferable	make sth known, communicate sth	lout	speaking, writing, and reading a foreign language well
grumpy	make sth public	pious	easily to annoy, unhappy, peevishly

VOCABULARY EXERCISE

Australianisms   [Based on #viii – #xi]

Australian English is famous for its use of Australianisms. These are words or phrases that are either used exclusively in Australia or have a special meaning there.
There are several strategies to form these Australianisms. Examples of the five most
frequent sources of Australianisms are given in the table below:

Australian English	Standard English
postie	postman
never never	inland Australia / desert areas / the Outback
rage	party
coldy	a (cold) beer
dingo	an Australian wild dog; an unreliable person or cowardly person
to be mad as a cut snake	to be furious, outraged, extremely angry
doco	documentary
evo	evening
greenie	member of the green party; conservationist, environmentalist
to be in full feather	to be fit as a fiddle or simply to be in good health
putt-putt	a small car
shout	a round of drinks in a bar
bizzo	business
woop woop	a very remote place / area / village / town

veggies	vegetables
unit	accommodation, usually a flat, suite or apartment
sunnies	sunglasses
smoko	a short break / a cigarette break
safe	storage container for food
arvo	afternoon
num-nums	delicious / good food
tea	supper
wombat	a distinctly Australian mammal; wordplay used as a term for egoistic men, i.e. someone who eats, roots (Australian English verb for having sexual intercourse) and leaves

EXERCISES

1. Form small groups of two to four people.
2. Try to identify the five different categories (i.e. strategies for forming Australianisms) represented in the table, explain how they are formed, and try to assign each of the words and phrases given in the table above to one of the five categories.
3. For each of the categories, discuss and explain why it might be difficult to understand these Australianisms not only for learners of English but also for all other English speakers outside of Australia.

 HOMEWORK

Discuss which of these categories of Australianisms might be hardest to understand. Give reasons for your opinion and provide examples supporting your point of view. (Write a minimum of 300 words!)

 LISTENING COMPREHENSION

Waltzing Matilda

Waltzing Matilda is probably one of Australia's most famous folk songs. It has even been called Australia's "unofficial national anthem" by the National Library of Australia. Its exact origin is unknown, but it was probably written by the Australian poet Banjo Paterson in 1895.

Sheep

Waltzing Matilda is an Australian slang expression meaning "to travel or wander with one's possessions in a bag or bundle (Matilda) on one's back". The song is about a wandering day labourer stealing a sheep for food. However, when the farmer arrives with the police to arrest the thief, he drowns himself in a nearby pond. The lyrics contain many distinctly Australian English words. [Based on #xii]

Look for the song on the Internet and listen to it.

Waltzing Matilda *by Banjo Paterson* [#3]

Oh there once was a swagman camped in the billabong,
Under the shade of a Coolibah tree,
And he sang as he looked at the old billy boiling,
Who'll come a'waltzing Matilda with me.

Who'll come a'waltzing Matilda my darling,
Who'll come a'waltzing Matilda with me,
Waltzing Matilda and leading a waterbag,
Who'll come a'waltzing Matilda with me.

Down came a jumbuck to drink at the billabong,
Up jumped the swagman and grabbed him with **glee**,
And he said as he put him away in the tucker bag,

"You'll come a'waltzing Matilda with me."
You'll come a'waltzing Matilda my darling,
Who'll come a'waltzing Matilda with me,
Waltzing Matilda and leading a waterbag,
Who'll come a'waltzing Matilda with me.

Down came the squatter a'riding his **thoroughbred**,
Down came policemen, one, two and three,
"Whose is the jumbuck you've got in the tuckerbag?
You'll come a'waltzing Matilda with me."

Chorus: You'll come …

But the swagman he up and he jumped in the water-hole,
Drowning himself by the coolibah tree,
And his ghost may be heard as it sings by the billabong,
Who'll come a'waltzing Matilda with me.

Chorus: Who'll come …

Vocabulary
Look up the words in bold face in a monolingual English dictionary.

ANALYSIS

1. *Waltzing Matilda* contains several typical Australian English words. With the help of the information given on the previous page and the lyrics of the song, try to give the standard English explanation or equivalent of these words and insert them into the table below.

Billabong

Australian English	British English
swagman	
waltzing	
Matilda	
billabong	
jumbuck	
tucker bag	
billy	
squatter	

2. Some of these typical Australian words are hardly used anymore outside of this song. Which ones do you think these are? Why? Give reasons. Have you ever seen any of these words before? Where? In which contexts?

COMPOSITION

1. Why do you think this song is often called the "unofficial national anthem of Australia"? What is so typically Australian about it? Discuss answers to these questions in a comment. (Write a minimum of 200–300 words!)
2. Discuss how a song can be a good medium to convey or represent the characteristics of a certain culture or country. (Write a minimum of 200–300 words!)

VIEWING AND READING COMPREHENSION

Andrew Denton interviews Steve Irwin

The following transcript is taken from an episode of the Australian talk show *Enough Rope*, which was hosted by the Australian comedian and media personality Andrew Denton. In this episode, which was broadcast on October 6, 2003, Andrew Denton talks to another very famous Australian, the conservationist, television personality, and wildlife expert Steve Irwin.

    This excerpt not only allows for interesting insights into the personal life and background of Steve Irwin, but also illustrates some of the most interesting aspects of Australian English pronunciation. Watch the video on YouTube by searching for "Steve Irwin Enough Rope Part 1".

> **INFO**
>
> Stephen Irwin (1962–2006) was an Australian wildlife conservationist and television personality. He became world-famous as the host of the television series *The Crocodile Hunter,* a wildlife documentary programme in which he usually presented and fearlessly approached dangerous and endangered species. He died in 2006 after being fatally pierced by a stingray barb while filming in Australia's Great Barrier Reef. [Based on #xiii]

[…]

Andrew: Steve Irwin …

Steve: Yes?

Andrew: … I'm looking forward to this, it'll be fun.

5 Steve: It will be. I'm on fire, mate. Let's get into it.

Andrew: We're already at the red level for energy and haven't got to the first question. The Australia Zoo, which is now Steve Irwin

10   Central on the Sunshine Coast …

Steve: Yeah, mate, that's where my heart beats from.

Andrew: This was started by your mum and dad …

15 Steve: Yeah.

Andrew: … back in the '70s. And it was hard, wasn't it? It was so hard sometimes, your mum would cry. What was so tough?

> **INFO**
>
> Andrew Denton (*1960) is an award-winning Australian comedian, television presenter, and producer. He hosted the ABC show *Enough Rope* from 2003–2008, which was a major success in Australia. [Based on #xiv]

Steve:	Well, mate, it was 1970 and, um, Dad was a **plumber** – really **well-to-do**

Steve: Well, mate, it was 1970 and, um, Dad was a **plumber** – really **well-to-do** plumber – he did really well in Melbourne. But he gave it all away to fol- 20 low his passion – reptiles. And Mum was a **maternity nurse** who actually wanted to follow her passion, which was **joey** kangaroos and **koalas** and **wombats** and **platypus** – raising them – you know, they're getting hit by cars all the time. So, together, they started the Beerwah Reptile Park in 1970. And it was tough times. We were on the main highway – like, the 25 Bruce Highway – but, um, it was the Beerwah Reptile Park. And at that stage, snakes were something you hit with a stick, you know, crocodiles were just evil, ugly monsters that killed people and koalas and kangaroos made, you know, great, um, fur coats.

Andrew: Yeah. 30

Steve: So it was hard times, mate.

Andrew: They weren't a bad barbecue either.

Steve: Ohhh!

Steve: Lucky enough, we're kind of … we're putting our foot on that kind of attitude, but, um … 35

Andrew: No, that was wrong, people.

Steve: And it was, yeah, tourism … Exactly. And I'm bigger than you, mate.

Andrew: Yeah.

Steve: Hey, um, tourism … Just kidding. Steady.

Andrew: This could be bad if you wrestle me to the ground … 40

Steve: Should we do that?

Audience: Yeah!

Steve: Yeah? Alright!

CHEERING AND APPLAUSE

Andrew: Tell you what … 45

Steve: (Laughs)

Andrew: … let's get a bit further in and we'll see how we go, alright?

Steve: Yeah.

Andrew: Because I want to oil up first …

Steve: (Laughs) Seriously, tourism, was, you know, it was in its **infancy** back 50 then and it was so tough that Dad had to go fishing on the sideline, he had to grow strawberries and **capsicums** to actually support, um, his … his passion, which was his wildlife **facility**.

Andrew: You grew up with the animals. They were your playmates.

Steve: Absolutely. Absolutely, Andrew. In my house, when I was growing up, 55 Mum would have 12, uh, **pouches**, you know, **make-believe** kangaroo pouches set up on the backs of chairs, virtually everywhere. So we'd have 12 little joeys, ranging from little **pinkies** all the way up to one-year-olds.

Um, you know, koalas hanging off the curtains, you know, with **gum-**
60   **leaves** stuck in there, **sugar gliders** gliding through. Like, you'd be walk-
ing down through the house … (To cameraman) Stay with me, mate …
the next minute, clack, you know, on your bare back you'd be … a pos-
sum – arggh! – ripped into you. And, of course, inside the house was just
snakesville.

65 Andrew: Really?

     Steve: Oh, crikey, mate! **Chock-a-block** full of snakes. Every wall that was
spare had snakes in it. You know, starting a reptile park, which then
became a **fauna sanctuary**, it was like, whatever you could **jam** in the
house, mate, 'cause everything needed to be close to your heart. […]

PRE-WATCHING ACTIVITIES

1. Carefully read through the transcript and familiarise yourself with the words
   in bold face (see the Vocabulary section below).
2. Can you find any non-standard features in the transcript?
3. Underline all instances of the following words in the transcript: mate, 1970,
   reptile, time, highway, kind, sideline, wildlife, my, house, pouch, glide, and
   crikey.

WHILE-WATCHING ACTIVITY

1. While listening to the interview at least two times, mark those letters and
   sounds in the transcripts which are pronounced differently than in standard
   English. Also try to describe how or in what way they differ when they are
   pronounced by Steve. Your underlined words will help you.

POST-WATCHING ACTIVITIES

1. Try to organise the notes you made while listening to the interview. Can you find any regularities or identify any Australian English pronunciation rules?
2. What else did you find notable about the interview and the style of speech? Discuss answers to this question with a partner and take notes.
3. Take a look at the following words: buy, late, mate, bay, mail, and fate. Which problems might come up when these words are pronounced by an Australian? Discuss with a partner.

COMPOSITION

1. Take a look at the results you have obtained so far and discuss why it might be very hard, especially for learners of English, to understand speakers of Australian English. (Write a minimum of 200–300 words!)
2. Do you think Steve's strong accent had a positive or rather a negative impact on his international career? Discuss this question critically in a comment and give reasons for your opinion. (Write a minimum of 200–300 words!)
3. Discuss whether Steve Irwin's appearance and attitude can be considered typically or only stereotypically Australian. Discuss the effects his behaviour, appearance, and way of speaking might have had on the way Australians and Australian English are perceived in the world. (Write a minimum of 200–300 words!)

Vocabulary

1. Look up the following words and expressions in a monolingual English dictionary: plumber, well-to-do, maternity nurse, infancy, capsicum, facility, pouch, make-believe, gumleaves, chock-a-block, spare, fauna, sanctuary, and jam.
2. The following words are used to describe Australian animals. Find out what these words mean and describe these animals in your own words: joey, koala, wombat, platypus, pinkie, and sugar glider.

 READING COMPREHENSION

Group work: Australian English

Carefully read through the text and the vocabulary. Form five groups and assign one of the question boxes following the text to each group.

While presenting your answers to one another, note the most important facts in a mind map called 'The major characteristics of Australian English'. You can find a template on page 148.

The English language as used in Australia […] has a short history, reflecting some 200 years of European settlement, and an even shorter period of **recogni-** [5] **tion** as a national variety, the term [Australian English (=AusE)] being first recorded in 1940. It is only since then that **features** of AusE have been regarded as distinctively and respectably Austral- [10] ian, instead of as evidence of colonial **decline** from the norms of the STANDARD ENGLISH of England.

Background. Initially, and uniquely, a majority of the British colonies in [15] Australia were penal. As they expanded and as free colonies were developed, immigrants using languages other than English were **insignificant**. Relations with the Aborigines were generally poor [20] and after an initial intake of words from their languages (such as *boomerang*, *dingo*, *kangaroo*, *koala*, *kookaburra*, *wombat*) were not **conducive** to **extensive borrowing**. The settlers were al- [25] most all Anglo-Celtic and geographical isolation was of great importance. The **preoccupations** of the colonists were the discovery and exploration of a new land, rich in exotic flora and fauna, and **pastoral** occupations such as raising [30] sheep and cattle under circumstances vastly different from 'the Old Country'. In the late 20c, however, Australians are **predominantly** urban and increasingly multicultural. The major areas of lexical [35] growth are international, as in computing and surfing. In the 19c, the situation was reverse.

Pronunciation. The most **marked feature** of the Australian accent is its [40] **homogeneity**, with no regional differences as marked as those in BrE and AmE, though recent studies have associated particular phonological characteristics with state capitals. There is, [45] however, a **social continuum** in which three varieties are generally recognized: *Broad Australian*, *General Australian*, and *Cultivated Australian*. Of these, Cultivated Australian most closely ap- [50] proaches British **RP** and Broad Australian most **vigorously** exhibits distinctive regional features. It is generally assumed that the Australian accent derives from the mixing of British and Irish accents in the early years of settlement. However, although most convicts and other settlers came from London, the Midlands, and Ireland, the influence of the original accents cannot be **conclusively quantified**. The present spectrum was probably established by the early 19c.

The major features of AusE pronunciation are: (1) It is **non-rhotic**. (2) Its **intonation** is flatter than that of RP. (3) Speech rhythms are slow, **stress** being more evenly spaced than in RP. (4) Consonants do not differ significantly from those in RP. (5) Vowels are in general closer and more frontal than in RP, with /i/ and /u/ as in *tea*, *two* **diphthongized** to /əi/ and /əʊ/ respectively. (6) The vowel in *can't dance* may be /æ/ or /a/. (7) The **schwa** is busier than in RP, frequently replacing /ɪ/ in unaccented positions, as in *boxes*, *dances*, *darkest*, *velvet*, *acid*. (8) Some **diphthongs** shift, RP /eɪ/ towards /ʌɪ/, as in *Australia*, *day*, *mate*, and /aɪ/ towards /ɒɪ/, as in *high*, *wide*. (9) Speakers whose first language is not English or who have a **bilingual background** (Aboriginal, immigrant) often use sounds and a delivery influenced by the patterns of the first or other language. (10) The name of the letter *h* is often pronounced 'haitch' by speakers wholly or partly of Irish-Catholic background.

Grammar and vocabulary. There are no **syntactic** features that distinguish standard AusE from standard BrE, or indeed any major non-standard features not also found in Britain, but there are many distinctive words and phrases. However, although AusE has added some 10,000 items to the language, few have become internationally active. The largest demand for new words has concerned flora and fauna, and predominant occupations like stock-raising have also required new terms. Because of this, AUSTRALIANISMS are predominantly naming words: single nouns (*mulga* an acacia, *mullock* mining refuse, *muster* a round-up of livestock), **compounds** (*black camp* an Aboriginal settlement, *black tracker* an Aboriginal employed by the police to track down missing persons, *black velvet* Aboriginal women as sexual objects, *red-back* a spider, *redfin* a fish, *red gum* a eucalypt), nouns used attributively (*convict colony* a penal colony, *convict servant* or *convict slave* a convict assigned as a servant).

The penal settlements. The first settlements were penal colonies and until 1868, when transportation **ceased**, a vocabulary similar to that in a slave society described the life of the convicts. A major distinction was maintained between *bond* and *free*, as in *free emigrant*, *free native*, *free labourer*, *free servant*, and the distinction between *free* and *freed*. The settlements were populated in part by convicts and the attendant military forces, in part by free settlers. Though convicts who had served their sentences or **obtained pardons** (known from 1822 as *emancipists*) became *free* in their own eyes and those of the law, they often had difficulty escaping the **stigma** of **servitude** and obtained only a measure of freedom, being known by the *exclusives* or *exclusionists* as *free convicts* or freed men.

Stock-raising. Concomitantly, the land was explored and opened up for settlement and the stock-raising industry was developing. *Squatters* (stock-raisers or *graziers* occupying large tracts of Crown land under lease or licence) moved inland from the *limits of location* (the frontier of settlement) into the *back country* or *back of beyond* in search of land suitable for *runs* (tracts of grazing land) or *stations* (ranches). They looked for *open* land (free from forest or undergrowth), seeking *open forest* or *open plains*, and using words like *brush* (dense natural vegetation), *bush* (the distinctive Australian natural vegetation), *mallee* or *mulga* (forms of natural vegetation giving their name to their habitat), and *scrub* (generally, poor vegetation) to describe features of an unfamiliar environment. The stock industry employed *overseers* or *superintendents* (both convict terms), *stockmen*, and *rouseabouts* (general hands). *Drovers* travelled stock long distances *overland*, the original *overlanders* driving stock from New South Wales to South Australia. The importance of sheep in opening up the country and establishing a frontier society was such that the occupational vocabularies of droving and shearing figure largely in Australian literature.

The goldfields. Gold was discovered in the 1850s, leading to movement between the Californian, Australian, and New Zealand goldfields. *Rushes* (first used of the sudden escape of a number of convicts and then of the sudden movement of a number of miners to a particular place or *goldfield*) followed when a *prospector* (*gold-finder*, *gold-hunter*, *gold-seeker*) made a *find* and established a *claim*. A number of mining terms originated in Australia, but many are shared with other varieties of English, and the importance of the discovery of gold, and of the rushes that followed, lies in the mobility it encouraged and the effect of this on the homogeneity of the accent.

Colloquialisms. A growing sense of national identity was fostered by involvement in the First World War. The line between formal and informal usage is perhaps less rigidly drawn in Australia than elsewhere, colloquialisms being more generally **admissible** than in Britain. In informal usage, the **suffixes** *-ie* or *-y* and *-o* or *-oh* are freely attached to short base words (*roughie* a trick, *tinnie* a can of beer, *bottle-oh* a bottle merchant, *plonko* an addict of *plonk* or cheap wine, *smoko* a work break) and **clippings** (*Aussie* an Australian, *arvo* an afternoon, *barbie* a barbecue, *Chrissy* Christmas, *compo* workers' compensation, *derro* a derelict or down-and-out, *reffo* a refugee).

Kinds of Australianisms. In terms of **origin** and structure, Australianisms fall into six categories: (1) Words from Aboriginal languages: *boomerang* a throwing weapon, *corroboree* a ceremonial dance, *jackeroo* a trainee farm manager, *kangaroo* a large **hopping marsupial**, *kookaburra* a kind of bird,

wombat a **burrowing marsupial**. (2)
Extensions of pre-existing senses: *bush*
215 natural vegetation, or rural as opposed
to urban life, *station* a garrison, colonial
outpost, tract of grazing land, ranch. (3)
Novel compounds: *bushman* someone
skilled in traversing the bush, *bush-*
220 *ranger* an armed bandit; *convict over-*
seer a convict appointed to supervise
other convicts, *convict police* convicts
appointed as police; *cattle/sheep station*
station for raising cattle or sheep, *station*
225 *black* an Aboriginal employed on a station; *stock agent* someone buying and
selling livestock, *stockman* someone
employed to tend livestock. (4) Novel
fixed phrases: *black bream*, *black swan*;
230 *colonial ale*, *colonial tobacco*; *native*
plum, *native potato*; *red ash*, *red cedar*;
white box, *white cockatoo*; *wild banana*,
wild spinach. (5) **Coinage**: *emancipist* a
freed convict, *go slow* a form of indus-
235 trial protest in which employees work to
rule (now international), *woop-woops*
remote country. (6) Words with greater
currency in Australia than elsewhere include new applications of words from
240 British regional dialects: *dinkum* reli-
able, genuine, *dunny* a privy, *larrikin* a
hooligan, *wowser* a killjoy.

Style and usage. **By and large**,
printed English is much the same as
245 elsewhere. [...] Where BrE and AmE
spelling norms differ, BrE is preferred:
honour, but *Labor* the name of the political party, *centre*, *licence*. The *-ise* spelling, as in *realise*, is generally preferred
250 to *-ize*.

Strine and stereotyping. Australian
usage has attracted comic stereotyping.

The term *STRINE* refers to a kind of stage
Australian in which vowels are **distort-**
ed and **syllables** reduced, as in *strine* 255
itself, **collapsing** the four syllables of
Australian to one, and in *Emma Chisit*,
a joke name **derived from** *How much*
is it? [...]

Social issues. Until recently, Aus- 260
tralia was determinedly assimilationist.
Although immigrant languages, such
as Greek and Italian are now accorded
the status of *community languages*, and
bilingualism is actively encouraged by 265
the government, the impact of these
languages on AusE has been negligible.
Two issues currently dominate the linguistic scene:

Multiculturalism. The arrival of im- 270
migrants (locally known as *migrants*)
is slowly **converting** a **homogeneous**
Anglo-Celtic society into a **multilin-**
gual, multicultural society that is more
or less tolerant of difference. A recent 275
development has been the publication of
a *National Policy on Languages* (J. Lo
Bianco. 1987), a report commissioned
by the Commonwealth Department of
Education in 1986, a key document for 280
federal and state initiatives to improve
the teaching of English as a first and a
second language, **promote bilingual-**
ism, especially in those whose only
language is English, and preserve and 285
foster the teaching of **community lan-**
guages, including Aboriginal languages.
Important also has been the increased
prominence of ABORIGINAL ENGLISH within the spectrum accessible to the average 290
Australian.

American, British, and New Zealand influence. Despite a new-found sense of independence (including the export of Australian films and television series), AusE is subject to the **media-borne influences** of BrE and AmE. By and large, because of traditional ties, there is less resistance to BrE than to AmE, particularly in pronunciation and spelling. Although it is 1,200 miles away, New Zealand is considered to be a close geographical, cultural, and linguistic neighbour. The constant movement of labour between the two countries **ensures** continuing exchange and sharing of features with NZE [New Zealand English].

[Tom McArthur and Roshan McArthur 2005: 53–55. #5; bold face added]

Vocabulary

1. Look up the following words and expressions in a monolingual English dictionary: recognition, feature, decline, insignificant, conducive, preoccupation, pastoral, predominantly, homogeneity, vigorously, conclusively, quantify, cease, obtain pardons, servitude, admissible, origin, (hopping or burrowing) marsupial, extension, by and large, distorted, collapse, derive from, convert, homogenous, foster, media-borne influence, and ensure.

2. Explain in your own words what the following linguistic terms and expressions mean or refer to. Consult a monolingual English dictionary if necessary: extensive borrowing, marked feature, social continuum, RP, non-rhotic, intonation, stress, diphthongize, schwa, diphthong, bilingual background, syntactic, compound, stigma, colloquialism, suffix, clipping, coinage, syllable, multilingual, promote bilingualism, and community language.

AUSTRALIAN ENGLISH: GROUP 1 (LL. 1–38)
Historical background of Australian English

1. For how long has English been spoken in Australia and for how long has Australian English been recognised as a variety of its own?
2. Assess the influence of other languages on the English spoken in the early colonial period of Australia.
3. Explain how Australian society has changed from the beginnings of European settlement to the present day.

AUSTRALIAN ENGLISH: GROUP 2 (LL. 39–88)

Australian English pronunciation

1. To what extent is Australian English different from / similar to British English in terms of social and regional variation?
2. Name and briefly explain the varieties of English typically distinguished in Australia as given in the text. Do you know any other varieties of English spoken in Australia?
3. Summarise and explain the major features of Australian English pronunciation as given in the text.

AUSTRALIAN ENGLISH: GROUP 3 (LL. 89–186)

Australian English grammar and vocabulary

1. What is unique about Australian English compared to other varieties of English / compared to British English?
2. Why has Australian English added so many new words to the English lexicon? How is this reflected in the kinds of words added to the lexicon by Australian speakers of English?
3. Why are penal settlements, stock-raising, and gold-mining so important for the history of Australia in general and Australian English in particular?

AUSTRALIAN ENGLISH: GROUP 4 (LL. 187–242)

Australian English colloquialisms and Australianisms

1. What can you say about Australian English in terms of formal and informal language use? Can you give examples?
2. Why are the suffixes -*ie*, -*y*, and -*o* so important in Australian English?
3. What are the six groups of Australianisms distinguished in the text? How are they formed? Give examples.

AUSTRALIAN ENGLISH: GROUP 5 (LL. 243–308)

Australian English style and usage

1. Which features of Australian English give rise to stereotyping and parody? Can you give examples?
2. Why and how has Australian society changed within the last decades?
3. To what extent is Australian English influenced by American, British, and New Zealand English? How do these varieties influence each other? Explain.

Mind map: The major characteristics of Australian English

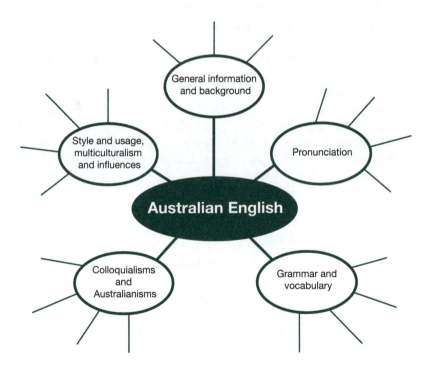

Sources

TEXTS

[1]   Cervi, David A. and Ruth Wajnryb. 1992. Coping with Aussie English. *English Today* 8:2, 18–21. © Cambridge University Press, reproduced with permission.

[2]   Foley, Kathy. 2009. "Learning to speak Aussie English". *The Sunday Times* [Dublin], April 05, 2009. <http://journalist.ie/2009/11/sunday-times-learning-to-speak-aussie-english/>, October 24, 2011. Reproduced with permission of *The Sunday Times* / NI Syndication.

[3]   Paterson, Banjo. 1895. "Waltzing Matilda". <http://en.wikisource.org/wiki/Waltzing_ Matilda_-_Unofficial_Anthem> (Public Domain), October 24, 2011.

[4]   Transcript of the ABC show *Enough Rope* with Andrew Denton and Steve Irwin, broadcast October 06, 2003. <http://www.abc.net.au/tv/enoughrope/transcripts/s960998. htm>, October 24, 2011. *Enough Rope* on the 6 October 2003 is reproduced by permission of the Australian Broadcasting Corporation and Zapruders Other Films Pty Ltd. © 2003. All rights reserved.

[5]   McArthur, Tom and Roshan McArthur (eds.). 2005. Australian English. In: *Concise Oxford Companion to the English Language*. Oxford: Oxford University Press, 53–55. © By permission of Oxford University Press.

PICTURES AND FIGURES

Ayers Rock: <http://commons.wikimedia.org/wiki/File:Ayers_Rock_-_Kuniya_walk_%28Rock_ climbing%29.jpg> (Public Domain), April 15, 2011.

Aborigines 1 (Drawing): <http://en.wikipedia.org/wiki/File:Indig2.jpg> (Public Domain), April 18, 2011.

Aborigines 2 (Photo): <http://en.wikipedia.org/wiki/File:Bathurst_Island_men.jpg> (Public Domain), April 17, 2011.

Wombat: <http://commons.wikimedia.org/wiki/File:Australia-wombat.jpg> (Creative Commons Attribution-ShareAlike 3.0), April 16, 2011.

Map of Australia: © Isabel Peters. Hamburg, 2011.

Kangaroo road sign: <http://en.wikipedia.org/wiki/File:Kangaroo_Warning_Sign.svg> (Public Domain), April 16, 2011.

Sheep: <http://en.wikipedia.org/wiki/File:Sheep_drenching.JPG> (Creative Commons Attribution-ShareAlike 3.0), July 16, 2009.

Billabong: <http://en.wikipedia.org/wiki/File:Billabong_-FWS.jpg> (Public Domain), April 11, 2012.

REFERENCES AND FURTHER READING

Burridge, Kate and Bernd Kortmann. 2004. Introduction: varieties of English in the Pacific and Australia. In: Kortmann, Bernd, Kate Burridge, Rajend Mesthrie, Edgar W. Schneider, and Clive Upton (eds.), *A Handbook of Varieties of English*, Vol. 2. *Morphology and Syntax*. Berlin/New York: Mouton de Gruyter, 547–559.

Collins, Peter and Pam Peters. 2008. Australian English: morphology and syntax. In: Burridge, Kate and Bernd Kortmann (eds.), *Varieties of English*, Vol. 3. *The Pacific and Australasia*. Berlin/New York: Mouton de Gruyter, 341–361.

Horvarth, Barbara M. 2008. Australian English: phonology. In: Burridge, Kate and Bernd Kortmann (eds.), *Varieties of English*, Vol. 3. *The Pacific and Australasia*. Berlin/New York: Mouton de Gruyter, 89–110.

Pawley, Andrew. 2008. Australian Vernacular English: some grammatical characteristics. In: Burridge, Kate and Bernd Kortmann (eds.), *Varieties of English*, Vol. 3. *The Pacific and Australasia*. Berlin/New York: Mouton de Gruyter, 362–397.

Schneider, Edgar W. 2007. *Postcolonial English. Varieties around the World*. Cambridge: Cambridge University Press, 118–127.

[i]   "Australia." The World Factbook. Central Intelligence Agency, 2011. <https://www.cia. gov/library/publications/the-world-factbook/geos/as.html>, September 22, 2011.

[ii]   "Australian Aboriginal languages." Encyclopædia Britannica. Encyclopædia Britannica Online Academic Edition. Encyclopædia Britannica, 2011. <http://www.britannica. com/EBchecked/topic/43873/Australian-Aboriginal-languages>, September 22, 2011.

[iii] "Australia." Encyclopædia Britannica. Encyclopædia Britannica Online Academic Edition. Encyclopædia Britannica, 2011. <http://www.britannica.com/EBchecked/ topic/43654/Australia>, September 12, 2011.

[iv]   "English language." Encyclopædia Britannica. Encyclopædia Britannica Online Academic Edition. Encyclopædia Britannica, 2011. <http://www.britannica.com/ EBchecked/topic/188048/English-language>, September 22, 2011.

[v]   "Australian Aborigine." Encyclopædia Britannica. Encyclopædia Britannica Online Academic Edition. Encyclopædia Britannica, 2011. <http://www.britannica.com/ EBchecked/topic/43876/Australian-Aborigine>, September 12, 2011.

[vi]   "Wombat." Encyclopædia Britannica. Encyclopædia Britannica Online Academic Edition. Encyclopædia Britannica Inc., 2012. <http://www.britannica.com/EBchecked/ topic/646897/wombat>, January 27, 2012.

[vii] "Platypus." Encyclopædia Britannica. Encyclopædia Britannica Online Academic Edition. Encyclopædia Britannica Inc., 2012. <http://www.britannica.com/EBchecked/ topic/464303/platypus>, January 27, 2012.

[viii] "Aussie slang." Australian Slang Dictionary – Ozzie Slang – Aussie Slang – Australian

Sayings – Australian Strine. <http://www.aussie-slang.com/html/australian_slang.html>, January 08, 2012.

[ix]   "Aussie glossary." <http://www.mudcat.org/aussie/display_all.cfm>, January 08, 2012.

[x]   "Aussie slang alphabetically." Aussieslang.org. <http://www.aussieslang.org/>, January 08, 2012.

[xi]   "Australian English." Wiktionary – the free dictionary. <http://en.wiktionary.org/wiki/Category:Australian_English>, January 08, 2012.

[xii] "Waltzing Matilda." National Library of Australia, 2011. <http://www.nla.gov.au/epubs/waltzingmatilda/index.php?p=home>, October 05, 2011.

[xiii] "Steve Irwin." Encyclopædia Britannica. Encyclopædia Britannica Online Academic Edition. Encyclopædia Britannica, 2011. <http://www.britannica.com/EBchecked/topic/1235358/Steve-Irwin>, October 06, 2011.

[xiv] "About Andrew." Australian Broadcasting Corporation, 2011. <http://www.abc.net.au/tv/enoughrope/about/about_andrew.htm>, October 05, 2011.

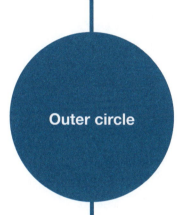

Outer circle

Chapter 6

Indian English

Introduction

As a variety, Indian English has been subsumed under various cover terms in the relevant literature: 'Asian English', 'Postcolonial English', and 'Non-native English'. All these labels point to different facets of the variety in question. In fact, some authors have voiced their concerns with respect to the label 'Indian English', as this umbrella term indeed masks a host of different forms of English (Hickey 2004: 542–543).

Perhaps one of the most prominent characteristics of Indian English is that it arose in a multilingual setting, similarly to other Asian Englishes. In other words, it developed some of its most important linguistic features in situations in which languages from different language families were used side by side and interacted with one another. Furthermore, Indian English emerged in the postcolonial era, mostly in classroom settings. Indian English is closely associated with contexts in which native speakers form a linguistic minority.

As Indian English is spoken by speakers sharing more than one common language, it abounds with patterns of code-switching, i.e. utterances containing linguistic material from different languages, e.g. *I looked in the almarija* [cupboard] *in the daftar* [office], *it's not there*. Having been introduced on the South Asian subcontinent in the early 17th century and having increased in importance after India's independence in 1947, Indian English has been undergoing constant change, in the course of which more and more speakers have become increasingly aware of their linguistic identity as speakers of Indian English as opposed to other World Englishes. English in India is still largely associated with education and higher socioeconomic status. Rural areas as well as lower strata of the society have largely remained unaffected by the influence of English.

This chapter familiarises you with the most essential characteristics of Indian English in the domains of pronunciation, grammar, and lexicon. The Reading Comprehensions (*Discovering Indian English*, *Why worry about small small things?*), the Viewing and Reading Comprehensions featuring an Indian student as well as Self-Study I and Self-Study II have been designed for this purpose. This chapter also features a Role-Playing Game discussing the importance of English in India and a Reading Comprehension activity addressing a debate about native speakers of Indian English (*Indian English: In search for the native speaker*). The text opening this chapter (*Indian English as a part of Indian history and culture*) introduces important details on the history of English on the subcontinent and its role in modern India.

 READING COMPREHENSION

Indian English as a part of
Indian history and culture

Indian English is a label used to describe a host of varieties. The variation that can
be observed within a particular variety of Indian English depends on a number of
factors such as user proficiency (language acquisition, years of instruction), the
region of India where the user comes from, and their ethnic background. These difficulties notwithstanding, it is possible to single out some features that make Indian
English a distinct variety. English as used in India can probably be best described as
a means of unifying India's cultural diversity. Read the following text to find out more
about the factors that can account for the special status English has in India.

[…] English was introduced into India
in the early 17th century (cf. Schneider
2007) but it was not until the beginning
of the 18th century that it was in regu-
5 lar use. […] British sailors and traders
were the first to bring English to India's
shores followed by **missionaries**, who
established English-medium schools.
[…]
10   In the second half of the 18th century, the British East India Company rose
to a prominent position in Bengal, thus
taking more and more power from the
Mogul emperor, and eventually became
15 responsible for civil government and
education. Since then, the Indian population has been divided into two large
groups as regards the question of whether or not English should remain the lan-
20 guage of education. Thus, **"orientalists"**
see English as a threat to **indigenous**
Indian culture and languages, whereas

"westernizers" believe that mastering
English was the best way to **gain access
to** Western knowledge (cf. Melchers and 25
Shaw 2003: 137). […]

In the 19th and the beginning of the
20th century English established itself
as the language of the elite. English has
become even more wide-spread since 30
India gained its independence in 1947.
Even the introduction of Hindi as one
of the official languages of India did
not stop English from becoming the
most **prestigious** means of communica- 35
tion among those well-to-do people and
those aspiring for more **prosperous positions** in life alike. English is thus the
principal language of higher education
and government, justice and legislation, 40
diplomacy and trade, journalism and
tourism.

There are basically two reasons for
this phenomenon. First and foremost,

English is perceived as a neutral language (as opposed to Hindi) by a vast majority of the population. As a result, it is the language in which people coming from different parts of India (for instance, Bihar and Tamil Nadu) are likely to **converse**. By contrast, Hindi is a language associated with a specific ethnic group. Introducing Hindi as a **lingua franca** implies that Hindus have a certain degree of privilege over other ethnic groups. It is for this reason that the introduction of Hindi as a national language **met with great resistance** on the part of many people in India. The second reason for English being so widespread in India is that it is a language normally associated with literacy, privileged social status and **economic prosperity**. To provide an example, mastering English is often the only way to get a well-paid job and have a career. […]

[Julia Davydova 2011: 29-31. #1; bold face added]

Vocabulary

1. Look up the following words and expressions in a monolingual English dictionary: missionary, indigenous, gain access to, prestigious, prosperous positions, converse, meet with great resistance, and economic prosperity.
2. Explain the following linguistic terminology in your own words. Consult a dictionary, if necessary: a host of varieties, user proficiency, and distinct variety.

COMPREHENSION

What are the primary reasons for English becoming a major means of communication in India?

ANALYSIS

Compare the status of English in India with that in Europe. What differences and similarities can you identify?

WORD ANALYSIS

1. What do the words "orientalists" and "westernizers" mean? Describe them in your own words. Use a monolingual English dictionary, if necessary.
2. What does the phrase "lingua franca" mean? See also Chapter 1 on English as a global language.
3. Explain the meaning of the word "variety" in your own words and give a few examples of different varieties of English.

ROLE-PLAYING GAME

Imagine that you are participating in the TV show *Voices of India* hosted by an Indian broadcasting company. The question addressed in the programme concerns the role of English in India. Is it a "language killer" or is it a "bridge builder" between people of different ethnic and linguistic backgrounds? Take on one of the roles suggested below and participate in the discussion, presenting the arguments from the point of view of the character you chose.

Role 1: You are a TV host who believes in promoting cultural and linguistic diversity while maintaining the status of English as a major uniting force in a multilingual context. Think of some arguments supporting your position. Since you are a TV host, prepare a list of questions that you will ask your guests.

Role 2: You are a 60-year-old professor of Hindu studies at the University of New Delhi. You are convinced that your compatriots should break away from the country's British heritage as soon as possible in order to preserve their cultural identity, which is an important part of who they are. Think of arguments to support this point of view.

Role 3: You are a Malayalam student who came all the way from Kerala to study at Jawaharlal Nehru University in New Delhi. You are certain that English is the only way to preserve the integrity of a multilingual country such as India. Give your arguments in favour of this opinion.

ROLE-PLAYING GAME

Role 4: You are a famous Indian politician who believes that bilingual education is the only way to support members of progressively thinking generations that have access to modern Western knowledge, which they can use for the good of their own culture and society. Think of several arguments to defend your position.

Role 5: You are a German student majoring in Asian studies. Your main focus is on India and its role in the global context. You are absolutely convinced that India simply cannot do without English if it wants to keep in pace with the rest of the world. Give your arguments to support this point of view.

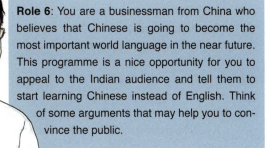

Role 6: You are a businessman from China who believes that Chinese is going to become the most important world language in the near future. This programme is a nice opportunity for you to appeal to the Indian audience and tell them to start learning Chinese instead of English. Think of some arguments that may help you to convince the public.

Drawings for the role-playing game

 READING COMPREHENSION

Discovering Indian English

The dialogues below feature different words, phrases, and grammatical features that can be encountered in the speech of Indian English speakers.

PRE-READING ACTIVITIES

1. There are many expressions in Indian English that come from local languages. In what domains of everyday life do you think the local words are most widely used? Explain.
2. The grammar of Indian English is different from that of standard English in many important ways. Which areas of grammar differ most, in your opinion? Try to give some examples.

WHILE-READING ACTIVITY

Read the dialogues below and underline a) the words and phrases that you believe to be authentic Indian English and b) the sentences and phrases that are different from standard English in terms of grammar.

1.

»   Tell me where are you going? I am waiting for you too long.

»   The Lajpat Nagar Market. Want something from there?

»   One small thing only. Bring me some veg pakoras, food is so good there. We can serve them before biryani for dinner. You love rice?

»   Haan, sounds good.

»   Shall we cook daal soup also?

»   We have cooked lentils last Friday, isn't it?

2.

»   Hello! Where are you belonging?

»   Bihar. Been here in Delhi not too long … had completed my MA in Bihar but now I am doing my MPhil in political science, second year. What about you?

»   I took my admission in JNU [Jawaharlal Nehru University] last year. Now I am in the second year of my BA studies. How are you liking it here in Delhi?

» Oh, I love it here. It's like very glamorous. The place where I belong is sort of very small but Delhi is fascinating.

3.

» What Indian food you prefer?
» Oh, I love Indian style of cooking: Love masaala food because of spice and love meat also. So saag goshth is one of my favourites. I love rice called chaaval in Hindi but often eat chapaati also because northern Indian bread is so very tasty – so I am in the habit of eating these things. And lassi is very good as a drink.
» Have you ever been to Rajasthan?
» Yes, but the food there though quite tasty is very greasy and oily also as they put a lot of desi ghee and that kind of thing into their cooking. Their most famous dish, daal baati, is spicy as it is made with ginger, chilli, and garlic and it is boiled in desi ghee, which is basically butter. So they are like small small things and you can get full in no time at all.

4.

» So you come here often, haan?
» Not often. I have family: wife and two children. Keeping me busy, not so much time for fun, isn't it? I started my family at really early age but my family very nice, beautiful wife, two good daughters too. What you call it? The apple of my eye. Yes!

5.

» Can you tell me where's Lotus Tempel is?
» Oh, it's too far from here, farther south. You can take a rickshaw, they will get you there. If you give them one hundred bucks more, will give you tour of the roundabouts.
» One hundred bucks, na?
» Yes, rupees, you know.

6.

» What are you doing for Diwali this year?
» Going to Bombay to see my family. After all, what a family holiday is good for if not to see your own family? Going to see your family once a year is important, don't you think?
» Not sure about my plans. I had been to Patna last week so may be in this week I will just stay here in Delhi and have some fun with my friends.

POST-READING ACTIVITIES I

1. Take a look at the Indian English words and phrases that you have under-
    lined. Try to guess from the context what these words mean.
2. Match the Indian English words and phrases that you saw in the text with
    their standard English explanations.

(i)	biryani	(a)	spice
(ii)	daal soup	(b)	Indian bread
(iii)	chapaati	(c)	lamb with spinach (from Punjab)
(iv)	masaala	(d)	lentil soup
(v)	saag goshth	(e)	Indian rice dish
(vi)	desi ghee	(f)	a kind of snack (usu. from vegetables)
(vii)	daal baati	(g)	small lentil balls (from Rajasthan)
(viii)	pakora	(h)	a kind of drink
(ix)	lassi	(i)	clarified Indian butter (grease)

POST-READING ACTIVITIES II

1. Take a look at the sentences that you identified as being different from
    standard English. Translate these sentences into standard English.
2. Based on what you found in the dialogues above, what are the major proper-
    ties of Indian English grammar?

ANALYSIS

Match the Indian English sentences on the left side with their standard English equivalents given on the right side of the page. Explain the differences you notice between Indian English and standard English in your own words.

Indian English	Standard English
I am here since two o'clock.	What is this made from?
You are going home soon, isn't it?	I drink very hot coffee.
What this is made from?	I have been here since two o'clock.
I am doing it often.	I was there ten years ago.
This sari cheap cheap.	You are going home soon, aren't you?
I drink hot hot coffee.	This sari is very cheap.
I have been there ten years ago.	I do it often.

SELF-STUDY I

Take a look at the recipe below. Underline the Indian English words that you already know with one colour. Use a different colour for the Indian English words that you are not familiar with. Check their meaning on the Internet. Make the dish at home.

Aloo Gobhi Masaala

450g / 1 lb potatoes, cut into medium chunks
Oil 3 tablespoons
1 teaspoon cumin seeds
1 green chilli chopped
450g / 1 lb cauliflower, broken into florets
1 tsp ground coriander
1 tsp jeera (cumin) powder
1/4 tsp chilli powder
1/2 tsp ground turmeric
1/2 tsp salt
Finely chopped fresh coriander (1/2 cup) for garnishing
Ginger julien strips 1 tablespoon

1. Take some oil in a heavy bottomed sauce pan and heat.
2. Add the potatoes cubes and shallow fry till done.
3. Now heat oil in the same sauce pan.
4. Add the jeera (cumin) seeds and fry till they start crackling.
5. Add the red chilli powder and stir for a minute.
6. Add the turmeric powder and stir for a minute.
7. Add the gobhi pieces (cauliflower florets) and fry.
8. Stir lightly.
9. Add the garam masaala.
10. Add coriander powder.
11. Add cumin (jeera) powder.
12. Stir for few minutes, lightly, rapid stirring will break the cauliflower florets.
13. Add the already fried potatoes cubes.
14. Add the salt.
15. Cook for another 5 minutes with minimal stirring.
16. Garnish with fresh chopped coriander.
17. Put the ginger juliens on top.

Serve with naan, rice or roti.

[Adapted from Punjabirecipes.gurudwara.net]

INFO

Some features of Indian English

(i) Different use of tense and aspect
- » I am using the Internet for two years.
- » I am often falling ill.
- » We have studied this chapter last week.

(ii) Different word order in questions
- » What you think of this dress?
- » I asked him where does he live?

(iii) The extended use of the question tag *isn't it*
- » We decided to stay longer, isn't it?
- » They are coming back, isn't it?

(iv) Repetition of words
- » hot hot coffee (very hot coffee)
- » small small things (very small things)
- » cheap cheap sari (very cheap sari)

SELF-STUDY II

Indian English is learnt as a second language in most parts of India. As a result, the grammar of Indian English is full of peculiarities. The following sentences represent authentic examples of Englishes spoken in different parts of the world. Determine which of the sentences given below are typical of Indian English.
- » You are after ruinin' me. [#i]
- » Sam didn't useta eat red meat, but he sure does anymore. [#ii]
- » You are going home soon, isn't it? [#iii]
- » She is now gone to dos properly na? [#iv]
- » Nobody don't like him. [#v]
- » You know what is Casanova? [#vi]
- » They give money very very. [#vii]
- » A lot of them ask me why don't I go into teaching. [#viii]
- » I wasnae liking it and the lassi I was going wi wasnae liking it. [#ix]
- » Com with us lah. [#x]
- » A: Is he in his office? – B: Sorry, […] left just now only. [#xi]

Why are these sentences (and not others) characteristic of this form of English? Explain.

Indian cuisine

It is probably not an exaggeration to say that Indian style of cooking enjoys an enormous popularity all over the world. This is due to its richness of ingredients and skilful use of different spices (*masaala*). Indian dishes often feature fresh vegetables: *gobhi* (cauliflower), *aloo* (potatoes), *daal* (lentils), and *saag* (spinach). *Chaaval* (rice) is usually served with these dishes. Traditional Indian butter is called *ghee*. It is clarified butter often made from buffalo's milk.

Indian food

Bollywood

India boasts one of the largest film audiences in the entire world. Although the beginning of the traditional film-making industry in India can be traced back to the 1930s, it is the most recent film productions such as *Om Shanti Om* (2007) featuring the megastar Shak Rukh Khan that have also become hits with European audiences. King Khan was a special guest at the Berlinale Festival in Germany in 2008.

Temple colours

Indian fashion

Indian jewelry

[Based on #xii – #xv]

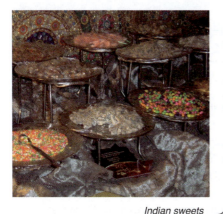

Indian sweets

Indian society

Indian society is subject to rigid social stratification. The caste system imposes different ranks on Hindu society as well as an elaborate complex of social codes that individuals must adhere to over the course of their entire lives. Perhaps the most controversial of all castes is the caste of *Achuta* or *Dalit*, otherwise known as the 'Untouchables'.

Languages in India

One of the most fascinating facets of this South Asian country is its linguistic diversity. There are two official languages in India – Hindi (official) and English (associate official), 22 regional languages, and hundreds of other native languages. The languages spoken in India belong to four different language families: Indo-European, Dravidian, Austro-Asiatic, and Tibeto-Burman. Hindi, Urdu, and Punjabi are Indo-European languages spoken in the North. Telugu, Kannada, Tamil, and Malayalam are Dravidian languages of the South. Bengali is the language of West Bengal, whereas Gujarati and Marathi are spoken in the western and central parts of the subcontinent. These are also Indo-European languages.

Languages in India

Kashmiri
Punjabi
Delhi● (New Delhi)
Hindi-belt
Gujarati and Sindhi
Marathi
Konkani
Kannada
Malayalam
Tamil
Telugu
Oriya
Bengali
Nepali
Assamese
English
Manipuri
Mizo
English

Indian fishing boat

[Based on #xvi – #xvii]

VIEWING AND READING COMPREHENSION

PRE-WATCHING ACTIVITY I

1. Take a look at the images shown on the preceding pages and describe what you see in these pictures.
2. What can they tell us about Indian culture? Here is a list of words that may help you to get started: bright, colourful, diverse, controversial, varied, complex, warm-hearted, and generous. (Use a thesaurus or a monolingual English dictionary to add to this list.)
3. Read the info-boxes on the preceding pages and draw a mind map that helps you to see the links between various aspects of Indian culture and the Indian way of life.

PRE-WATCHING ACTIVITY II

India, also known as *Bharat*, has 22 national languages. English is an associate official language of the Republic of India. Discuss the following questions with a partner or in groups:

1. What role does English play in India?
2. In what domains of everyday life is English used in this country?
3. In what ways is the English spoken in India influenced by Indian culture? Think of Indian food and the languages spoken in India.

In this video, Ramesh, a student from Jawaharlal Nehru University, one of the most prestigious universities in India, is going to talk to you about Indian culture.

Listen to Ramesh's story at www.awe.uni-hamburg.de. [#2]

Student from Jawaharlal Nehru University

WHILE-WATCHING ACTIVITY I

Listen to his story again and fill in the gaps below.

Indian culture is _____
India has a population of _____
The North of India and the South of India _____
India gave birth to three major religions: _____
with the addition of some special minor religions such as_____
People have migrated to India from _____
In India, there is a mainstream Hindu culture and there are _____
"Indian culture" or a "culture of the East" is merely a _____
The community, the family, and the village _____
The West focuses on _____, whereas India is
concerned with _____
Summarise the major facts about India and Indian culture as they are reported by
the speaker in the video.

WHILE-WATCHING ACTIVITY II

Listen to Ramesh's story again while following along in the transcript below. The
transcript is an excerpt from his story. Find the words which are pronounced differently than in Received Pronunciation and mark them in the text.

Ramesh: Hello! My name is Ramesh and I am a student of Jawaharlal Nehru University. I am **pursuing** my M.Phil. in Centre for European Studies and I am going
to talk to you about a little bit on Indian culture. The first thing that I have to say is
Indian culture is not one **single entity**, it's not a sort of a … **monolithic** sort of a
thing: It's **vibrant**, it's diverse and let's face it, not … I mean you cannot just give it
a term "Indian culture" because there is a lot of differences. India is a huge country
with a population of more than a billion people. We are as good as a billion different
understandings of what you may wanna simply call as Indian culture. The North of
India, the South of India, and in all four directions we have differences feature so
vast and so vibrant that the South of India may not exactly go in tandem with the
cultural **leanings** of North of India. And within each regions there are subcultures and
there are different languages and there are different ways of understanding the same
religion. Hinduism may be the biggest religion in India but it is not the only religion.
India is a country which gave birth to three big religions, that is Hinduism, Sikhism,
Buddhism, and some small … some special side religions like Jainism.

POST-WATCHING ACTIVITY I

1. What is your general impression of the language of this particular speaker? Is he a fluent speaker of English? Explain.
2. What features of his language did you find interesting, confusing or difficult to understand? How do they differ from standard British English?
3. As you can see, Ramesh's pronunciation differs in many ways from that of standard British English speakers. Where do you think might these special features come from?

POST-WATCHING ACTIVITY II

Considering what you have learnt about Indian culture so far, what are the differences and similarities between Indian culture and the culture of your home country? Fill in the gaps in the table below. Use as many new words that you have learnt as possible.

	Indian culture	Home culture
Drinks	*lassi*	*beer*
Food		
Languages		
Family		
Religion		
Migration		
…		

POST-WATCHING ACTIVITY III (ADVANCED)

1. Which sounds are different in Indian English compared to Received Pronunciation?
2. Try to determine some specific rules for Indian English pronunciation.

CREATIVE WRITING

Imagine that you are on a trip around India. You have seen quite a lot and met many people. Write an essay on "My India" in which you convey your impressions about the country and its people to the reader. Comment on how Indian people use English and describe the impressions their English has made on you.

PROJECT

In his speech, Ramesh mentions different religions that play important roles in India. Find out more about Hinduism, Islam, Sikhism, Buddhism, and Jainism in India. Describe the following aspects of these religions: rituals, ceremonies, pilgrimages, and festivals. Include native Indian words in your descriptions of these religions. Use the following sources as a starting point for your research:

» http://en.wikipedia.org/wiki/Religion_in_India
» Wandel, Reinhold (ed.). 2008. *India. A Unity in Diversity*. Berlin: Cornelsen Verlag.

Vocabulary

Look up the following words and expressions in a monolingual English dictionary: pursue, single entity, monolithic, vibrant, and leanings.

READING COMPREHENSION

PRE-READING ACTIVITY FOR *WHY WORRY ABOUT SMALL SMALL THINGS?*

Take a look at the text given below and underline all the words that are repeated.

» What meanings do these words express in a sentence?
» Translate this small text into standard English.

A silk trader while talking to a customer:

> This sari house good good. Very cheap price. Many many quality of sari, Sir. Banaras sari the best sari. Supply all city. Make by hand. First they make art on paper. Then they put on silk. About fifty fifty thousand handloom. Some silk best quality. Some silk bad quality. Country go wash colour finish. Sari about three hundred to five thousand rupees. This make of nice ladies dress. One sari make two long dress and one half dress. Sari six yard. Some tourist give order. I like this size this size. They give little advance and we make. Sometime your sari is old. About fifty fifty year old. Then sari is broken. Then you can fire gold and make money half.

[Raja Ram Mehrotra 1997: 49. #3]

Why worry about small small things?

The structure of Indian English sentences often mirrors those available in the speaker's native language. The text given below explains why so many Indians repeat one and the same word within a single sentence.

Because English and Indian languages differ widely in behaviour, some of our ways of expression can never be recreated in English. *Indlish* sounds **ludicrous**
5 when we recreate the reduplication that all Indian languages permit either for musical effect or for emphasis:

Hindi
• *chhoti chhoti baaten* (trivial issues/ trifles) [...]   10
Bengali
• *chhoto chhoto katha* (trivial issues/ trifles) [...]

15 **Oriya**
- *bada bada katha* (big talk) [...]

Tamil [...]
- *vanna vanna pookkal* (colourful flowers) [...]

20 **Malayalam**
- *kochchu kochchu karyangal* (trivial issues/trifles) [...]

Telugu
- *chala chala bagunadi* (very very
25 good) [...]

Kannada
- *hannu hannu muduka* (grand old man) [...]

Marathi
30 • *chotya chotya goshti* (trivial issues/ trifles) [...]

All those expressions are idiomatic and lend music to our regional languages.
35 The translation alongside each is **inadequate**: it carries neither the music nor the effect, and almost nothing of the connotation. No translation can convey the **flavour** of any of those expressions.
40 English does not permit reduplication for meaningful effect. The few examples that English does permit achieve little more than meaningless sound-effects in:

45

- finger rhymes for babies (*this little pig said wee wee wee*)
- animal sounds (*baa-baa/moo-moo/ meow-meow/quack-quack*)
50 • nursery rhymes (*twinkle twinkle little star/hey diddle diddle, the cat and the fiddle*) [...]

English permits the replication (not re-duplication) of a sound-effect (*hickory* 55 *dickory dock .../... and there in the wood a piggy wiggy stood*), or the close repetition of words in songs (*in a tiny house by a tiny stream, where a lovely girl had a lovely dream*). 60

In some poems, words are repeated for heightened effect (*In vain I weep to him that cannot hear, and* weep *the more because I* weep *in vain*: Coleridge), or a whole line is repeated in refrain (*For I* 65 *have promises to keep, and miles to go before I sleep. And miles to go before I sleep*: Robert Frost).

In English, the closest to reduplication would be those few rhyming pairs 70 used in informal adult speech to emphasise an idea, usually derogatory. Unlike the Indian expression that repeats the identical word, the English word pairs with: 75

1. a word that replicates the sound of the first, but with a change in the initial consonant (*argy-bargy*; *fuddy-duddy*; *fuzzy-wuzzy*; [...] *heebie-* 80 *jeebies*; [...] *itsy-bitsy*; [...] *nitty-gritty*; *razzle-dazzle*; *roly-poly*; *teeny weeny*)
2. a word that begins with the same consonant sound, but changes a 85 vowel within (*dilly-dally*; *flip-flop*; [...] *mish-mash*; [...] *tip-top*; *tittle-tattle*; *whim-wham*; *wiggle-woggle*; *wishy-washy*).

90

Often, only the first word may carry the meaning intended; the second may have no meaning or existence independent

of the combination (*fuzzy-wuzzy*). With
a few, neither of the pair may have a
meaning, and neither is used alone (*fud-dy-duddy*). [...]

Readers will at once recognise that
all Indian languages have such **imita-tive** rhyming pairs too, made with simi-lar changes in the initial consonant or
vowel sounds: such a term for *things
around you*, for instance, would be *aas
paas* (Hindi); *aashay paashay* (Ben-gali); *pakha pakhi* (Oriya); *sutta mutta/
akkaa pakkaa* (Kannada); *ikkada ak-kada* (Telugu); *akkam pakkam* (Tamil);
aviday ividay (Malayalam); *aazu baazu*
(Marathi), etc.

But Indians often recreate in English
the reduplication they are accustomed to
use in their languages, and this has led
to what Englishmen consider a comical
feature of *Indlish*. In its list of features
of Indian English, the *Oxford Com-panion to the English Language* (OUP,
1992) includes 'Reduplication used for
emphasis and to indicate a distributive
meaning: *I bought some small small
things*; *Why don't you give them one one
piece of cake?*' Because they never use
reduplication, and only rarely a replica-tion, Englishmen are unable to under-stand why Indians use such expressions
as [...] 'Such *little little* things can cause
big big problems'/'I want a *same same*
dress as yours'/'She was saying *some
some* things'/'Why don't you pay them
ten ten rupees each?'

Reduplication **enlivens** Indian lan-guages. But let's recognise that if Eng-lish doesn't permit it, we mustn't import
it. That can only make such 'transla-tions' ludicrous.

[Jyoti Sanyal 2007: 310-315. #4; bold
face added]

Vocabulary

Look up the following words and expressions in a monolingual English dictionary:
ludicrous, inadequate, flavour, imitative, and enliven.

COMPREHENSION

1. Describe the meaning of the term 'reduplication' in your own words and give
   examples of reduplication in Indian English.
2. What is the source of reduplication in the English spoken by people in India?
3. What strategies does English have that are similar to reduplication? Give
   examples from the text. Moreover, think of examples of your own.

ANALYSIS

1. Describe the main ways in which languages of India differ from English.
2. Comment on the similarities found between English and Indian languages.

ROLE-PLAYING GAME

Imagine that you are a linguist invited to a talk show with the title: "The Future of Indian English: Maintaining the British Standard or Emancipating from Colonial Ties?!" Work with a partner and make up a dialogue in which you discuss with another linguist whether Indian English should maintain its "original flavour" or should orient itself more closely on the standard language.

DISCUSSION

Do you agree with the author that non-native speakers should not import features from their mother tongue into English? Explain.

SELF-STUDY (ADVANCED)

Imagine that you are a linguistics student doing research on reduplication in Indian English. Write a short article in which you describe the major strategies of reduplication, its primary functions or meanings, and the contexts – both linguistic and social – in which reduplication occurs. The following article may help you to get started with your research:

Mehrotra, Raja Ram. 1997. Reduplication in Indian Pidgin English. *English Today* 13:2, 45–49.

Your paper should have the following structure:

1. Introduction
2. Main body
   2.1.   Point 1
   2.2.   Point 2
   2.3.   Point 3, etc.
3. Conclusion

 READING COMPREHENSION

Indian English: In search of the native speaker

Indian English is spoken by different groups of people in India. It is a means of communication amongst professors and lecturers at Indian universities and can also be heard at markets or bazaars, in various shops, and on the streets in big cities. Some people in India start learning English very early on in life, while others come in contact with the language much later. The linguistic situation in India is so complex that it is not always easy to say who is a native speaker of English.

In the boxes below, you will read stories about different people. Read the texts and decide (i) how well these people can speak English, (ii) what their first language is, (iii) under what circumstances they learnt these languages, and (iv) how the context of language acquisition in India is different from that in Europe. Work in pairs or in groups.

Vivek comes from a Christian family. His father is an Evangelic priest in Bangalore, Karnataka, which is in the South of India, and his mother is a nurse at a Red Cross hospital. Ever since he was a young boy, Vivek has been engaged in various social activities. He helped his mother out looking after patients at the hospital. He went on Christian missions with his father where he met people from all over the country. Although English was the language of communication in the family, Vivek also grew up speaking Kannada, the major regional language of Karnataka. Because the educational system in India requires a child to acquire three languages, Vivek also had to learn Hindi, a major language of northern India. He can now speak Hindi fairly fluently and even uses it now and again when he takes trips around India with his father.

Drawings of Vivek, Prija, and Raj

ANALYSIS

Analyse the linguistic situation in India and compare it to that in Europe. What differences and similarities can you identify?

Prija was born in a Vaishya family in West Bengal. Bengali was the language spoken in her family and at school. But Prija was very interested in other languages. While growing up in the city of Kolkata, she would listen to people speaking Hindi or English on the streets, trying to understand what they were talking about. Prija was a very bright girl and always applied herself at school. As a result she was able to go and study in Delhi. Her first years at the university were hard ones. She had to improve her English to be able to write papers, which are written obligatorily in English at Indian universities. Despite great emotional strain and an immense working load, Prija did not give up and managed to get her M.A. and M.Phil. degrees. She is currently working on her Ph.D. project, which is about the influence of British poetry on Indian English writers and poets.

Raj was born in New Delhi. His father was a Punjabi Sikh and his mother was a Hindu Brahmin. Both Punjabi and Hindi were spoken in the family, so Raj learnt both languages from the very beginning. Being a businessman, his father was very eager for his son to receive a proper education and spared no expense for it. Raj went to an English-language kindergarten when he was three. He later went to a primary school where the lessons were conducted in English. After finishing at an English-medium private school in Delhi, Raj decided to study abroad and went to the United States, where he earned a degree in medicine at the University of Pennsylvania. Raj intends to stay in the United States but is currently looking for a native Punjabi wife in his home country. He intends to raise his future children conscious of the Punjabi language and culture.

COMPREHENSION

Summarise some important characteristics of the linguistic situation in India.

DISCUSSION

1. What does the term 'native speaker' mean? Is it possible to be a native speaker of more than one language? Give examples and discuss in pairs or in groups.
2. Think of criteria that may help you classify speakers of a language into native and non-native speakers. Discuss these criteria with a partner or in groups.
3. What are the advantages or perhaps disadvantages of living in a multilingual society, meaning a society in which three or more languages are spoken?

VIEWING AND READING COMPREHENSION

Indian English and Indian culture: Bombay and New Delhi

PRE-WATCHING ACTIVITY I

1. Take a look at the map and find the cities of Bombay (also known as Mumbai) and New Delhi (Delhi). What are the differences between the two in terms of geographic location?

Map of India

2. Do you think that the cultures of people living in cities so far away from each other differ from one another? What do you think these cultural differences might be?
3. If you were invited to go to India, would you rather go to New Delhi or to Bombay? Explain your choice.

PRE-WATCHING ACTIVITY II

Some speakers of Indian English pronounce words like *school* and *station* as /ɪskul/ and /ɪsteʃan/, thus adding a vowel before the two initial consonants.

Furthermore, words like *tea* and *dark* are pronounced as /ʈiː/ and /ɖɑːk/, the tip of the tongue being curled back when the consonants /t/ and /d/ are pronounced.

Finally, the word *are*, as in *we are*, is trilled in Indian English so that you can hear people say /ar/ instead of /ɑː/.

What do you think are the reasons for these differences in pronunciation?

In the following video, Ramesh, the student from Jawaharlal Nehru University whom you have already met, will tell you about the differences between Bombay (Mumbai), which happens to be his native city, and New Delhi, the capital of India.

You can find the video at www.awe.uni-hamburg.de. [#5]

Student from Jawaharlal Nehru University

WHILE-WATCHING ACTIVITY I

Take notes while listening to his story and be ready to answer the following questions:

- » Why are there so many bureaucrats and ministers in New Delhi?
- » Why is the Central Bank located in Bombay?
- » What is the difference in work ethic between Bombay and New Delhi?
- » In which city do people have a business-like attitude?
- » Where are the tallest buildings in the country located?
- » In which city is the way of working becoming more "American"?
- » Which city is better planned in terms of infrastructure?
- » What are the differences between Bombay and New Delhi in terms of climate?
- » How does Ramesh describe the people from Bombay?

The differences between
Bombay and New Delhi

WHILE-WATCHING ACTIVITY II

Listen to Ramesh's speech one more time and read the transcript given below.
Pay close attention to the pronunciation of the words in bold face:

Ramesh: Well, I am from Bombay.
Interviewer: Wow, that's interesting!
Could you describe the differences between Bombay and New Delhi?
5 **Ramesh:** Okay … New Delhi is the
capital of India. It's the seat of power.
It has historically been the political
capital of India. But Bombay has been
a commercial capital. It's the biggest
10 economic city of India. And historically
the job opportunities have been **there**.
It's now that India is growing and you
know … Delhi is also doing pretty good
on the economic **bit**. So Bombay has a
15 commercial culture but Delhi has **more**
of a political culture. You have bureaucrats, you have ministers, you have …
Because it's a seat of power all the min-
istries and everybody of the government
20 is mostly in Delhi, while Bombay has
more of the banking, the Central Bank is
there, companies have their headquar-
ters in Bombay so it's **more** of a commercial **way** of life. There's a difference
25 in the **work ethics**: I mean previously,
when India was still a slow growing
country economically, Delhi had a very
slow sort of a **work ethic**. But Bombay

because of … being a commercial capital and because people used to travel for 30
business, Bombay has had a **work ethic**
which is quite fast and which probably
compares to the European or the American **way** of **work**. But Delhi is **more** of
an Asian sort of a slow moving bureau- 35
cratic **work** culture. Obviously, now
things have been changing … The economy … since it is doing **well**, there's a
lot of migration of professionals from
within East to cities. But the man on the 40
street in Bombay is **more** likely to be …
is **more** likely to have a **business-like**
attitude, he will value time, while Delhi
has a sort of a slow culture. I shouldn't
call it **lazy** but yeah … It will be slow 45
compared to what Bombay is. Bombay
is **more globalised**, we … I mean because people have been **travelling** to
… **travelling** abroad, they bring those
values back and when a guy sees New 50
York open till 24 hours a day, I mean he
wants Bombay to be like that because
he's been **there** and he wants it here. So
Bombay is **more** open in the sense that
the shops are open longer, the **working** 55
hours are longer. In Delhi it's **more** of

a government … Delhi still holds on to the idea that you open at maybe ten and shut by five. And at the **street** level,

60 at a very basic level, Delhi still has a **work** culture which is slow. Bombay is small, it's an island city: Unfortunately that means that we cannot expand horizontally, we can only expand vertically.

65 So you have the tallest buildings in the **country** are in Bombay. Well, Delhi because it's not an island, it's a **way** up north, it's **more** of … it has **more** of an urban **sprawl**. I mean, there's huge sub-

70 urbia that **develops** and the **expansion** is horizontal rather than vertical. So Delhi is turning out **more** into the American **way** of **working** and you have people **travelling** 60–80 hundred kilometres,

75 people driving that long to get to **work**. But Bombay because of the concentration it's **more** of … the maximum that you may travel is maybe 50 km in a day and … Because Bombay was … it was

80 the commercial capital even during the British times – the British built transport systems for Bombay which were **more** enorm when compared to what Delhi has. And the legacy of those transport

85 systems **continues** although it's very crowded and because of rural migration into the city. Migration has happened in Delhi **as well** but because Delhi has … I mean, you can build **roads more** eas-

90 ily than you can build **railways** in India. So the expansion of **railways** in Bombay has been tougher, while in Delhi, because it is the seat of the central government the expansion has been easier

95 because the central government holds power. While Bombay is the state capi- tal, Delhi is a national capital. So hav- ing … being close to the powers, the high powers, means some **advantages**, one of them being that Delhi is **more** 100 planned. Bombay was planned by the British in the 1900s. After 1947 Indians

Bombay

were down and we sort of messed it up. And well, Delhi still has some planning that goes in and Bombay has multiple 105 decision-making bodies, while in Delhi it can be finally the right of the central government which **works**. Bombay is a seaport … it is one of the biggest ports in the **country**. So there's a lot of port 110 movement that happens **there**. Well, Delhi is land-locked and **way** off from the sea. The weather in Bombay … I

mean, since I come from Bombay I pre-
115 fer Bombay weather, but we have some
of the most intense spells of rain in the
world. We have three months of enormous amount of rain, while Delhi has
more of the climate of the plains, where
120 it is **cold**, very **cold** in winter because of
the winds blowing from the Himalayas,
the Himalayan Mountains up north, and
very hot in summer. And the difference
between the people of Bombay and the
125 people of Delhi – **as** I have experienced
– is that Bombay has been a city which
has been built by migrants but Delhi
has been built by a government and
the kings. So since the migrants built
130 it, they have sort of … they retained a
charm and they retained a love for the
city which may not be visible in their
contribution to making a city infrastructure better off. But they somehow on a
135 people-to-people basis … I mean Bombay people are **more** generous, **more**
helpful, compared to what Delhi is and
… The other difference … One major
contribution to what makes Bombay
140 what it is today – I mean kind-hearted
and professional people – is that it's in
the **West**, western region of India, it has
the state of Gujarat to its north. This
state has people who are entrepreneurial
145 and they brought this **entrepreneurial
culture** to Bombay, while Delhi has
bureaucrats and the general profile of a
Delhiete would be that he is in the city

to make money and get out **as** soon **as**
is possible. Maybe he is a bureaucrat 150
who is here for two years, five years on
a transfer basis because employees of
government of India keep getting trans-
ferred. So a Delhiete may be in the city
for maybe three years, five years, not all 155
of them but quite a few of the elite are
in the city for some time and then they
move out. But in Bombay the guy is
there he will probably be **there** for the
rest of his life. Also, because Bombay 160
is an island and because we cannot expand horizontally, the real estate prices,
the price of a house in Bombay, is **as**
probably **as** expensive **as** in New York,
or in London or in Frankfurt. Delhi pric- 165
es have also risen but not **as** much **as**
what you have in Bombay, where it can
be crazy if you want me to put it that
way. So huge differences, huge cultural
differences … Delhi is surrounded by 170
states which are … which have borne
the brand of **partition** with Pakistan,
which have borne the brand of invasions
from kings of central **Asia**. So it's **more**
of a **martial culture** out here. But Bom- 175
bay is **more** of a business and economic
culture, safe and far away from the invading kings and the invading hordes.
So Bombay is **more** concentrated on the
business and the economy, it's basically 180
on money while Delhi that is basically
power.

Vocabulary

Look up the following words and expressions in a monolingual English dictionary:
business-like attitude, globalised, expansion, entrepreneurial culture, partition, and
martial culture.

QUESTIONS

» How is the word *bit* pronounced?

» How are the words *there*, *country*, *travelling*, *sprawl*, *street*, *more*, and *martial culture* pronounced? What do they all have in common in terms of pronunciation?

» How are the words *way*, *work(ing)*, *as well*, and *West* pronounced?

» What is the pronunciation of the word *ethics*?

» How is the word *as* pronounced?

» In what way does the pronunciation of the words *railway*, *roads*, *lazy*, and *cold* differ from that of Received Pronunciation?

» Based on your observations, try to describe the vowel and consonant system of Indian English as presented by this speaker.

» Have you noticed any peculiarities in the way the words *develops*, *continues*, *advantages*, *partition,* and *Asia* are stressed? Are these words stressed in a different way compared to Received Pronunciation? If yes, what exactly are those differences?

» What other interesting linguistic features did you notice in Ramesh's speech?

POST-WATCHING ACTIVITY I

In pairs or groups, summarise the major differences between New Delhi and Bombay.

POST-WATCHING ACTIVITY II

Create a mind map illustrating the most important differences between standard British English and Indian English.

Sources

TEXTS

[1]   Davydova, Julia. 2011. *The Present Perfect in Non-Native Englishes. A Corpus-Based Study of Variation*. Berlin/Boston: Mouton de Gruyter, 29–31. Reproduced with permission of Mouton de Gruyter.

[2]   The interview stems from own data collection conducted at Jawaharlal Nehru University, New Delhi between October 29, 2007 and November 19, 2007. We are grateful to the interviewee for consenting to publish the interview.

[3]   Mehrotra, Raja Ram. 1997. Reduplication in Indian Pidgin English. *English Today* 13:2, 49. Cambridge: Cambridge University Press, reproduced with permission.

[4]   Sanyal, Jyoti. 2007. *Indlish. The Book for Every English Speaking Indian*. New Delhi: Viva Books Private Limited, 310–315. Abridged version reproduced with permission of Viva Books Private Limited.

[5]   The interview stems from own data collection conducted at Jawaharlal Nehru University, New Delhi between October 29, 2007 and November 19, 2007. We are grateful to the interviewee for consenting to publish the interview.

PICTURES AND FIGURES

Drawings for the role-playing game: © Isabel Peters. Hamburg, 2012.

Indian food: © Julia Davydova. Hamburg, 2011.

Temple colours: © Isabel Peters. Hamburg, 2012.

Indian jewelry: © Julia Davydova. Hamburg, 2011.

Indian fashion: © Julia Davydova. Hamburg, 2011.

Indian sweets: © Julia Davydova. Hamburg, 2011.

Languages in India: © Isabel Peters. Hamburg, 2012.

Indian fishing boat: © Isabel Peters. Hamburg, 2012.

Drawings of Vivek, Prija, and Raj: © Isabel Peters. Hamburg, 2012.

Map of India: © Isabel Peters. Hamburg, 2011.

Student from Jawaharlal Nehru University: © Isabel Peters. Hamburg, 2011.

Bombay: © Isabel Peters. Hamburg, 2011.

REFERENCES AND FURTHER READING

Bhatia, Tej K. 2008. Major regional languages. In: Kachru, Braj B., Yamuna Kachru, and
    S.N. Sridhar (eds.), *Language in South Asia*. Cambridge: Cambridge University
    Press, 121–131.

Davydova, Julia. 2011. *The Present Perfect in Non-Native Englishes. A Corpus-Based
    Study of Variation*. Berlin/Boston: Mouton de Gruyter, 29–42.

Hickey, Raymond. 2004. South Asian Englishes. In: Hickey, Raymond (ed.), *Legacies of
    Colonial English. Studies in Transported Dialects*. Cambridge: Cambridge University
    Press, 536–559.

Mehrotra, Raja Ram. 1997. Reduplication in Indian Pidgin English. *English Today* 13:2,
    45–49.

Schneider, Edgar W. 2007. *Postcolonial English. Varieties around the World*. Cambridge:
    Cambridge University Press, 161–173.

Ohrem, Michaela. 2008. Berlinale Special: King Khan erobert Deutschland. *INDIEN
    Magazin. Reise Kultur Entertainment* February 2008, 56–71.

O'Neill, Tom. Untouchables. *National Geographic* June 2003, 2–22. In: Wandel, Reinhold
    (ed.), *India: Unity in Diversity*. Berlin: Cornelsen, 58–61.

[i]   Filppula, Marku. 2004. Irish English: morphology and syntax. In: Kortmann, Bernd,
        Kate Burridge, Rajend Mesthrie, Edgar W. Schneider, and Clive Upton (eds.), *A
        Handbook of Varieties of English*, Vol. 2. *Morphology and Syntax*. Berlin/New York:
        Mouton de Gruyter, 75.

[ii]   Murray, Thomas E. and Beth Lee Simon. 2004. Colloquial American English:
        grammatical features. In: Kortmann, Bernd, Kate Burridge, Rajend Mesthrie, Edgar
        W. Schneider, and Clive Upton (eds.), *A Handbook of Varieties of English*, Vol. 2.
        Morphology and Syntax. Berlin/New York: Mouton de Gruyter, 230.

[iii]   Bhatt, Rakesh M. 2004. Indian English: syntax. In: Kortmann, Bernd, Kate Burridge,
        Rajend Mesthrie, Edgar W. Schneider, and Clive Upton (eds.), *A Handbook of
        Varieties of English*, Vol. 2. *Morphology and Syntax*. Berlin/New York: Mouton de
        Gruyter, 1021.

[iv]   Hosali, Priya. 2004. Butler English: morphology and syntax. In: Kortmann, Bernd,
        Kate Burridge, Rajend Mesthrie, Edgar W. Schneider, and Clive Upton (eds.), *A
        Handbook of Varieties of English*, Vol. 2. *Morphology and Syntax*. Berlin/New York:
        Mouton de Gruyter, 1040.

[v]   Wolfram, Walt. 2004. Urban African American Vernacular English: morphology and
        syntax. In: Kortmann, Bernd, Kate Burridge, Rajend Mesthrie, Edgar W. Schneider,
        and Clive Upton (eds.), *A Handbook of Varieties of English*, Vol. 2. *Morphology and
        Syntax*. Berlin/New York: Mouton de Gruyter, 332.

[vi]   Davydova, Julia, Michaela Hilbert, Lukas Pietsch, and Peter Siemund. 2011.

Comparing varieties of English: problems and perspectives. In: Siemund, Peter (ed.), *Linguistic Universals and Language Variation (Trends in Linguistics)*. Berlin/New York: Mouton de Gruyter, 307.

[vii]   Mehrotra, Raja Ram. 1997. Reduplication in Indian Pidgin English. *English Today* 13:2, 47.

[viii]   Davydova, Julia, Michaela Hilbert, Lukas Pietsch, and Peter Siemund. 2011. Comparing varieties of English: problems and perspectives. In: Siemund, Peter (ed.), *Linguistic Universals and Language Variation (Trends in Linguistics)*. Berlin/New York: Mouton de Gruyter, 306.

[ix]   Miller, Jim. 2004. Scottish English: morphology and syntax. In: Kortmann, Bernd, Kate Burridge, Rajend Mesthrie, Edgar W. Schneider, and Clive Upton (eds.), *A Handbook of Varieties of English*, Vol. 2. *Morphology and Syntax*. Berlin/New York: Mouton de Gruyter, 54.

[x]   Wee, Lionel. 2004. Singapore English: morphology and syntax. In: Kortmann, Bernd, Kate Burridge, Rajend Mesthrie, Edgar W. Schneider, and Clive Upton (eds.), *A Handbook of Varieties of English*, Vol. 2. *Morphology and Syntax*. Berlin/New York: Mouton de Gruyter, 1068.

[xi]   Bhatt, Rakesh M. 2004. Indian English: syntax. In: Kortmann, Bernd, Kate Burridge, Rajend Mesthrie, Edgar W. Schneider, and Clive Upton (eds.), *A Handbook of Varieties of English*, Vol. 2. *Morphology and Syntax*. Berlin/New York: Mouton de Gruyter, 1027.

[xii]   Ohrem, Michaela. 2008. Berlinale Special: King Khan erobert Deutschland. *INDIEN Magazin. Reise Kultur Entertainment* February 2008, 56.

[xiii]   "Bollywood." Encyclopædia Britannica. Encyclopædia Britannica Online Academic Edition. Encyclopædia Britannica, 2012. <http://www.britannica.com/EBchecked/topic/72209/Bollywood>, February 8, 2012.

[xiv]   Shehzad Husain and Rafi Ferdenandez. 1998. *Best-Ever Cook's Collection. Indian*. Bristol: Parragon, 6, 10.

[xv]   Schroeter, Andreas and Patrick Uecker (eds.). "bab.la. Wörterbuch. Vokabeltrainer. Übersetzung" [Hamburg], June 2007. <http://de.bab.la/woerterbuch/hindi-englisch/>, February 9, 2012.

[xvi]   O'Neill, Tom. Untouchables. *National Geographic* June 2003, 2–22. In: Wandel, Reinhold (ed.), *India: Unity in Diversity*. Berlin: Cornelsen, 59.

[xvii]   Bhatia, Tej K. 2008. Major regional languages. In: Kachru, Braj B., Yamuna Kachru, and S.N. Sridhar (eds.), *Language in South Asia*. Cambridge: Cambridge University Press, 32–34, 122–124.

Outer circle

Chapter 7

Nigerian English

Introduction

Nigeria is a country in West Africa marked by enormous linguistic diversity. There are nine official languages, with more than 400 indigenous African languages spoken in the country of 140 million inhabitants (cf. Faraclas 2004: 828). Given this linguistic heterogeneity, English plays an important role as a link language, or lingua franca, in Nigeria.

Having been introduced in West Africa in the 16th century through trade, English began to spread in the mid-19th century as a result of missionary activities and commercial interests (cf. Schneider 2007: 199–200). The expansion of English is linked to both institutional contexts and informal settings.

Firstly, English was taught by missionaries in schools, which gave rise to the second-language variety of Nigerian English. This is an indigenised variety of English which developed mainly in the classroom setting through second-language acquisition. Similar to other Englishes of the outer circle, its development is generally associated with fairly high levels of bilingualism, influence from Nigeria's indigenous languages, and non-standard features of British English (cf. Alo and Mesthrie 2004: 813).

Secondly, English was widely used by people speaking different mother tongues in informal contexts such as trade and everyday communication. This situation gave rise to Nigerian Pidgin English, which is actually a variety of Afro-Caribbean English Lexifier Creole spoken by over 50 per cent of the Nigerian population, with this figure likely to increase to 80 per cent in the present decade (cf. Faraclas 2004: 828). Many features of Nigerian Pidgin English are derived from so-called 'substrate languages'. This term refers to the African languages that influenced English.

This chapter considers some of the most salient features of Nigerian English in the domains of pronunciation, lexicon, and grammar. *A quick guide to Nigeria* provides a succinct anthropological and cultural overview of Nigeria. The song *Beng Beng Beng* reveals the flavour of Nigerian English sounds, whereas the Reading Comprehension *Civil Peace* by Chinua Achebe introduces and allows you to practise peculiarities of Nigerian English words and phrases as well as some pronunciation and grammar rules. The article from *Daily Trust Nigeria* looks not only at some typical grammatical features, but also those related to the organisation of (written) discourse in Nigerian English. A short exercise closing the chapter illustrates some features of Nigerian Pidgin English.

A quick guide to Nigeria

Map of Africa

What kind of country is Nigeria?

Nigeria is a federal republic consisting of 36 states and one Federal Capital Territory, which is – as in other federal republics such as the USA – a state or district of its own. Nigeria is situated in the West of Africa and shares borders with Benin, Chad, Cameroon, and Niger. The capital city is Abuja.

The country gained independence from the United Kingdom in 1960 and has had a complicated history with a bloody civil war and constant alternation between democracy and military coups d'etat. Indeed, the 2007 elections resulted in the first transfer of power between civil governments in the country's history. Ever since Nigeria returned to democracy in 1999, the situation in the country, both politically and economically, has improved.

Nigeria's economy is rapidly growing, as the country has a rich supply of natural resources such as oil and minerals.

Map of Nigeria

Who lives in Nigeria?

Nigeria is the most populous country in Africa but just how populous it is, is not exactly clear. It has been estimated that about 155 million people lived in Nigeria in 2011, belonging to more than 250 different ethnic groups.

Of these many different ethnicities, the Hausa and Fulani, the Yoruba, the Igbo, and the Ijaw are the biggest, and also the most influential groups in political terms.

About half of the population, especially in the North of the country, is Muslim, while Christians make up 40 per cent of the population. The remaining Nigerians either adhere to traditional native religions or have no religion at all.

Which languages do people speak?

According to experts' estimates, more than 400 different languages are currently spoken in Nigeria. The most important native languages of Nigeria are Hausa, Igbo, and Yoruba, each of which is spoken by about 18 million native speakers. The non-native languages spoken in Nigeria include Arabic, French, and, of course, English. Although not actually stated in any law or government statute, English is often referred to as an official language of Nigeria.

Nevertheless, English is widely used for business, commerce, education, and official purposes of all kinds. It is a lingua franca in the national media and among the educated classes that helps to make communication within the country easier.

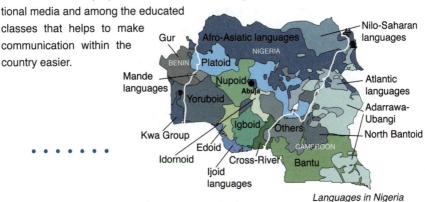

Languages in Nigeria

The happiest people in the world?

Although Nigeria still has to struggle with social and economic inequality, crime, and sectarian violence, a study carried out by the British *New Scientist* magazine (October 2003), in which 65 countries were analysed from 1999 to 2001, found that Nigerians were the happiest people on the planet. The report stated that family life and culture were more important to Nigerians than the country's problems and material wealth.

Nigerian flag

What's Nollywood?

Analogous to the American film industry, often referred to as *Hollywood*, and the Indian film industry called *Bollywood*, the Nigerian film industry has been called *Nollywood*.

The country's booming film industry has grown to such an extent within the last two decades that it has become the second largest film industry on the planet with regard to the number of films produced each year. In 2006, for example, the Indian film industry produced 1,091 feature films, followed by 872 Nigerian productions, while the American film industry only produced 485 movies.

However, basically all Nollywood films are produced and distributed directly as videos, as this helps to reduce costs and there are hardly any formal cinemas.

Only 44 per cent of all Nigerian films are produced in English. The remaining 56 per cent are produced in local languages.

What about Nigerian culture?

Nigeria's most famous authors are perhaps Wole Soyinka and Chinua Achebe. While the former was the first black African Nobel Laureate in Literature, Chinua Achebe is celebrated particularly for his most famous novel *Things Fall Apart*, which has been sold more than eight million times.

Furthermore, dance and music are crucial parts of Nigerian culture with each ethnic group having its own traditions and customs. Contemporary Nigerian music often fuses elements of Western music with traditional indigenous elements.

All in all, the ethnic diversity of Nigeria is reflected in the rich and diverse culture of the country.

[Based on #i – #ix]

EXERCISES

1. Form groups and assign two or three boxes from the previous pages to each member of the group. Report the content of your boxes to your fellow group members.
2. Imagine you are on a students' exchange to Nigeria. After your first month, you write to your grandparents about your experiences so far. Compose a letter based on the boxes given above. (Write a minimum of 200–300 words!)

HOMEWORK

Answer the following questions about Nigeria in full sentences. You may consult the websites listed below.

> » Who is the current president?
> » Where does the word *Nigeria* come from?
> » What are the biggest cities and where are they located?
> » When did Nigeria become a colony?
> » Can you name three famous Nigerians? Why are they famous?

> » https://www.cia.gov/library/publications/the-world-factbook/geos/ni.html
> » http://news.bbc.co.uk/2/hi/africa/country_profiles/1064557.stm
> » http://en.wikipedia.org/wiki/Nigeria

EXPLORING NOLLYWOOD

1. Go to YouTube and look for one of the channels featuring *Nollywood* films.
2. Pick out a movie or part of a movie and prepare a short presentation in which you answer the following questions:

> » What is the film about?
> » How is it different from *Hollywood* or *Bollywood* films?
> » Which features do you think make it Nigerian?
> » What language is used?
> » Which linguistic particularities can you identify?

 LISTENING COMPREHENSION

BENG BENG BENG

by Femi Kuti

Femi Kuti

Many Nigerian pop songs are sung in Nigerian English. A prominent example of such a pop song is *Beng Beng Beng* by Femi Kuti. Nigerian pop music has transported Nigerian English to many parts of the world.

Notes

INFO	EXERCISES
Olufela Olufemi Anikulapo Kuti (*1962), more commonly known as Femi Kuti, is perhaps one of the most famous contemporary Nigerian musicians. He is the son of the afrobeat pioneer and political activist Fela Kuti. In 1978, Femi joined his father and became a member of his band. In 1985, he started his solo career with his own band. Like his father, Femi has been socially and politically active throughout his career. [Based on #x – #xii]	1. Listen to this song on the Internet. Listen to it several times and try to understand what it is about. 2. Transcribe the song lyrics. 3. After listening to this song, what can you say about Nigerian English pronunciation? Take notes while listening to the song and give examples.

ANALYSIS

1. Try to find the standard English explanation for the Nigerian English words and expressions in the table given below. The following links might be helpful:
   » http://www.ngex.com/personalities/babawilly/dictionary/default.htm
   » http://naijalingo.com/index.php
   » http://www.nigeriandictionary.com/language.php?lang_id=63&char=

2. Can you find any other features that might be typical of Nigerian English?

Nigerian English	Standard English
na	
-o	
oya	
dey	
kai	
ego	
wahala	
wey	
wahala	

[Based on #xiii – #xvi]

COMPOSITION

1. Imagine how the lyrics of this song might look if they had been written by a British or American artist. Rewrite the song lyrics from a more European or American perspective and add at least two stanzas. (Write a minimum of 200–300 words!)
2. Consider the lyrics, the melody, and the subject of the song and discuss whether you think that this song represents Nigerian and African culture or is simply a pop song. (Write a minimum of 200–300 words!)

 READING COMPREHENSION

Civil Peace

by Chinua Achebe

The following passage is taken from the short story *Civil Peace* (1972) which is set shortly after the end of the civil war in Nigeria (1967–1970). It tells the story of Jonathan, his wife Mary, and their three children, who luckily survived the war and quickly manage to start a new existence by opening a small bar. However, the family's fortune is put to the test when someone suddenly knocks on the door one night …
[Based on #vii – #ix]

[…] He was normally a heavy sleeper but that night he heard all the neighbourhood noises die down one after another. Even the night watchman who
5 knocked the hour on some metal somewhere in the distance had fallen silent after knocking one o'clock. That must have been the last thought in Jonathan's mind before he was finally carried away
10 himself. He couldn't have been gone for long, though, when he was violently awakened again.

'Who is knocking?' whispered his wife lying beside him on the floor.
15 'I don't know,' he whispered back breathlessly.

The second time the knocking came it was so loud and **imperious** that the **rickety** old door could have fallen down.
20 'Who is knocking?' he asked then, his voice **parched** and trembling.

'Na tief-man and him people,' came the cool reply. 'Make you hopen de door.' This was followed by the heaviest knocking of all.   25

Maria was the first to raise the alarm, then he followed and all their children.

'*Police-o! Thieves-o! Neighbours-o! Police-o! We are lost! We are dead! Neighbours, are you asleep? Wake up!* 30 *Police-o!*'

This went on for a long time and then stopped suddenly. Perhaps they had scared the thief away. There was total silence. But only for a short while.   35

'You done finish?' asked the voice outside. 'Make we help you small. Oya, everybody!'

'*Police-o!   Tief-man-o!   Neighbours-o! we done loss-o! Police-o! …*'   40

There were at least five other voices besides the leader's. Jonathan and his family were now completely paralysed by terror. Maria and the children **sobbed inaudibly** like lost souls. Jonathan 45 **groaned** continuously.

The silence that followed the thieves' alarm vibrated horribly. Jonathan all but

begged their leader to speak again and
50 be done with it.

'My frien,' said he at long last, 'we
don try our best for call dem but I tink
say dem all done sleep-o … So wetin
we go do now? Sometaim you wan call
55 soja? Or you wan make we call dem for
you? Soja better pass police. No be so?'

'Na so!' replied his men. Jonathan
thought he heard even more voices now
than before and groaned heavily. His
60 legs were **sagging** under him and his
throat felt like sand-paper.

'My frien, why you no de talk again.
I de ask you say you wan make we call
soja?'

65   'No'.

'Awrighto. Now make we talk business. We no be bad tief. We no like for
make trouble. Trouble done finish. War
done finish and all the katakata wey de
70 for inside. No Civil War again. This time
na Civil Peace. No be so?'

'Na so!' answered the horrible chorus.

'What do you want from me? I am
75 a poor man. Everything I had went with
this war. Why do you come to me? You
know people who have money. We …'

'Awright! We know say you no get
plenty money. But we sef no get even
80 anini. So derefore make you open dis
window and give us one hundred pound
and go commot. Orderwise we de come
for inside now to show you guitar-boy
like dis …'

85   A **volley** of automatic fire rang
through the sky. Maria and the children
began to **weep** aloud again.

'Ah, missisi de cry again. No need
for dat. We done talk say we na good
tief. We just take our small money and 90
go nwayorly. No molest. Abi we de
molest?'

'At all' sang the chorus.

'My   friends,'   began   Jonathan
hoarsely. 'I hear what you say and I 95
thank you. If I had one hundred pounds
…'

'Lookia my frien, no be play we
come play for your house. If we make
mistake and step for inside you no go 100
like am-o. So derefore …'

'To God who made me; if you come
inside and find one hundred pounds,
take it and shoot me and shoot my
wife and children. I swear to God. The 105
only money I have in this life is this
twenty-pounds *egg rasher* they gave me
today…'

'OK. Time de go. Make you open
dis window and bring the twenty pound. 110
We go manage am like dat.'

There were now loud murmurs of
dissent among the chorus: 'Na lie de
man de lie; e get plenty money … Make
we go inside and search properly well 115
… Wetin be twenty pound? …'

'Shurrup!' rang the leader's voice
like a lone shot in the sky and silenced
the murmuring at once. 'Are you dere?
Bring the money quick!'   120

'I am coming,' said Jonathan **fum-
bling** in the darkness with the key of the
small wooden box he kept by his side on
the **mat**. […]

[Chinua Achebe. Copyright © 1972,
1973. #1; bold face added]

INFO

Chinua Achebe (*1930) is one of the most famous contemporary Nigerian authors. A typical characteristic of his style of writing is his orthographic reproduction of the way people speak in Nigeria. This is also one of the main reasons why this Nigerian author is so interesting to us here.

Vocabulary

1. Look up the following words and expressions in a monolingual English dictionary: imperious, rickety, parched, inaudibly, sag, volley, molest, egg rasher, dissent, fumble, and mat.
2. Investigate the meaning of the following words describing human sounds and construct a sentence with each of them: sob, groan, and weep.

A) NIGERIAN ENGLISH WORDS AND PHRASES

1. Read through the text and take a close look at the vocabulary.
2. Take a look at the memory cards on the next page. With the help of the text and a partner, try to find out which cards belong together.
3. When you have found the matching pairs, write them down in the table given below.

Nigerian English	Standard English

CIVIL PEACE EXERCISE: VOCABULARY MEMORY

[Based on #xiii – #xvi]

✂

na	**3rd person object pronoun equivalent to** *him / her / it*	**-o / o**	**oya**
trouble(s) / problem(s) / turmoil	**soldier (n.)**	**wetin**	**comparative/ superlative marker often in the sense of 'better than' / 'more than'**
soja	**pass**	**emphasis marker attached to the end of words or sentences**	**who / that**
commot	**it is; am / are / is**	**katakata**	**wey**
question word in a yes / no question similar to the English question tag *isn't it*	**abi**	**come out / leave**	**am**
what (is)	**come on / let's get it on (idiomatic)**		

B) NIGERIAN ENGLISH PRONUNCIATION

1. Take a look at the following words and phrases from the text, especially those containing letters in bold face. Based on these examples, can you come up with any pronunciation rules for Nigerian English? Work with a partner.
2. Can you think of any other standard English words that might be pronounced differently according to your rules? Give five examples.

" "Awright!"

"My frien'"
"we don try our best for call **d**em
but I **t**ink say **d**em all done sleep-o"

"So **d**erefore make you open **d**is window"

"We no be bad tief"   **"Lookia my frien'"**

"But we se**f** not get even anini".

"

C) NIGERIAN ENGLISH COMPOSITION

1. As was mentioned in the introduction to this chapter, Nigeria is a country with more than 400 native languages. In a comment, discuss whether you think English is a useful and necessary bridge builder between people of different cultural and linguistic backgrounds or whether the use of English prevents the establishment of a native Nigerian lingua franca. (Write a minimum of 200–300 words!)
2. How might Chinua Achebe's story go on? Continue the dialogue or the story. (Write a minimum of 200–300 words!)
3. Take another look at the differences in pronunciation, vocabulary, and grammar discussed above and below. In a comment, explain which of these, in your opinion, are hardest to understand. Give reasons and examples illustrating your opinion. (Write a minimum of 200–300 words!)

D) NIGERIAN ENGLISH GRAMMAR

The boxes below contain Nigerian Pidgin English phrases taken from the text. Work with a partner and try to answer the following questions:

1. Take a look at the sentences in 1. and 2. How do they differ from one another? Try to give their standard English translations. Can you determine any rules based on these sentences? It might be helpful to check the context in which these sentences appear.
2. Take a look at the sentences in 3. and 4. What do they have in common and how are they different from one another? Can you give their standard English translations? Can you come up with any rules based on these sentences?

1. "Make we help you small."
   "Make we go inside and search properly well."

2. "Make you hopen de door."
   "Make you open dis window and bring the twenty pound."

3. "Ah, missisi de cry again."
   "My frien, why you no de talk again."
   "Na lie de man de lie; e get plenty money ..."

4. "You done finish?"
   "Trouble done finish."
   "We don try our best for call dem but I tink say dem all done sleep-o ..."

E) NIGERIAN ENGLISH TRANSLATION

Try to translate the text from lines 51 to 84 into standard English. Your notes on Nigerian English vocabulary and pronunciation will be very helpful.

READING COMPREHENSION: NIGERIAN ENGLISH NEWSPAPER

The following text is taken from *The Daily Trust*, a newspaper based in the Nigerian capital Abuja. Carefully read the text, and answer the questions and exercises below.

Pastor bags six months for swindling lady

Written by Usman A. Bello, Tuesday, 15 April 2008

An Abuja magistrate's court yesterday sentenced a 40 year-old pastor to six months imprisonment without fine option for swindling a woman of the sum of N450,000.

The court also ordered the pastor, Dominic Udemgba to refund the said amount to the woman.

The prosecutor had earlier informed the court that the pastor **conspired with** one Regina Obinna (who jumped bail) to swindled one Mrs Amaka Aguike Anih of the sum of N450,000.

He said Mrs Anih petitioned the commissioner of police on February 12, 2005, that she took her sick husband to Regina Obinna's clinic in Gwagwa for **medical attention** and that instead of given him medical attention she said he had a spiritual problem and referred them to Rama Temple India for prayers. "On getting to Rama Temple, Pastor Dominic Udemgba asked them to pay N9,000 for prayer, after diagnosing that the problem was from their village," he said.

He explained further that after paying N9,000, the pastor deceived them to part with another N450,000 in order to purchase a vehicle for the pastor for **spiritual cleansing**.

The prosecutor said immediately after the last **batch of money** was given to the pastor, he vanished.

City News learnt that the case was first mentioned in June 2006, when the accused persons pleaded not guilty and were granted bail.

The case suffered several adjournments due to the disappearance of the second accused person (Regina Obinna), who jumped bail.

The disappearance of one of the accused persons then

prompted the counsel of the pastor to seek for separate trial.

While delivering Judgment yesterday, the **presiding** 60 **magistrate**, Ndukwu Chukwu condemned the action of the pastor and said his actions have shown that he uses his temple to deceive and collect money 65 from people, adding that all elements of cheating has been proven against the him by the prosecutor.

In another case, a 25 year- 70 old man was arraigned for **allegedly** threatening a lady for refusing his love proposal.

The man, David Balogun, was said to have threatened to 75 deal with one Comfort Momoh, after she **declined** his friendship request.

The prosecutor, Phanuel Masi told the court that on 80 April 10, one Comfort Momoh reported to the police that the accused **traced** her to where she lives at Lugbe village and threatened that he would organize a gang to kill her for 85 refusing his love advances.

The accused denied the charge when the charge sheet was read out in court and he sought for bail which was not 90 **objected to** by the prosecutor.

The presiding magistrate, Rosemary Kanyip granted him bail in the sum of N30, 000 and a surety in like sum.   95

"The surety must reside within the jurisdiction of the court with a fixed address," the magistrate ordered and adjourned the case to May 5 for 100 hearing.

[From *Daily Trust* (Abuja/Nigeri). #2; bold face added.]

Vocabulary

1. Look up the following words and expressions in a monolingual English dictionary: swindling, conspire with, medical attention, spiritual cleansing, batch of money, prompt, presiding magistrate, allegedly, decline, trace, and object to.
2. The text shown here features many words related to court and the legal system. Underline these words in the text and look up their definitions in the dictionary, if necessary. Write one sentence of your own with each word.

EXERCISES

1. In the table below, you can find Nigerian English sentences taken from the
    above newspaper article. Try to find all linguistic features that you would not
    expect in a British or American newspaper article (look carefully at the tenses,
    the word order, and for places where something might be missing) and give their
    standard English equivalents.
2. Assess the extent to which this article is typically Nigerian or African and discuss
    how it would differ from an American or British article covering the same or a
    similar topic. (Write a minimum of 200–300 words!)

Nigerian English	Standard English
An Abuja magistrate's court yesterday sentenced a 40 year-old pastor to six months imprisonment without fine option for swindling a woman of the sum of N450, 000.	
The prosecutor had earlier informed the court that the pastor conspired with one Regina Obinna (who jumped bail) to swindled one Mrs Amaka Aguike Anih of the sum of N450, 000.	
[...] that she took her sick husband to Regina Obinna's clinic in Gwagwa for medical attention and that instead of given him medical attention she said he had a spiritual problem and referred them to Rama Temple India for prayers.	
"On getting to Rama Temple, Pastor Domnic Udemgba asked them to pay N9, 000 for prayer, after diagnosing that the problem was from their village," he said.	

The disappearance of one of the accused persons then prompted the counsel of the pastor to seek for separate trial.	
While delivering Judgment yesterday, the presiding magistrate, Ndukwu Chukwu condemned the action of the pastor and said his actions have shown that he uses his temple to deceive and collect money from people, adding that all elements of cheating has been proven against the him by the prosecutor.	

 HOMEWORK

Search for a Nigerian news article on the Internet.

1. Analyse how it would differ from a European or American article covering the same or a similar topic.
2. Look for differences in grammar and vocabulary.
3. Be prepared to present your article and its peculiarities in class.

The following web links will be helpful:
- » http://dailytrust.com.ng/
- » http://www.sunnewsonline.com/
- » http://www.newswatchngr.com/
- » http://www.ngrguardiannews.com/

Nigerian Pidgin English

In Nigeria, we find very different ways of speaking English. Standardised Englishes coexist besides Nigerian English and Nigerian Pidgin English. In general, it is quite difficult to draw a clear distinction between Nigerian English and Nigerian Pidgin English, as elements of Pidgin English can occur in the speech of nearly any Nigerian speaker. The text below, however, is a clear example of Nigerian Pidgin English:

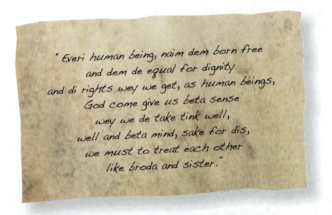

" Everi human being, naim dem born free
and dem de equal for dignity
and di rights wey we get, as human beings,
God come give us beta sense
wey we de take tink well,
well and beta mind, sake for dis,
we must to treat each other
like broda and sister. "

[From *Universal Declaration of Human Rights in Nigerian Pidgin English. Article 1. #3.*]

EXERCISES

1. Try to translate the above text into standard English and note the distinct Nigerian Pidgin English expressions along with their standard English equivalents in a separate list. The following web links will be very helpful:
    »   http://www.ngex.com/personalities/babawilly/dictionary/default.htm
    »   http://naijalingo.com/
2. Explain why there is even a Nigerian Pidgin English translation of this text. Work in pairs.
3. In a comment, discuss whether you believe the right to express oneself in one's native language is a universal human right or whether it would be better if people used as few languages as possible in order to make communication easier. (Write a minimum of 200–300 words!)

Sources

TEXTS

[1] Achebe, Chinua. 1972/1973. Civil Peace. In: Achebe, Chinua. *Girls at War*. Ibadan: Heinemann, 86–89. Copyright © 1972, 1973, Chinua Achebe, used by permission of The Wylie Agency (UK) Limited.

[2] Bello, Usman A. "Pastor bags six months for swindling lady". *Daily Trust Online* [Abuja], April 15, 2008. <http://news.dailytrust.com/content/view/4226/32/>, April 15, 2008. Reproduced with permission of Daily Trust Abuja/Nigeria.

[3] "Universal Declaration of Human Rights in Nigerian Pidgin English". The Office of the United Nations High Commissioner for Human Rights (OHCHR), Geneva/Switzerland, 1996–2011. <http://www.ohchr.org/EN/UDHR/Pages/Language.aspx?LangID=pcm>, July 01, 2011. Reproduced with permission of the Office of the United Nations High Commissioner for Human Rights (OHCHR).

PICTURES AND FIGURES

Map of Africa: © Isabel Peters. Hamburg, 2011.

Map of Nigeria: © Isabel Peters. Hamburg, 2011.

Languages in Nigeria: © Isabel Peters. Hamburg, 2011.

Nigerian flag: © Isabel Peters. Hamburg, 2011.

Femi Kuti: <http://commons.wikimedia.org/wiki/File:FemiKuti.jpg> (Creative Commons Attribution-ShareAlike 3.0), February 07, 2012.

Notes: © Isabel Peters. Hamburg, 2011.

REFERENCES AND FURTHER READING

Alo, Moses A. and Rajend Mesthrie. 2004. Nigerian English: morphology and syntax. In: Kortmann, Bernd, Kate Burridge, Rajend Mesthrie, Edgar W. Schneider, and Clive Upton (eds.), *A Handbook of Varieties of English*, Vol. 2. *Morphology and Syntax*. Berlin/New York: Mouton de Gruyter, 812–827.

Faraclas, Nicholas. 2004. Nigerian Pidgin English: morphology and syntax. In: Kortmann, Bernd, Kate Burridge, Rajend Mesthrie, Edgar W. Schneider, and Clive Upton (eds.), *A Handbook of Varieties of English*, Vol. 2. *Morphology and Syntax*. Berlin/New York: Mouton de Gruyter, 828–853.

Gut, Ulrike. 2008. Nigerian English: phonology. In: Mesthrie, Rajend (ed.), *Varieties of English*, Vol. 4. *Africa, South and Southeast Asia*. Berlin/New York: Mouton de Gruyter, 35–54.

Schneider, Edgar W. 2007. *Postcolonial English. Varieties around the World*. Cambridge: Cambridge University Press, 199–212.

[i]   "Nigeria." The World Factbook. Central Intelligence Agency, 2011. <https://www.cia.
        gov/library/publications/the-world-factbook/geos/ni.html>, October 24, 2011.

[ii]   "Nigeria." Encyclopædia Britannica. Encyclopædia Britannica Online Academic
        Edition. Encyclopædia Britannica Inc., 2011. Web. <http://www.britannica.com/
        EBchecked/topic/414840/Nigeria>, October 26, 2011.

[iii]   "Nigeria country profile." The BBC, 2009. <http://www.bbc.co.uk/news/world-
        africa-13949550>, January 31, 2012.

[iv]   Gut, Ulrike. 2008. Nigerian English: phonology. In: Mesthrie, Rajend. (ed.), *Varieties
        of English*, Vol. 4. *Africa, South and Southeast Asia*. Berlin/New York: Mouton de
        Gruyter, 35–54.

[v]   "Nigeria tops happiness survey." The BBC, 2003. <http://news.bbc.co.uk/2/
        hi/3157570.stm>, January 31, 2012.

[vi]   "Nigeria surpasses Hollywood as world's second largest film producer." United
        Nation's News Centre [New York/USA], May 05, 2009. <http://www.un.org/apps//
        news/story.asp?NewsID=30707&Cr=nigeria&Cr1=>, October 24, 2011.

[vii]   "Chinua Achebe." Encyclopædia Britannica. Encyclopædia Britannica Online
        Academic Edition. Encyclopædia Britannica Inc., 2012. Web. <http://www.britannica.
        com/EBchecked/topic/3493/Chinua-Achebe>, January 31, 2012.

[viii] Ogbaa, Kalu. 1999. *Understanding Things Fall Apart: A Student Casebook to Issues,
        Sources, and Historical Documents*. Westport, CT: Greenwood Press.

[ix]   "Chinua Achebe's Biography and Style." The University of North Carolina. <http://
        www.unc.edu/~hhalpin/ThingsFallApart/achebebio.html>, January 31, 2012.

[x]   "Biography." Femi Kuti. <http://www.myspace.com/femikuti>, January 31, 2012.

[xi]   "Biography of Femi Anikulapo Kuti". The Shrine. The Unofficial Website for Fela Kuti
        and Afrobeat Music. <http://www.afrobeatmusic.net/html/femi_bio_.html>, January 31,
        2012.

[xii]   "Fela." Britannica Book of the Year, 1998. Encyclopædia Britannica Online Academic
        Edition. Encyclopædia Britannica Inc., 2011. Web. <http://www.britannica.com/
        EBchecked/topic/203842/Fela>, October 26, 2011.

[xiii] "Babawilly's Dictionary of Pidgin English Words and Phrases." <http://www.ngex.com/
        personalities/babawilly/dictionary/default.htm>, January 31, 2012.

[xiv]   "Naija Lingo: Nigerian Pidgin English." <http://naijalingo.com/index.php>, January 31,
        2012.

[xv]   "Pidgin English." nigeriandictionary.com. <http://www.nigeriandictionary.com/
        language.php?lang_id=63&char=>, January 31, 2012.

[xvi]   "Index:Nigerian Pidgin." Wiktionary, the free dictionary. <http://en.wiktionary.org/wiki/
        Index:Nigerian_Pidgin>, January 31, 2012.

Outer circle

Chapter 8

South African English

Introduction

The sociolinguistic situation in South Africa is quite complex. Therefore, South African English can best be described as a heterogeneous variety marked by considerable internal differentiation. There are five major ethnic population groups within the country – Africans, Afrikaners, Whites, Coloureds, Indians – and different varieties of English often play the role of identity markers (cf. Schneider 2007: 174–175). We can at least identify White South African English and Black South African English as distinct forms of English spoken in South Africa. In addition, there is a contact variety called 'South African Indian English' rooted in the speech of Tamil, Telugu, and Hindi-speaking populations of indentured labourers who settled in the Natal area between 1860 and 1911 (Mesthrie 1992: 7). This form of English is distinct from Indian English and South African English.

The first contacts with English can be traced back to the beginning of the 19th century, when the British established control over the Cape region in 1815, thereby seizing power from Dutch colonists, who had occupied the area since 1652 (cf. Schneider 2007: 175). The Dutch, who had lived in the territory for generations, had assimilated to the indigenous culture to a considerable extent and developed their own variety of Dutch (Afrikaans), as contacts with their ancestry in Europe were barely maintained. The 19th century saw an increase in bilingualism with English playing a decisive role. Contact between speakers of Afrikaans and English was much more frequent than that between Europeans and Africans. Most Africans came into contact with English via missionary schools, as interpersonal communication with the European population was largely sporadic. During the Apartheid years in the 20th century, English began to enjoy increasing popularity among the African population as a language associated with liberation and solidarity.

A quick guide to South Africa provides a linguistic and sociocultural overview of South Africa. The Listening Comprehensions *South African culture* and *English in South Africa: A part of South African culture?* present authentic reports from South African students. The subsequent group discussion builds on the previous activities with the purpose of systematically organising students' knowledge of attitudes towards English in South Africa. The Reading Comprehension *Newspaper cuttings* presents students with clippings from authentic South African articles from newspapers and the Internet. A text titled *South African English* focuses on the issues of attitudes towards language and how English has helped to shape South African identity. The chapter is rounded off with a mind map on South African English.

A quick guide to South Africa

Which languages do people speak?

• • • • • •

South Africa has eleven official languages: Zulu (IsiZulu), Xhosa (IsiXhosa), Afrikaans, Pedi (Sepedi), English, Tswana (Setswana), Sotho (Sesotho), Tsonga (Xitsonga), Swati (siSwati), Venda (Tshivenda), and Ndebele (isiNdebele).

According to 2001 National Census figures, the three most widely spoken of these eleven languages are Zulu (23.8%), Xhosa (17.6%), and Afrikaans (13.3%).

This means that although English is used as a national lingua franca in many domains, such as science, economy, government, and education, it was the mother tongue of only 8.2 per cent of the South African population in 2001.

Rainbow

Why 'Rainbow Nation'?

The concept of the 'Rainbow Nation' was "invented" by the former Archbishop of Cape Town, Desmond Tutu, to describe South Africa after the end of Apartheid. The term was coined to draw attention to as well as encourage unity among people from different races and cultures in a country once identified with the strict division of different ethnicities.

Flag of South Africa

Do they really have robots on street corners?

Actually they do, as traffic lights are often called *robots* in South Africa. Other distinct South African terms include *bakkie* for a 'pick-up truck', *takkies* for 'sneakers', and *braai* for a 'barbecue'. Moreover, an insect may be called a *gogga* and an alcoholic drink a *dop*. Due to this distinct flavour, many people think that the variety of English spoken in South Africa is *lekker* (i.e. 'nice', 'cool', 'great')!

Map of South Africa

Who lives in South Africa?

South Africa is a nation of over 49 million people with different origins, cultures, languages, and beliefs.

In terms of ethnicity, around 79 per cent are African, nine per cent are of European descent, nine per cent are 'coloured' – the South African designation for people of mixed African, Asian, and European descent – and 2.5 per cent are Indian or Asian.

Dancing children

However, these rather broad categories can be further subdivided, as considerable cultural and linguistic differences exist within these communities.

As an example, the cultural and linguistic diversity within the African community is nicely illustrated by the country's nine official languages with African origin.

The European population is similarly diverse, with inhabitants with roots in different European countries such as Great Britain, the Netherlands, and Germany. The most important distinction within the European community is that between the so-called Afrikaners, who speak Afrikaans and are mainly the descendents of Dutch, German, and French settlers, and the English-speaking groups, whose ancestors were largely British colonists, but who also may have roots in other European countries such as Italy or Portugal.

Who is Nelson Mandela?

Nelson Mandela (*1918) is a South African politician. He was the first president of South Africa who was elected in a democratic election. He served one term as president and was in office from 1994–1999. Before he became president, Mandela was an anti-Apartheid activist. As a consequence of his struggle against Apartheid, he spent 27 years in prison. After his release from prison in 1990, Mandela helped to lead South Africa's peaceful transition towards a multicultural democracy. For his efforts, he was awarded the Nobel Peace Prize in 1993.

What's Apartheid?

Apartheid, an Afrikaans term meaning 'separateness', was a political system of racial segregation that was established in 1948 and maintained until 1990 in South Africa.

This system of the systematic segregation of different ethnic groups had its roots in the colonial history of South Africa in which the separation of different ethnic groups and the predominance of the European settlers had an inglorious tradition. After winning the 1948 election, the National Party implemented their programme of Apartheid, which expanded the already existing segregation policies into a system of racism and white domination, assigning each inhabitant to a certain racial group.

The system of Apartheid was closely connected to the Afrikaans language as it was the preferred language of the Apartheid regime. English, in contrast, was used as a lingua franca by black liberation organisations such as the African National Congress (ANC) during the struggle for freedom, and has often been considered the language of liberation.

Apartheid was slowly removed following negotiations from 1990 to 1993, culminating in the 1994 elections, the first in South Africa in which every citizen had the right to vote.

CITY OF DURBAN
UNDER SECTION 37 OF THE DURBAN
BEACH BY-LAWS, THIS BATHING AREA IS
RESERVED FOR THE SOLE USE OF
MEMBERS OF THE WHITE RACE GROUP.
STAD DURBAN
HIERDIE BAAIGEBIED IS, INGEVOLGE
ARTIKEL 37 VAN DIE DURBANSE
STRANDVERORDENINGE, UITGEHOU VIR
DIE UITSLUITLIKE GEBRUIK VAN LEDE
VAN DIE BLANKE RASSEGROEP.
IDOLOBHA LASETHEKWINI
NGAPHANSI KWESIGABA 37 SOMTHETHO
WAMABHISHI ASETHEKWENI, LENDAWO
ICCINELWE UKUSETSHENZISWA
NGAMALUNGU OHLANGA OLUMHLOPHE
KUPHELA.

Sign

[Based on #i – #xiv]

COMPOSITION

1. Using the boxes given above, discuss why English was and still is so important in South Africa. Explain whether you think that it is good that English is used as a national lingua franca or if you can imagine some disadvantages that might come along with this language use. Answer these questions in a comment. (Write a minimum of 200–300 words!)

2. Based on the boxes given above, write a short article for a travel guide about South Africa. (Write a minimum of 200–300 words!)

DISCUSSION

1. Form groups and assign two to three boxes to each of the group members. Report the content of your boxes to your fellow group members.
2. Discuss the content of the boxes in your groups. What did you already know and what is new? Can you add something? What else do you know about South Africa?
3. Note the most important facts from the boxes and from your discussion in a small mind map.

 HOMEWORK

Find answers to the following questions and write them down in full sentences:

- » What do John Maxwell Coetzee, Frederik Willem de Klerk, and Nelson Mandela have in common?
- » What or who is meant by the phrase *Bafana Bafana* and what does it actually mean in English?
- » What are the three biggest cities in South Africa and where are they located?
- » What are *townships*?
- » When did South Africa become a British colony and when did it gain its independence?
- » Who are Thabo Mbeki and Jacob Zuma?
- » What is *Soweto* and what does it mean?
- » What is the difference between *now*, *now now*, and *just now* in South African English?

These links might be helpful:
- » https://www.cia.gov/library/publications/the-world-factbook/geos/sf.html
- » http://www.southafrica.info/about/
- » http://www.bbc.co.uk/news/world-africa-14094760
- » http://www.britannica.com/EBchecked/topic/555568/South-Africa

LISTENING COMPREHENSION

South African culture

In the boxes below, you find statements provided by South African
students from different social and ethnic backgrounds. All of them
report their opinions of South African culture. Before listening
to the corresponding audio files, care-
fully read through the boxes and the
vocabulary.

You can find the audio file at
www.awe.uni-hamburg.de. [#1]

South African provinces

1. "I can, ok – here in South Africa we
have nine official languages. Ok, we –
we have Sesotho, Xhosa, isiZulu, English, Boers, isiNdebele, Sepedi, and –
and I have forgot the two and then. So,
all those – all those people practising
– practising their, their things. The way
they wear is different from the Zulus on
that time. But now, we just, we're wearing the Western styles. But if maybe Zulus have their ceremonies – ceremony,
there you can see that this people are
the Zulu and then this people are the
Sesotho. The way they dance if they
have the ceremony. […] There is those
cultures in South Africa, but – but we all
people understand that we have to respect one another's culture and one another's culture, ya."

2. "South African culture? I think
it's a big mix of different things.
Ehm, so, like, we'll go to the sta-
dium and watch rugby, which is a
very Afrikaans culture and then
we'll go down, ehm, to – we'll
go home and watch British Television, ehm, that's kind of in my
environment. That's my exposure
of – of South African culture. But
then also, like, we watch soccer,
ehm, and some South African
soccer, which is very much a Zulu
and a, you know, that kind of a
culture. So, I think South African
culture is a very mixed, ehm, variety of different people and different things that – that brings it out,
ya. That makes it what it is."

South African countryside

3. "What is South African culture? Ehm, I think diversity. The fact that we're so **cosmopolitan** and we can just **intermingle with** everyone. The fact that we have such a rich history and a lot of change that happened. I think that's South African culture."

4. "In general I think there's no – there – I don't think there is a general South African culture. There's mixed cultures and somewhere around the line some people meet, you know, half way and some people don't. You know what I mean? Like, for instance, you'll find a lot of African people perhaps meeting with, ehm, **Caucasian** people and they kind of – you know what I mean? But – but perhaps you won't find African people meeting with Indians, especially since there's a lot of – there's a lot of conflict that happened in South Africa. So – especially with, like, the Zulus and the Indians, in that sense – they really – it's very rare that you find them – really **hitting it off**. So in that sense there are **culture divisions**, but I think, ehm … South Africa's got so much cultures. That's – I don't know. South African culture is just – it's like they say, the Rainbow Nation."

5. "It show where do I come from. Actually, and I appreciate, you know, there's appreciate, that I'm a Zulu-speaking person. I'm dark in colour. I've got my hair different. Every-thing, you know. I – I appreciates that. That's how God made me and I have to be happy and enjoy it. And appreciation of the difference that we have. You know, it's so nice to see other people. I love to see Indians, see Whites people. It's, it's great, it's amazing. Ya, especially, if you're united in something, you know, I agree that this is good thing. I'm happy."

Cape Town

6. "Uuuh, South African culture's great, it's just wonderful, I'm so proud to be South African, I'm so proud to be black. I love my country. See, the thing is with South Africa, it's so **diverse**, it's diverse in many aspects, not only in language, and culture and lifestyle. But it's diverse in the sense that people with their different backgrounds form a **common ground** and learn and … And within their common ground, they form a culture on its own, so for me, I think that's … – 'Cause I mean, we could cause a whole lot of conflict – if I as a Sotho, don't like a Zulu girl, you know, or if someone lives in Umhlanga and I live in Clermont, I have a problem with them or something like that. But South Africans somehow find a common ground and learn to relate and respect each other in that sense at most times."

PRE-LISTENING ACTIVITIES

Work with a partner:
1. Carefully read through the boxes and try to find all non-standard features of English and give their standard English equivalents. In which box(es) do you find most of them?
2. Try to match the statements above to the profiles of the students on page 220–221. Give at least five reasons to support your opinion.
3. Underline all instances of the words 'especially' and 'culture' as well as all words with *th*-sounds.

WHILE-LISTENING ACTIVITY

While listening to the audio files at least two times, mark those letters and sounds in the boxes which are pronounced differently than in Received Pronunciation. Also try to describe how or in what way they differ from Received Pronunciation and from the other speakers. Your underlined words will be helpful.

POST-LISTENING ACTIVITIES

1. Try to organise the notes you made while listening to the interview. Can you identify any regularities and determine any rules? Can you find any similarities between the individual speakers?
2. Which of these speakers are most difficult to understand? Give reasons to support your opinion.
3. Reconsider your assignment of the statements to the portraits of the students. Were your initial judgements correct?

EXERCISES

Summarise the most important aspects of South African culture as mentioned above. Discuss what these statements have in common and in what ways they differ.

COMPOSITION

1. "South African culture is just – it's like they say, the Rainbow Nation." In a comment, discuss whether you think the designation Rainbow Nation is a good term to describe the cultural diversity of South Africa. Give reasons to support your opinion. (Write a minimum of 200–300 words!)
2. Imagine that you are one of the students portrayed on page 220–221 and that you have just spent your first week at the university in Durban. Write a letter / e-mail to your family describing your impressions of the people of various cultural backgrounds, the different ways of speaking English, and maybe even your problems understanding your new fellow students. (Write a minimum of 200–300 words!)

SELF-STUDY

Pick one of the cultures mentioned above and find out more about it. Take notes and prepare yourself to present your results to your fellow students in a 3–5 minute presentation.

Vocabulary
Look up the following words and expressions in a monolingual English dictionary: cosmopolitan, intermingle with, Caucasian, hit it off, culture divisions, diverse, and common ground.

Sesi was born and raised in Johannesburg. Her native language is Sesotho and in addition to English, she also speaks Zulu. She has been speaking English since she was three years old. Nowadays, her family speaks more English than Sesotho so that her younger sisters and brothers have the chance to practice it as much as possible. English is seen as a tool to get ahead. She studies psychology at the University of KwaZulu-Natal in Durban.

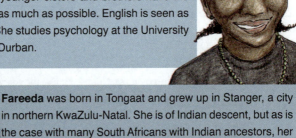

Fareeda was born in Tongaat and grew up in Stanger, a city in northern KwaZulu-Natal. She is of Indian descent, but as is the case with many South Africans with Indian ancestors, her native language is English. Apart from that, she also speaks a bit of Zulu and Afrikaans. She is studying social work in order to help the victims of crime and poverty in South Africa.

Anna was born in Zimbabwe and also spent the first years of her childhood in that country. However, due to the political unrest there, she and her family emigrated to South Africa, where she has been living in Durban ever since. Her native language is English, but she also speaks Afrikaans and a bit of Zulu. Now she is a student at the University of KwaZulu-Natal in Durban. Her subjects are English and media studies. What she likes most about South Africa is the cultural diversity of the country.

Dumisani was born and raised in a small village near Durban. His native language is Zulu and he is very proud of his Zulu origins and the traditions and values of his culture. He has now been learning English for twelve years and speaks English at university, although no English is spoken in his family and he hardly ever speaks English with his friends, since most of them are Zulus as well. He is studying community development at the University of KwaZulu-Natal in order to help poor African communities and the people living there to further develop and to have a better chance to succeed.

Jim was born in Kimberley in the Northern Cape Province and also spent parts of his childhood there. As a teenager, his family moved to Richards Bay. His native language is Afrikaans, but his dad insisted very early that he should learn English. That is why he always went to English schools and why English is often spoken in his family. Jim has now been learning English for 16 years. He studies philosophy in Durban.

Andrew was born in Durban and also spent most of his life there. His native language is English and he also speaks Afrikaans fairly well. He admits that he has never thought about learning an African language. He studies biology, neurosciences, and linguistics at his university.

Mandla was born and raised in a small town in central Kwa-Zulu-Natal. His native language is Zulu, which is the only language spoken in his family. Although he has been learning English for 14 years, he is not too happy with his skills, saying that his English schooling, especially in primary school, was rather poor. As he comes from an underprivileged background, he not only wants to succeed in life but also wants to help other people who do not have the same opportunities as he has had. Thus, he is studying law at his university in order to become a lawyer and help other people.

Mbali was born and raised in a small town in the North of KwaZulu-Natal. Her native language is Zulu, which is the only language spoken in her family. She is very dissatisfied with her command of English, for which she blames the poor schooling she received in school. Thus, she is constantly trying to improve her English. At university, she is studying law in order to become a judge.

Drawings of South African students

 LISTENING COMPREHENSION

English in South Africa:
A part of South African culture?

In the boxes below, you find statements from South African students as to whether they think that English is a part of South African culture and how they perceive the status and importance of English in their country. Carefully read through the boxes and the vocabulary and answer the questions given below. You can find the audio file at www.awe.uni-hamburg.de. [#2]

"Yes, I do think it is. Sometimes unfairly so, because so few people, actually, in South Africa, can speak English. So, the fact that it's spoken in university and that it is the language of university is quite a – a highly contested subject, because not a lot of people can actually speak it fluently. But ya, I do think, because it's such a – such a part of South African **tertiary education** it will naturally be part of culture."

"No. […] If you're tracing back from our roots you found that, eh, English was not appearing here in South Africa. So, it is something new. Even our parents they don't know how to speak English. Even if I'm going at home in my, in my community, local people around me, they don't – even say one words of English, because English is a new thing, ya."

"Yes, a lot. Because English now is became **injected** even to Zulu speakers, you know. You find that some Zulu speakers who are from those schools which are called "Model Cs", you know, they started English from 'cratch up until grade twelve, so the others don't even know their language is Zulu. They don't even know Zulu, so it's became, English became South African culture to a larger extent because there is that mentality as well, that if you know English, you are **superior**. If you know English, you are better, you know. So that's what I can mention about English being a culture in South Africa. Yeah, I can say that they do need it, but they don't necessarily have to take English as the main thing or as the main language. But we do need English, because it's the communication language. Even to other countries or even to other languages, we use English just for communication. But others are misusing English because they even use English, even though there's no necessary. 'Cause you can find that you are the Zulu, I'm the Zulu. You supposed to speak isiZulu, but you keep on speaking English, you know? Ya."

"Well, I suppose – it depends what you take to be South African culture. It – it has to be a part of South African culture at some point, because, ehm, well, it's the national language and it's – it's – it does have a – well – ya. Ya, there's a lot of people who **resent** it as a – as a national language, but it – it played a big part in – in the struggle as well with – with, ehm, the Afrikaans regime at the time. The – the Africans used English as a – as a sort of neutral language of communication. That – that was – that was one sort of, ehm, politically neutral sort of thing that it did. It was useful. Ehm, but you can't – you can't avoid the fact that it is part of South African culture, because it just – as I said, it's the national language. It's used in all – all sorts of different environments and circumstances. Ya."

"Ah, perhaps not traditionally, but it has become a part of South African culture. Ehm, a lot of things, I would say, wasn't traditionally a part of South African culture. When I say traditionally, I mean in – in an **indigenous** sense. But it – ya, it's – English has become a part of South African culture. I mean you have – just the other day I was back home in Richards Bay and there was kids playing on a tree. And it was two African girls and they spoke the most beautiful English. And I complimented her and she said 'What else would I be speaking?', you know. And I was like 'Wow, don't you speak Zulu?' And she said 'No'. – I really like kids. I'm really interested in kids, you know. – And she said 'No'. 'cause I – I took my niece out to the park. She said 'No, we don't speak Zulu. You know, I can't even say a word in Zulu'. And so I think English has become part of South African culture, you know. It's – it's become something that I think 90 per cent of South Africans use every day, you know. That's – it's – it's – we – we – English is one with us now, you know what I mean? It's one – it's our – one of our eleventh official languages. It's part of that Rainbow Nation. So I would say English is a part of South African culture."

Vocabulary

Look up the following words and expressions in a monolingual English dictionary:
tertiary education, injected, superior, resent, indigenous, and ostracised.

"Yes, I think, I think it plays a major part, see, 'cause there's this distinguish-ment here in South Africa, that according to the rankings of education, especially in high school, if you go to – if you been to a private school, it's assumed that you have a better education than a person that been to high school in a rural area. And with English, it's like, those private schools are usually described as the white schools, so you get a black person who suddenly develops a white ac-cent. And they're called "coconuts" in society or you know there is those weird names, because it's assumed that they're tryin' to be white. Whereas, if a person from a rural area can't really speak English two hours they get to university, they are **ostracised** for being unintelligent. It's – there's a great misconception with English in South Africa that if you don't know English, it's assumed that you're un-intelligent, which is not true. So I think, in that sense, English plays a major role."

EXERCISES I

Work with a partner:

1. Carefully read through the boxes and try to find all non-standard features of English and give their standard English equivalents. In which box(es) do you find most of them?
2. Do certain non-standard features occur more often than others? Can you identify any regularities or similarities between the speakers?
3. Based on the information in the boxes, what arguments can you think of for and against English being a part of South African culture?
4. Try to match the statements above to the profiles of the students on page 220–221. Give at least five reasons for your opinion.

EXERCISES II

Work with a partner:

1. While listening to the audio files at least two times, mark those letters and sounds in the boxes which are pronounced differently than in Received Pro-nunciation. Also try to describe how or in what way they differ from Received Pronunciation and from the other speakers.
2. Which of these speakers are most difficult to understand? Give reasons.
3. Do the different speakers remind you of any other varieties of English?
4. Think again about the statements you attributed to the various students. Were your initial judgements correct?
5. To what extent do you think the students' judgements are justified? Discuss this question with a partner and note your results.

COMPOSITION

1. Imagine that you are an exchange student in South Africa. One day, you hear two friends discussing the status and role of English in South Africa. Pick two of the above monologues with opposing opinions and use them as a starting point for a dialogue, in which your friends debate this issue. Try to contribute to the discussion by expressing your own personal opinion. Write a dialogue illustrating this scene. (Write a minimum of 200–300 words!)

2. The concept of the 'Rainbow Nation' expresses the idea of peaceful unity within a multicultural society. In a comment, critically evaluate if you consider this term appropriate as a metaphor for South African society. (Write a minimum of 200–300 words!)

3. Imagine that you are a South African student and a native speaker of Zulu who thinks that it is both absolutely unfair and a form of discrimination for students to be taught in English, not only in many schools but also at most universities in the country. Write a letter to the current president of South Africa in which you complain about this situation and try to convince him or her that it has to be changed. (Write a minimum of 200–300 words!)

4. Imagine that you are a journalist for a British newspaper and you have to write an article about the English language in South Africa. In an opinion piece, summarise the status of and different attitudes towards English in South Africa, also expressing your personal opinion. In addition, come up with an appropriate headline. You may either write this article from the point of view of a broadsheet newspaper, like *The Times* or *The Guardian*, or from the point of view of a tabloid newspaper, such as *The Sun* or *The Daily Mirror*. (Write a minimum of 200–300 words!)

GROUP DISCUSSION:
ENGLISH IN SOUTH AFRICA: A PART OF SOUTH AFRICAN CULTURE?

English is one of the eleven official languages of South Africa and is the native language of about 3.5 million people or about 8.2 per cent of the population. Attitudes towards English differ throughout South Africa, however, with many people disagreeing on whether or not it is a necessary part of South African culture.

What do you think:
» Is English a part of South African culture?
» Do people really need English in South Africa?

Work with a partner and discuss these questions on the basis of what you already know about South Africa and with the help of the figure below. Come up with a list of as many pros and cons as you can think of.

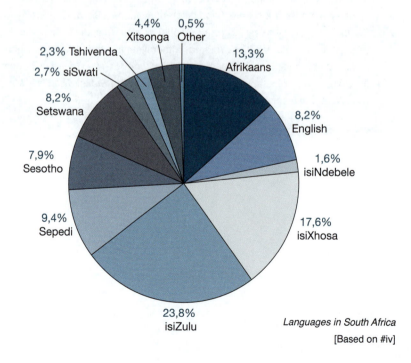

Languages in South Africa
[Based on #iv]

Pros	Cons

READING COMPREHENSION

Newspaper cuttings

The boxes on this page contain
headlines and articles from
South African newspapers and
online publications. All of them
contain at least one word, phrase
or grammatical structure that is
typical of South African English.
Carefully read through the boxes
and the vocabulary.

Letter to the editor:
Re: Cape liquor wars loom

The new law comes at a rather
bad time. Liquor sales are already suppressed due to the **recession**. People visit **shebeens**
as a means of socializing after
work. No one person will go and
buy a quart of beer and drink it
alone at home. Our shebeens are
equivelent to pubs in the UK.
Pubs can be found in every village in the UK. These pubs are
situated in residential area, they
are convenience as thr drinkers
does not have far walk home.
Most importantly the 2010 soccer tourist want to visit shebeens
during their stay in SA. [#3]

What Is Clever?

[...] But how do you really judge how
clever someone is? Stephen Hawking discovered something amazing and
incomprehensible to the mere **mortal
mind**, but how clever is he?

Can he **hold a good argument
against** the free distribution of **antiretroviral drugs**, for example, or make a
case for Hitler? Is he capable of concep-
tualising future computer revolutions, or
finding cures for mysterious illnesses,
or indeed just a way to escape the 5pm
traffic heading out of the city towards
the southern suburbs along the Eastern
Boulevard?

That one's a **tantalising mystery**
that has defeated even the greatest traffic
planner's minds, and if Hawking is such
a genius why doesn't he fix it? Could he,
is the more **pertinent question**?

Or is his intelligence merely restricted to scientific theory – theories that as-
tound and delight but which never actually have any practical application in the
real world?

It's one thing having a theory that
little green men exist on Mars, but how
does that knowledge help us if we
don't go to Mars and say howzit?

"Howzit, okes. You must come
to South Africa, hey. Have a lekker
braavleis and a sponsor's brew, my
bru. Kap some lekker choons, watch
some lekker rugby, lag ourselves stuk-
kend, my china." [...] [#4]

Dagga 'ticket' for on-duty traffic cop

A Cape Town traffic cop faces disciplinary action after he was caught in possession of dagga while on duty.

The officer was caught in Athlone on Tuesday afternoon, apparently by Neighbourhood Watch members, and taken to Manenberg Police Station. [...] [#5]

Car dealer in hijack horror

July 22 2009 at 06:42am
By Angelique Serrao

It was a 70km hell-ride that has left him **traumatised**, the "**ferocious**" faces of his hijackers forever etched in his mind.

He was hijacked by two men dressed as policemen, stuck in the boot of their car, before being dumped in the veld in Bapsfontein without a cellphone. [...] [#6]

Vocabulary

1. Look up the following words and expressions in a monolingual English dictionary: recession, sheebeen, mortal mind, hold a good argument for / against, antiretroviral drugs, find cures for, tantalising mystery, pertinent question, traumatise, and ferocious.

2. The text *What Is Clever?* features some words and expressions useful for talking about theories. Find these words and expressions in the text and compose one sentence with each of them.

COMPOSITION

1. Imagine that you are a correspondent for a British newspaper. Pick one of the articles given above and rewrite it for a British audience. If necessary, make up some additional details or add information in order to be able to write a minimum of 200 to 300 words.

2. Write a comment in which you discuss which of these articles might be the hardest to understand for someone who is not from South Africa due to differences compared to standard English. Give reasons and examples to support your opinion. (Write a minimum of 200 to 300 words!)

EXERCISES

1. Take a look at the boxes on the previous pages. Can you find any grammatical structures that you would not expect in a standard English newspaper? What are they? Explain what makes them different and give their standard English equivalents.

2. Work with a partner and try to find all words and phrases in the boxes which can be considered typically South African in that they are only used in South Africa or have a special meaning there. Write them down in the table given below together with their standard English counterparts.

3. Which boxes might have been authored by native speakers of English and which by non-native speakers? Give reasons for your assumptions.

South African English	Standard English

READING COMPREHENSION

South African English

by Cynthia Schweer

Americans, like all citizens of former British colonies, are well positioned to understand the rebellious need to **modify the language** of our **imperial**
5 **ancestors**. We **former colonies** are just **defiant teenagers** at heart; my own time spent in London resembled a wayward child being sent home to reflect on her linguistic sins. Many a Brit would **chas-**
10 **tise** me **for** the grave errors in spelling or pronunciation that I claimed as proper English. But even the most subversive of Americans will find instruction in the South African tactics described below.

15
Tactic No. 1: Linguistic Expediency
The English language was not created with efficiency in mind. In fact, it can be argued that many proper English (read:
20 British) speakers actually delight in us- ing as many words as possible to say as little as possible. While some may de- fine this sort of **speech marathon** as ev- idence of good breeding, South Africans
25 go the extra mile to fight the tradition.

One tactic is combining words: the art of forgoing proper pronunciation to eliminate the need for **extraneous words**. Texans (like myself) understand
30 that merging words into catch-all phras- es saves energy, while still getting the

point across. "Y'all" is a great example. Amazingly, South Africans rival Texans at the art of word combining. Case in point: the uniquely South African phrase 35 *Howzit?*. *Howzit* consolidates "How are things going?", "Are things ok with you?", and "Exactly how are you on this fine day that we're having?" *Howzit* can be used in most any social or work-relat- 40 ed situation – both formal and informal. It's efficiency a Texan can take pride in.

Alternatively, defiant English speak- ers may choose to simply eliminate words altogether. South Africans have 45 taken this to a laudable scale, often re- ducing phrases to a single word. For example, the service industry in South Africa has been modernized by the re- duction of the **antiquated phrase** "It's 50 my pleasure" to simply, *pleasure*. Usu- ally said with the utmost cheeriness, the word efficiently acts as the American phrase "You're welcome." Furthermore, by simply changing the intonation to in- 55 dicate disdain or utter indifference, the *pleasure* can take on a host of different meanings, including (again, most often evident in the service industry), the con- cept that the pleasure in question is dis- 60 tinctly *not* a pleasure.

Tactic No. 2: Strategic Incomprehensibility

65 One of the most productive ways to **distort language** is to use it in a way that is **structurally incomprehensible** to outsiders. While Americans have used this tactic in the past, the prevalence 70 of American English in Hollywood has seriously undermined its effectiveness. Fortunately, our South African counterparts have been secretly adopting incomprehensible English phrases for the past 75 two centuries, virtually unbeknownst to the rest of the world, creating a **treasure trove of dissident vocabulary**.

Visitors to South Africa are forever puzzled by the use of the phrase *Izzit?*. 80 Similar to *Howzit?*, this phrase combines the words "Is" and "It" to form a frequently used question. The twist here, however, is that *izzit* can be used in almost any situation, regardless of 85 grammatical integrity. You might say: "Geez, it's pretty hot outside today," and the South African would reply, with a questioning look: "*Izzit?*" Or, you might remark, "South Africans seem to like 90 beer even more than Americans", which would **prompt a hearty handshake** and an "*Izzit!*" from your average South African. In an act of desperation, you could yell, "Under my rental car agree- 95 ment, it states that I should receive 100 free kilometers per day!" to which the South African car rental representative would dismissively say "*izzit*," and turn to the next customer.

100 South Africans have also creatively turned a casual national attitude toward punctuality into a collection of incomprehensible phrases regarding time. The word *now* spans the timeframe of "this very instant" all the way to "the 105 very distant future." In order to **clarify things**, South Africans use the phrase *just now* to mean "sometime in the near future" and *now now* to mean "very soon, though I may change my mind". 110 Just bear in mind: if the word *now* is used, you can be very secure that you will have to wait a long while.

Tactic No. 3: Alternative Language 115 Adoption

Finally, for English speakers who have exhausted all known tactics for subverting their native language, it's appropriate to adopt other languages in order to 120 thoroughly confuse the outsider. Like most former colonies, South Africa is fortunate enough to have had multiple aspiring imperialist groups cross its shores, thereby allowing South Africans 125 to draw upon several linguistic traditions. Most prominent, of course, is Afrikaans, itself a prime example of how a language (in this case Dutch) can be thoroughly exploited and modified by 130 a **raucous colony**. Any true South African can effectively **sprinkle** Afrikaans **words** liberally **into** his or her English speech, creating a slang that is virtually **unintelligible** to proper English speak- 135 ers.

The use of Afrikaans words is most **prevalent in** social situations, thereby easily allowing South Africans to **assert** their **national identity** and exclude non- 140 South Africans from the conversation at will. For example, as a visitor to this country, you will most likely be invited to a *braai* by the first South African that 145 you meet as you step off the plane. As an English-speaker, you will not understand that this is an informal barbecue, as opposed to some form of Apartheid-era torture for tourists. If your hospita-150 ble South African truly would like to include you at his *braai*, he will explain to you the origins of the word; if not, he will simply laugh and move on.

Afrikaans slang words are often 155 used **in conjunction with** phrases described above. English speakers beginning to comprehend the **vast irregularities of** South African **speech** will thus be **confounded** yet again. The use of 160 *lekker* (literally interpreted: nice; figuratively interpreted: cool); is frequently employed in this pursuit. A typical conversation, therefore could go something like this:

165 **South African #1:** Howzit?
South African #2: Lekker. Howzit?
South African #1: Lekker. It's pretty hot outside today.
South African #2: Izzit? Should we go 170 have a beer just now, then?

South African #1: Lekker. Now now.
South African #2: Ok, I'll see you later then.
South African #1: Ja, at the braai, now.   175

Fortunately for the English-speaking former colonies of the world, the **devolution of the English language** should continue apace in South Africa. In the 180 last decade, the government has **deemed** 11 languages to be officially South African, and there should be no **abatement** in the resulting **cross-contamination**. Even more encouraging, South Africans 185 are increasingly crossing continents for both work and travel, thereby spreading their unique version of the language abroad. As revolutionary English-speakers, it is essential that we do not rest on 190 our laurels and allow proper English to drift back into common use. Through the use of tactics such as those employed by our counterparts in South Africa, the **insurgency** will not be in vain.   195

[From *Flakmagazine Online*. #7; bold face added.]

Vocabulary

1. Look up the following words and expressions in a monolingual English dictionary: modify the language, imperial ancestors, former colonies, defiant teenagers, chastise sb for sth, prompt a hearty handshake, clarify things, raucous colony, sprinkle words into, prevalent in, assert national identity, in conjunction with, confound, deem, abatement, cross-contamination, and insurgency.

2. Explain in your own words what the following expressions mean. Consult a dictionary, if necessary: speech marathon, extraneous words, antiquated phrase, distort language, structurally incomprehensible, treasure trove of dissident vocabulary, unintelligible, vast irregularities of speech, and devolution of the English language.

COMPREHENSION

1. In your own words, summarise the most important characteristics of South African English as given in the text and explain how it differs from British English. Give examples.
2. What factors do you think have led to the differences between British English and South African English?

ANALYSIS

1. Compare the author's attitude towards British English with that expressed towards South African English and give reasons and examples supporting your opinion. (Write a minimum of 200–300 words!)
2. Analyse the overall style in which this article is written and give examples and reasons for your opinion. (Write a minimum of 200–300 words!)
3. "As revolutionary English-speakers, it is essential that we do not rest on our laurels and allow proper English to drift back into common use." Explain what the author means with this statement and also try to identify her general attitude towards standard English as opposed to different non-standard varieties of English. Give reasons and examples to support your assessment. (Write a minimum of 200–300 words!)

COMPOSITION

1. Imagine that you are a South African reader. Write a review of this article in which you discuss what you like and do not like about it. Consider not only what is said in the text, but also try to think of other important aspects, facts, influences, and groups of people that the author did not mention in her text. (Write a minimum of 200–300 words!)
2. "Fortunately for the English-speaking former colonies of the world, the devolution of the English language should continue apace in South Africa." Explain in your own words what the author means with this statement and critically discuss in a comment whether or not you share her view. Give reasons for your opinion. (Write a minimum of 200–300 words!)
3. This article was undoubtedly written from a North American perspective. Now imagine that you are a British journalist who has to adapt this text for a British audience. Rewrite the first 61 lines of this article and try to look at South African English from a typically British (English) point of view.

SOUTH AFRICAN ENGLISH: TRANSLATION EXERCISE

1. Try to give possible standard English translations of the different instances of "Izzit" that you can find below.
2. Translate these short dialogues into standard English.

> South African #1: "Geez, it's pretty hot outside today,"
> South African #2: "Izzit?"

American #1: "South Africans seem to like beer even more than Americans."
South African #3: "Izzit!"

Tourist #1: "Under my rental car agreement, it states that I should receive 100 free kilometers per day!"
South African #4: "Izzit."

REPETITION EXERCISE: SOUTH AFRICAN ENGLISH MEMORY

Take a look at the memory cards given below. Work with a partner and try to find the
matching pairs. Write down the correct pairs.

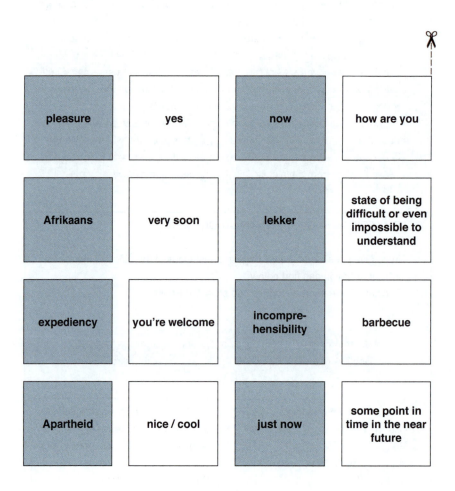

pleasure	yes	now	how are you
Afrikaans	very soon	lekker	state of being difficult or even impossible to understand
expediency	you're welcome	incompre-hensibility	barbecue
Apartheid	nice / cool	just now	some point in time in the near future

ja	can express meanings ranging from 'this very moment' to 'the distant future'	izzit	former system of racial / ethnic segregation
howzit	language that has developed from Dutch	braai	all purpose answer, similar to *Really?*
now now	state of being effective / useful / suitable		

REPETITION EXERCISE: SOUTH AFRICAN ENGLISH TABOO

Explain in your own words what the following terms and phrases mean. You are not allowed to use the terms and phrases themselves.

defiant	resemble	breeding	go the extra mile
merge	catch-all	case in point	intonation
undermine	puzzled	yell	timeframe
aspiring	shore	consolidate	at will
exploit	figurative	pursuit	devolution

REPETITION EXERCISE: MIND MAP SOUTH AFRICAN ENGLISH

Work with one or more partners and sum up all facts and aspects that you have learnt about South African English in a mind map. You may use the template below as a starting point and add as many branches and subbranches as necessary. Prepare yourselves in order to be able to present the results of your discussion in class.

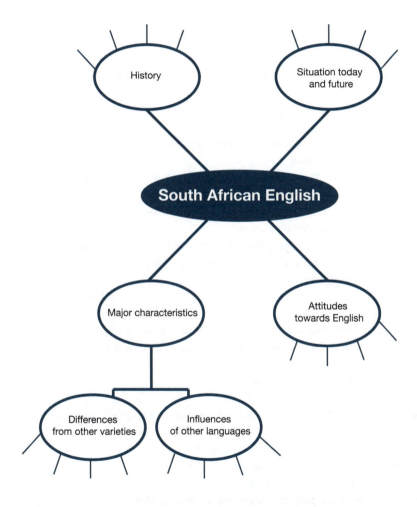

Sources

TEXTS

[1]   The transcripts stem from own data collection conducted in Durban, South Africa, between September 30, 2008 and October 15, 2008. We are grateful to the interviewees for consenting to publish the transcripts.

[2]   The transcripts stem from own data collection conducted in Durban, South Africa, between September 30, 2008 and October 15, 2008. We are grateful to the interviewees for consenting to publish the transcripts.

[3]   "Letter to the editor". 2009. *Mail and Guardian Online* [Johannesburg/South Africa], January 19, 2009. <http://www.mg.co.za/article/2009-01-19-cape-liquor-wars-loom>, August 12, 2009. Reproduced with permission of Mail and Guardian Online.

[4]   Tagg, Luke. 2005. "What Is Clever". *The Daily Smoke*, March 17, 2005. <http://www. thedailysmoke. co.za/smokes/article434.asp>, September 01, 2009. Reproduced with permission of Luke Tagg.

[5]   Sanidueb, Leila. 2009. "Dagga 'ticket' for on-duty traffic cop". *The Saturday Star Online* [Johannesburg/South Africa], August 22, 2009. <http://www.security.co.za/fullStory. asp?NewsId=13548>, September 01, 2009. Reproduced with permission of Independent Newspapers (Pty) Limited.

[6]   Serrao, Angelique. 2009. "Car dealer in hijack horror". *The Star Online* [Johannesburg/ South Africa], July 22, 2009. <http://www.iol.co.za/news/south-africa/car-dealer-in-hijackhorror-1.450537>, September 01, 2009. Reproduced with permission of Independent Newspapers (Pty) Limited.

[7]   Schweer, Cynthia. 2003. "South African English". *Flakmagazine Online*, November 09, 2003. <http://www.flakmag.com/misc/saenglish.html>, August 12, 2009. Reproduced with permission of Flakmagazine.

PICTURES AND FIGURES

Rainbow: <http://www.clker.com/clipart-14387.html> (Public Domain), November 01, 2011.

Flag of South Africa: <http://en.wikipedia.org/wiki/File:Flag_of_South_Africa.svg> (Public Domain), November 01, 2011.

Map of South Africa: © Isabel Peters. Hamburg, 2011.

Dancing children: © Georg Maier. Hamburg, 2008.

Sign: <http://en.wikipedia.org/wiki/File:ApartheidSignEnglishAfrikaans.jpg> (Public Domain), November 01, 2011.

South African provinces: © Isabel Peters. Hamburg, 2011.

South African countryside: © Georg Maier. Hamburg, 2008.

Cape Town: © Georg Maier. Hamburg, 2008.

Drawings of South African students: © Isabel Peters. Hamburg, 2012.

Languages in South Africa: © Isabel Peters. Hamburg, 2011.

REFERENCES AND FURTHER READING

Bowerman, Sean. 2008. White South African English: morphology and syntax. In: Mesthrie, Rajend (ed.), *Varieties of English*, Vol. 4. *Africa, South and Southeast Asia*. Berlin/ New York: Mouton de Gruyter, 472–487.

Kamwangamalu, Nkonko M. 2006. South African Englishes. In: Kachru, Braj B., Yamuna Kachru, and Cecil L. Nelson (eds.), *The Handbook of World Englishes*. Malden/ Oxford/Carlton: Blackwell, 158–171.

Mesthrie, Rajend. 1992. *English in Language Shift. The History, Structure and Sociolinguistics of South African Indian English*. Cambridge/New York/Oakleigh: Cambridge University Press.

Mesthrie, Rajend (ed.). 2008a. *Varieties of English*, Vol. 4. *Africa, South and Southeast Asia*. Berlin/New York: Mouton de Gruyter.

Mesthrie, Rajend. 2008b. Black South African English: morphology and syntax. In: Mesthrie, Rajend (ed.), *Varieties of English*, Vol. 4. *Africa, South and Southeast Asia*. Berlin/New York: Mouton de Gruyter, 488–500.

Mesthrie, Rajend. 2008c. Indian South African English: morphology and syntax. In: Mesthrie, Rajend (ed.), *Varieties of English*, Vol. 4. *Africa, South and Southeast Asia*. Berlin/New York: Mouton de Gruyter, 501–520.

Schneider, Edgar W. 2007. *Postcolonial English. Varieties around the World*. Cambridge: Cambridge University Press, 173–189.

[i]   "South Africa." The World Factbook [Washington, DC/USA]. Central Intelligence Agency, October 21, 2011. <https://www.cia.gov/library/publications/the-world-factbook/geos/sf.html>, November 01, 2011.

[ii]   "South Africa." Encyclopædia Britannica. Encyclopædia Britannica Online Academic Edition. Encyclopædia Britannica Inc., 2012. Web. <http://www.britannica.com/ EBchecked/topic/555568/South-Africa>, February 28, 2012.

[iii]   "South Africa country profile." The BBC, 2012. <http://www.bbc.co.uk/news/world-africa-14094760>, February 28, 2012.

[iv]   "Census 2001 at a glance". Statistics South Africa. <http://www.statssa.gov.za/ census01/html/CInBrief/CIB2001.pdf>, January 09, 2012.

[v]   "The languages of South Africa". Brand South Africa, 2012. <http://www.southafrica. info/about/people/language.htm>, February 28, 2012.

[vi]   "South African English is lekker!". Brand South Africa, 2011. <http://www.safrica.info/ travel/advice/saenglish.htm>, November 01, 2011.

[vii]   Silva, Penny. 1997. South African English: oppressor or liberator? In: Lindquist, Hans, Staffan Klintborg, Magnus Levin, and Maria Estling (eds.), *The Major Varieties of English. Papers from MAVEN 97, Växjö, 20–22 November 1997*. Växjö: Växjö University Press, 69–78.

[viii] "South Africa's Rainbow Nation". South African Tourism, 2011. <http://www.
        southafrica.net/sat/content/en/za/full-article?oid=16667&sn=Detail&pid=732>,
        February 28, 2012.

[ix]   "The Rainbow Nation". The Editors Inc. <http://www.southafricaataglance.com/south-
        africa-rainbow-nation.html>, February 28, 2012.

[x]   "World Cup 2010: Football in the Rainbow Nation." Encyclopædia Britannica.
        Encyclopædia Britannica Online Academic Edition. Encyclopædia Britannica Inc.,
        2012. Web. <http://www.britannica.com/EBchecked/topic/1687317/World-Cup-2010>,
        February 28, 2012.

[xi]   "The Rainbow Nation". Brand South Africa, 2011. <http://www.southafrica.info/pls/
        cms/cm_show_gallery?p_gid=2363&p_site_id=38>, February 28, 2012.

[xii]   "apartheid." Encyclopædia Britannica. Encyclopædia Britannica Online Academic
        Edition. Encyclopædia Britannica Inc., 2011. Web. <http://www.britannica.com/
        EBchecked/topic/29332/apartheid>, November 01, 2011.

[xiii] "Apartheid South Africa". South Africa Travel Online. <http://www.southafrica.to/
        history/Apartheid/apartheid.htm>, November 01, 2011.

[xiv]   "Nelson Mandela." Encyclopædia Britannica. Encyclopædia Britannica Online
        Academic Edition. Encyclopædia Britannica Inc., 2012. Web. <http://www.britannica.
        com/EBchecked/topic/361645/Nelson-Mandela>, February 28, 2012.

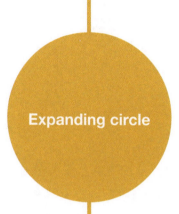

Expanding circle

Chapter 9

English in Europe

Introduction

In contrast to countries in South and Southeast Asia as well as those in various parts of Africa, English in Europe is not used as a means of communication between different ethnic groups within one country. Its function is restricted to the domain of international communication, as English is regarded as an important lingua franca for travelling, business, and academic discourse.

In countries such as Germany, France, the Netherlands, and Russia, to mention just a few, English is typically taught in schools as the first foreign language. Other subjects are usually taught in the respective native language, although some schools have started to offer bilingual models of education. Contact with English occurs primarily through the media such as television and the Internet. Some countries broadcast English television shows and films in the original version with subtitles in the native language.

The degree of contact with English varies considerably from speaker to speaker. As a result, the Englishes spoken in Europe can be conceived of as a bundle of varieties exhibiting considerable differentiation reflecting the individual speakers' proficiency in English. Similarly to other non-native forms of English, these varieties demonstrate many non-standard features that can be traced back to the speakers' mother tongues. The influence of the mother tongue, also known as first language influence, permeates phonology (pronunciation), morphology, syntax, and vocabulary. However, not all non-standard properties result from contact with the speakers' native languages. Some of them can be attributed to second-language acquisition strategies and are frequently associated with processes of simplification (i.e. reduction, omission) and overgeneralisation or regularisation (i.e. when a non-native speaker of English says *goed* instead of *went*).

This chapter familiarises you with the specific properties of some European Englishes starting out with a Brainstorming exercise. The interview with Luc, a French-speaking engineer, reveals some aspects of English as it is used by many speakers of French. The activity *How do Germans speak English???* introduces features typical of German English, as does the Listening Comprehension *Mey English Song*. The exercise *German creations of English words* points out some persistent 'false friends' in English-German vocabulary. The Reading Comprehension *Understanding Russian culture and the English spoken in Russia* then introduces some salient aspects of this English variety. The chapter also features two texts: One of them deals with the topic of the expansion of English on a global scale and is meant as a revision exercise, while the other text addresses the role of English in Europe.

Introducing English in Europe

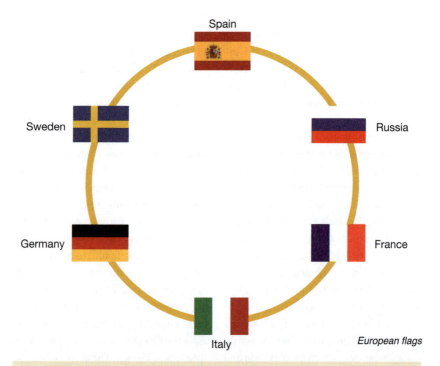

European flags

English as a world language: History, current status, perspectives

The following text traces the current expansion of English to its historical roots. It summarises the major steps in the expansion of English from the 5th century A.D. through the 21st century.

The history of a language, like the history of a human life, can be full of **vagaries** and unpredictable turns. When the Angles, the Saxons, and the Jutes
5 reached the shores of England in the 5th century, little did they realise that they were sowing the linguistic seeds that 1,500 years later would produce a **colossal** tree spreading its roots through
10 the entire planet – the English language. What was originally an **obscure** tongue spoken by a rude civilisation is now a language with a sociocultural, political, and economic legacy so robust and di-
15 verse that it seems almost impossible to challenge or surpass.

To start with, a Brazilian pilot requesting permission to land in the Netherlands performs his commands in Eng-
20 lish. In order to inform the international scientific community about a new and exciting discovery in the field of quantum mechanics, a Swiss physicist writes a paper in English, thereby preferring it
25 to German, his mother tongue.

Twelve years ago, the famous Russian singer Alsou won second place in the Eurovision Song Contest. Journalists speculated at the time that this was due to her **impeccable** English **accent** and
30 the fact that her producer had the financial resources to secure good English lyrics for the song.

Surprisingly enough, during the time of the Iron Curtain, Soviet propaganda
35 was often publicised in English, not Russian. A prominent example of the Soviet attempts to control the world through or with the help of English are speeches made by Vladimir Posner. A living leg-
40 end of Russian television, this journalist was born into a Russian / French family in 1934. He grew up predominantly in New York, where he lived until the age of 14. After his family moved to Mos-
45 cow in 1952, Posner studied biology before deciding to take up a career in journalism. While broadcasting during the Cold War, Posner skilfully and convincingly employed his competencies as
50 an English native speaker to reach out to the audiences all over the world and to present the position of the Soviet Union.

The role played by English in the modern world can be compared to that
55 of Latin during ancient times or that of

Russian during the Soviet era. English is needed in academia, in trade and commerce, as well as in diplomacy and media, to give just a few examples. In fact, there are only few domains involving global communication in which the use of English is not requested or may even be undesired. In her article 'English: Out to conquer the world', Susanna McBee (1985) cites Donald Bowen, professor of English at the University of California, who puts the history of the expansion of English in a nutshell: "It is really amazing," he says "that one dialect spoken in one small place has become so important around the world".

The complex and exciting history of the English language is also a **testimony** to its global spread, the first attempt at which was made as early as in the 12th century, when the Anglo-Norman nobility headed by Henry II and their English soldiers and servants invaded Ireland. A much more important step, however, was made five centuries later. In 1607, the English established their first colony in Jamestown, Virginia, thereby bringing English to what is now the United States of America. A little bit earlier, in the mid-16th century, English was introduced to the Guinea coast in West Africa. The early 17th century saw the introduction of English to the Indian subcontinent and in the Caribbean, where it began to rival with Spanish and Portuguese. The expansion of English in Southeast Asia began late in the 18th century. In Australia, the first English settlements were established in 1788, with the European population becoming the dominant social group, in contrast to colonies in Africa and Asia.

With the rise of American influence in science, politics, and technology in the second half of the last century, English moved to centre stage on the international scene, while other established lingua francas such as French and German retreated into the shadows.

Will there ever be another language that achieves a degree of global spread similar to that of English? While current prognoses should never be taken for granted, some analysts may want to argue that Chinese and Arabic have the political and economic potential to establish themselves as linguistic giants.

Moreover, the end of the Cold War induced a wave of migration on a worldwide scale. Many large European cities play host to communities from Russia and from other countries in Eastern Europe. The Polish Embassy in Dublin reports an estimate of approximately 100,000 people with Polish roots currently living in the city.

The languages spoken in such communities play a far greater role than English. While English still plays a major role in education and other social domains, its omnipresence is not necessarily self-evident, as linguistic dominance is not inherent in a language itself, but is rather the result of historical and sociocultural processes, political configurations, and economic developments.

[Written by Julia Davydova based on #i – #vii.]

Vocabulary

Look up the following words and expressions in a monolingual English dictionary: vagaries, colossal, obscure, impeccable accent, and testimony.

COMPREHENSION

1. Describe the major phases in the spread of English as explained in the text.
2. Which factors have contributed to the enormous popularity of English in the countries of the expanding circle? Give examples.

DISCUSSION

Certain international airlines offer their services on board in several different languages including German, French, and Russian, to mention just a few. Based on what you know about the role of English in the countries of the expanding circle and throughout the world, explain what you see to be possible motivating factors underlying the airlines' policy. Work in pairs.

ACADEMIC WRITING

You have been asked to give an academic contribution on the gradual expansion of English as a lingua franca and its consequences for the role that English plays in various parts of the world today.

» What aspects of this topic would you like to highlight in your presentation? Draw a mind map collecting your ideas. Think of the linguistic vocabulary that you will use while presenting this topic. Here are some suggestions: inner circle, outer circle, expanding circle, English-based Pidgins and Creoles, English as a second language, and English as a foreign language.
» Read the text from David Crystal's book *English as a Global Language* (2003: 59–60) introduced in Chapter 1 again and see how it fits with what you learnt about the global expansion of English from the text on the previous pages.
» Now write a short academic essay. (Write a minimum of 500 words!)

 READING COMPREHENSION

English in the expanding circle:
Focus on Europe

As a world lingua franca, English enjoys a special status in countries where it is not a native language of the **dominant social group** or an official or a co-official lan-
5 guage of the country. This is true for all countries in continental Western Europe, Russia, China, Japan, and South America. In these countries, English is taught as a first foreign language in schools and is
10 regarded as an important language in academic spheres as well as in international diplomacy and communication.

In Western Europe and in Russia, English has spread into more informal
15 domains as well. English is widely used on the Internet in chat forums and on blogs. It is seen as a link language uniting those who do not share the same mother tongue. It is also used in the **linguistic**
20 **repertoire** of individuals as a means of expressing and reconstructing various **identities** such as heavy metal fans, computer freaks, fashion girls, and many others.

25 English has permeated various domains of popular culture in the countries of the **expanding circle**. Many popular songs and lyrics are written in English; some cinemas offer the original English
30 version of films in addition to the more traditional dubbed versions. Lifestyle magazines in English can be found nearly anywhere.

English generally plays an important role in advertising, too, as promoting 35 products in this language is associated with prestige, high quality, globalisation, and internationalisation. The increasing dominance of the English language in advertising has, however, clashed with 40 language ideologies and language policies established in some countries of the expanding circle. To give one example, the predominant use of English in advertisements can have legal consequences in 45 Russia, where the law requires the use of Russian, the language of the state, in advertising. In France, in addition, English advertisements were never en vogue in the first place as this nation is well known 50 for the pride it takes in its **linguistic and cultural heritage**.

Although the domains allotted to English may vary slightly from country to country in the expanding circle, at- 55 titudes towards this language can generally be described as highly positive. A substantial amount of evidence including academic research suggests that different population groups associate English with 60 good education, prestigious social status, and better opportunities in life.

Because of the enormous popularity of English as a foreign language, the countries of the expanding circle have 65 started to develop their own forms of

English known as 'Learner Englishes'. As a result, many Learner Englishes have become the subject of academic scrutiny, 70 as these forms of English exhibit distinct features in phonology, morphosyntax, and lexis. Speakers thus often employ **native words** in their English in order to talk about various aspects of their culture 75 such as cuisine, architecture, history, and lifestyle. English has also been making inroads in the languages spoken in Europe and in the expanding circle at large, mainly through borrowed vocabulary.

[Written by Julia Davydova based on Melchers and Shaw 2003: 178–191 and #viii.]

Vocabulary

Look up the following words and expressions in a monolingual English dictionary: dominant social group, linguistic repertoire, identity, and linguistic and cultural heritage.

WORD ANALYSIS

1. Find the expression "native words" in the text. From the context, try to guess what this expression means. Then consult a dictionary, if necessary. Translate this word into your native language.
2. Describe the meaning of "expanding circle" in your own words. Give examples.

COMPREHENSION

» On the whole, what is the status of English in Europe?
» Describe the domains in which English is used in Europe.

DISCUSSION

1. Why has English achieved such enormous currency in the countries of Western Europe? Explain.
2. Do you think that the popularity of English is likely to continue? Give your reasons.
3. Do you think that English is likely to penetrate into domains other than those described in the text in the countries of the expanding circle? Explain.
4. Discuss the pros and cons of English spreading around the globe and penetrating into an increasing number of spheres of social life in the countries where it is not spoken as a native language.

VIEWING COMPREHENSION

Cultural differences across Europe. The case of French English

In this interview, Luc, an engineer from French-speaking Switzerland, talks about cultural differences across Europe.

Watch this interview at www.awe.uni-hamburg.de. [#1]

French-speaking engineer

PRE-WATCHING ACTIVITY

The following sentences contain non-standard features frequently found with non-native speakers of English. Identify these features and transform the sentences into standard English.

> » I very like it.
> » In such big city.
> » And here it's more easier to …
> » There's a lot of little shop where you can buy something to eat and then to take away.
> » I think here a lot of people are drinking a lot of beer.
> » It's a very busy city. A lot of people are going everywhere and every time.
> » I am very interesting about the history of Berlin.
> » Lyon is probably, I think, the seven city in France but it's ten times less people than in Paris.
> » You don't have too much big building.
> » And I think in France it's very more important to have a regular meal at midday.
> » It was very interesting experience.

Take notes while you are watching this video so that you are able to answer the following questions.

1. Summarise Luc's impressions of Hamburg.
2. Describe the differences between German and French culture as portrayed by the speaker.
3. Summarise the major facts about Berlin mentioned by the speaker.
4. What is Luc's favourite city in France and why does he like it?

Interviewer:	You know, how do you like it here in Hamburg?
Luc:	Mmmm … I think it very nice, nice city. I very like it. I go … I think I go almost every year here. It's quiet. I like to be here. I like the people here. It's very friendly, friendly people.
Interviewer:	So, what do you like about Hamburg?
Luc:	I think it's most … most the people who live here. And it's a big city; there is a lot of things to do. I very like to be here. In such big city. I very like it. To walk and to meet people or to go to … shopping, to go out on the evening, sometimes, to have some beers, something like that.
Interviewer:	Does it also have something to do with German culture? Do you like it?
Luc:	Ehmm. The German culture? I don't know. I like it. I used to be in Germany. And it was very interesting experience. And I like it. And, I think it's a bit different here in Hamburg than other city in Germany and I don't know if it's really a German culture or something to do with the inhabitants of the cities.
Interviewer:	In what way's Hamburg different?
Luc:	I think the people here are very open-minded. I have the feeling. I don't know if it's true or wrong but I have this feeling when I am in Hamburg.
Interviewer:	So do you think it's because there are so many foreigners here or …?
Luc:	It's probably a part of it but I think … I don't know I think maybe … It's difficult to explain for me because it's more a feeling or something like that and … I don't know, I think … eh the people, for example, from Munich are not so open-minded are not so free or a bit … I don't know … They don't care about other. And here it's more

easier to [...] with other people ... it's quite ... I like the feeling, I like the people here.

30 Interviewer: So do you think there are differences between French culture and German culture?

Luc: Okay. If you mean something like to drink or to eat, I think there is a lot of difference. I think ... I have the feeling German people like to eat every time during the day and you are very free. There's a lot of
35 little shop where you can buy something to eat and then to take away. And I think in France it's very more important to have a regular meal at midday or in the evening for dinner. And for the drink, I think here a lot of people are drinking a lot of beer. And in France it's not very usual to drink beer for the meal or with the meal or something like
40 that. It's more like wine or water but almost never ehm, yeah never with beer.

Interviewer: Is there a French city that you could compare to the city of Hamburg? You know, in terms of spirit, in terms of cultural flair?

Luc: No, actually, in a way every city is different for me and it's very dif-
45 ficult to say this city is almost like the other city. I never had, I never had this feeling before. That Berlin is like Paris, no, it's every different or like Lyon or some other city like Marseille. Every cities are something different, like ...

Interviewer: Yeah, that's right we also were in Berlin once, right, together. We
50 went to Berlin, you know, like a couple of years ago. Do you remember?

Luc: Yeah, I remember a little bit.

Interviewer: So do you think Berlin is different from Hamburg?

Luc: Yes, very different. Ehm.

55 Interviewer: What are these differences?

Luc: Yeah, it's quite ... Actually it's quite difficult to say. I think for me ...

Interviewer: I think it's is more crowded, right? More crowded?

Luc: I didn't have this feeling in Berlin. I think it's a very big city. I think it's almost three or five millions people are living there. But it's not
60 such a busy city like the big capital in Europe like Paris or London. It's very busy city. A lot of people are going everywhere and every time. And you don't have this feeling in Berlin, I think it's very wide. You don't have too much big building. A little bit right now and what is very different with Berlin is you have a lot of things, a lot of things
65 coming from the Second World War and after from the Cold War and I think you can feel it. Right now it's maybe a little bit different but I was ten years ago in Berlin and it was very interesting. You can see a

lot of part of the war and you can very ... yeah probably feel what the
people were feeling during this time, during the Cold War and I am
very interesting about this part and I think in Hamburg, for example, 70
to compare with Hamburg, you don't have this ... you don't see anything about it. I think the history of ... I am very interesting about the
history of Berlin and you don't have the same history in Hamburg.
It's not so strong like this one. It's a difference, for example! Big difference!   75

Interviewer: That's interesting. Let us talk about France a little bit. So what is your
               favourite city in France?
Luc: I think it's not very original but my favourite city is ... Paris.
Interviewer: (laughs) Why Paris? What is so special about Paris?
Luc: I think yeah ... If you want to see only one city in France, you have 80
               to go to Paris because the most beautiful buildings are there and yeah
               it's the most beautiful city in France, of course. And then you can see
               a lot of history, a lot of museums. Very, very different and special
               and it's a big city in France. You have nothing to compare with other
               big city. It's very a big difference. Like Lyon is probably, I think, the 85
               seven city in France but it's ten times less people than in Paris, for
               example. Paris very is a big city.

WHILE-WATCHING ACTIVITY II

Listen to this interview once again while looking at the transcript given above.
Find the words that are pronounced differently than in standard English and mark
them in the text. Pay close attention to the way Luc pronounces the names of the
European cities.

SELF-STUDY

1. The speech of this English language learner exhibits some non-standard
   features. Read the transcript and identify these non-standard properties of
   English. Think of the English quantifiers *much* and *many*, strategies for the
   formation of the comparative forms of English adjectives, and the differences
   between the forms *interested* and *interesting*.
2. Describe in your own words how the use of these language features as produced by this speaker differs from that found in standard English. Consult an
   English grammar reference book, if necessary.

How do Germans speak English???

When coming to Germany or speaking with Germans, many people from English-speaking countries are often surprised and impressed by the large number of Germans who speak English. However, they often notice a typically German accent and certain kinds of non-standard features that may occur in the English speech of Germans.

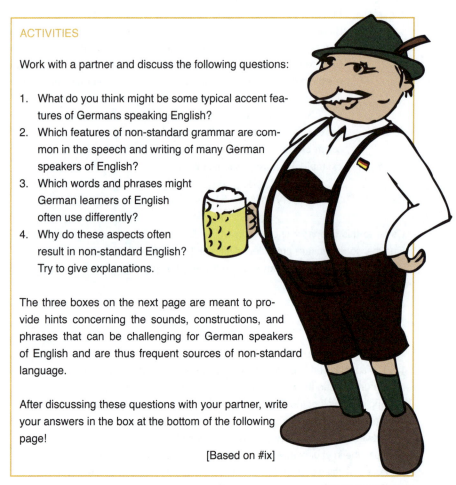

ACTIVITIES

Work with a partner and discuss the following questions:

1. What do you think might be some typical accent features of Germans speaking English?
2. Which features of non-standard grammar are common in the speech and writing of many German speakers of English?
3. Which words and phrases might German learners of English often use differently?
4. Why do these aspects often result in non-standard English? Try to give explanations.

The three boxes on the next page are meant to provide hints concerning the sounds, constructions, and phrases that can be challenging for German speakers of English and are thus frequent sources of non-standard language.

After discussing these questions with your partner, write your answers in the box at the bottom of the following page!

[Based on #ix]

Stereotypical German

Pronunciation

think, that, this, that, tooth, through, three

wine, vine, vet, wet, vow, wow, vile, while

ant, and, bag, back, rude, root, ride, rite, love, laugh, rib, rip

English: so, go, know, old, boat
German: Boot, Not, so, Tod

English: bad, bed, fat, fed, Pat, pet, pan, pen vs. German: Fett, Bett, nett, etc.

Grammar

Gestern sind wir im Kino gewesen.

Nachher gehe ich ins Schwimmbad.

Ich kenne ihn schon seit zehn Jahren.

Bis morgen habe ich die Hausaufgaben gemacht.

Stör deinen Vater jetzt nicht! Er arbeitet gerade.

Wenn ich du wäre, würde ich jetzt gehen.

Ich war noch nie in New York.

Vocabulary

German: Handy, Beamer, Barkeeper, Oldtimer, Showmaster, Body Bag, Schatten, Schnecke, leihen

Eventuell gehen wir heute ins Kino.

Mein aktueller Chef ist wirklich sehr nett.

Es gibt drei Kirchen im Dorf.

Das gibt es doch gar nicht.

Was gibt es Neues?

Pronunciation: _____
_____
_____
_____

Grammar: _____
_____
_____
_____

Vocabulary: _____
_____
_____
_____

1. In a comment, discuss which kinds of non-standard features (pronunciation, grammar or words and phrases) might cause the greatest difficulties in communication between native speakers of English and German speakers of English. (Write a minimum of 200–300 words!)
2. "Ze masters of ze vorld!" This is a headline from the British tabloid newspaper *The Sun* [#x]. Discuss why every British reader will understand immediately who is meant by this phrase and try to explain what this article may (exactly) be about. You may also refer to the picture on page 256. Give reasons and examples to support your opinion. (Write a minimum of 200–300 words!)
3. Imagine that you are a correspondent for a North American newspaper living in Germany and that you have to write an article for your newspaper about the use of English in Germany and by Germans. Summarise where, in which contexts, and why Germans use English and also describe to your readers the peculiarities of the English used and spoken by many Germans. (Write a minimum of 200–300 words!)

German creations of English words

Interestingly enough, Germans have created some English words of their own. Take a look at them and answer the questions below.

Beamer, Messie, Showmaster, Handy, Flipper, Oldtimer, Public Viewing, Body-bag, Horror-Trip [Based on #xi – #xiv]

» Work with a partner and give an exact dictionary-style English definition of what these words mean in German!
» Consult your dictionary: Can you find any differences?
» Try to give the standard English equivalents of these words.

LISTENING COMPREHENSION

Here you can see the lyrics from a song by Reinhard Mey, a German singer-songwriter, written in German English.

Listen to this song on the Internet!

Notes

QUESTIONS AND EXERCISES

1. Summarise in your own words what this song is about.
2. Work with a partner and try to find all of the features, phrases, and expressions that you would not expect in a standard English text and try to give their standard English equivalents.
3. In a short comment, discuss what exactly makes this song sound so German. (Write a minimum of 200–300 words!)
4. What would this song look like if it was written by a native speaker? Try to translate it completely into standard English.

M(e)y English Song

I think that I make something wrong,
I once must make an english song,
'Cause in my radio everyday
I hear them english music play
And all the radio peoples stand
On songs, they cannot understand!

So I sing english now that's really animally strong
And your can hear my english song all day long
Out your loudspeaker at home or riding in your car
All over this, our land, wherever you are
From the SFB to the WDR.

A poor little sausage was I,
When I in german sang, oh my …
I could not english, but quite cool,
I learned it at the Folks-High-School.
Now my producer says me, "Well,
What do we now for records sell!"

So I sing english now …

You reach the german music-freak
Now only if you can english speak,
And if you will a song outbring,
You better should it english sing!
And people flip out, say I you my friend,
Even if they only railwaystation understand!

So I sing english now, that's really animally strong
And you can hear my english song all day long
Out your loudspeaker at home or riding in your car
All over this, our land, wherever you are
From the SFB to the WDR.
And you can even me
On TV see,
Sometimes at ZDF,
Sometimes on ARD,
Oh Babe, oh yeah!

[*M(e)y English Song* by Reinhard Mey. #2]

READING COMPREHENSION

Understanding Russian culture and the English spoken in Russia

PRE-READING ACTIVITIES

1. Take a look at the short texts and pictures below. What aspects of Russian culture and the Russian way of life do they reveal?
2. What other aspects of Russian culture are you aware of?
3. Discuss the texts in pairs and draw a mind map summarising your ideas.

Traditional Russian cuisine is perhaps best described as nourishing but somewhat heavy. This is largely due to the abundant use of *smetana* (sour cream) in traditional dishes such as Russian *borshtch* (beetroot soup) and *pel'meni* (meat dumplings). Many Russians also love *draniki* (fried potato pancakes), which can be served with tomatoes and vegetable ragout. Russian *khleb i sol'* (bread and salt) are symbols of abundance, prosperity, and good will.

Russian food

Russian churches are symbols of the Russian Orthodox religion, which has always advocated the inseparability of Russian cultural and spiritual values.

Russian church

Russian tea party

Russians are also known for (and proud of) their **tea parties** (*russkiye chayepitiya*), which they see as an opportunity to socialise with their family and close friends. Traditional Russian pastries associated with these social occasions include *sushki*, *baranki*, and *bubliki*, all of which are variations of dry bread rings, *pryaniki* (gingerbread cakes), and *varenje* (self-made jam).

Many Russians are self-confessed lovers of books and literature. There are very few homes in Russia that don't boast collections of works by **Leo Tolstoy** and **Fyodor Dostoyevsky**. This alone explains the enormous popularity of the screen adaptations of *War and Peace*, directed by Sergey Bondarchuk (1965–1968) and *The Idiot*, directed by Vladimir Bortko (2003).

The notion of **Russian spaces** is yet another idea enshrined in the Russian mentality, as Russians' perception of time and space has always been influenced by the enormous expanses of this wondrous land.

Russian spaces

WHILE-READING ACTIVITIES

The short text excerpts below introduce you to some Russian learners of English sharing their views on and knowledge of Russian culture [#3]. Read these texts and underline

» the words and phrases that strike you as representative of the English spoken in Russia, and
» the sentences and phrases that differ from standard English in terms of grammar.

Nadja: [...] "Some people think that Russian culture is *borshtch*, *vodka*, and *pel'meni*. But it's not all like that. Russian culture is very big and rich. It's not all *khleb i sol'* as some people think. Sometimes people think that there are bears on Russian street but it's not true. Russian cuisine is interesting. We can cook *borshtch* and *shtchi*, and *selyodka pod shuboj*, and *salat Olivier*. That sounds French but it's Russian. It's a Russian salad made of meat, carrots, potatoes, and we season it with mayonnaise. And *selyodka pod shuboj* is made with herring, beetroots and it's some sort of salad too. In English language we do not find these words because they have not like these and then, of course, we do have sightseeing. There is *Kreml'* in Moscow. There is St Petersburg and I also must say that Russian people they are known for the width of their heart."

Alexej: "Russian culture is very much like Russian history. For example, many centuries ago before Christians religion our country has another religion. This is a pagan religion. And many traditionals and customs we have from this time. Russian person is a [...] very kind person and willing to help but he may be sometimes lazy but if it's necessary he can do his work in the best way. So I think Russian culture stayed as it is but maybe it now has more Western features."

Lena: "So, as for me, Russian culture is the 19th century. The 19th century is important to us because of the great Russian writers such as Tolstoy or Dostoyevsky. I especially like Tolstoy. He is such a great writer. Yeah, and what about our times, Russia has start to copy American and European cultures and their traditions and I think it's very sad. I think Russia [...] begin to forget its old traditions. So, for example, for me reading Russian literature is much more interesting than playing computer games or searching the web."

Drawings of Russian students

POST-READING ACTIVITIES

1. Take a look at the Russian words that you underlined while reading the text. From the context, try to guess what these words mean.
2. Match the Russian words that you have encountered in the texts so far with their standard English explanations. You can find the Russian words and the English explanations in the boxes below.
3. Based on what you have read in the short texts given above, what are the major characteristics of the grammar of Russian English that you can identify from this cohort of speakers?

(a) fried potato pancakes	(i) borshtch
(b) an important historical site in Moscow	(ii) pel'meni
(c) ginger bread cakes	(iii) smetana
(d) dried bread rings	(iv) khleb i sol'
(e) Russian meat salad	(v) russkiye chayepitiya
(f) bread and salt	(vi) baranki
(g) sour cream	(vii) pryaniki
(h) beetroot soup	(viii) draniki
(i) Russian tea parties	(ix) salat Olivier
(j) meet dumplings	(x) Kreml'

INFO-BOX CODE-SWITCHING

Have you ever heard – on the bus or simply in the street – people speaking more than one language? Well, if you have, you have been witness to what is called 'code-switching' in the study of language contact. Code-switching is a term that is used to describe a situation in which more than one language is spoken by two or more people.

The possible motivations behind code-switching are numerous. Some people code-switch to show that they belong to a particular social or ethnic group. Another potential motive may be a person's desire to adjust to the language of the people he or she is interacting with.

Code-switching can be found among bilingual or multilingual speakers. 'Bilingual' means that the person can speak two languages, while 'multilingual' implies the ability to speak more than two languages.

LANGUAGE ANALYSIS

You might have noticed that Russian students use Russian words while speaking English, a process that linguists refer to as 'code-switching'.

1. Do you ever use any words from your native language while speaking English? Under what circumstances?
2. Why do you think code-switching is so wide-spread?
3. In certain cultural domains, having some working knowledge of the languages of non-native speakers of English (Russian, German, French, etc.) becomes important. What do you think these domains are? Explain.

PROJECT

Write an article assessing the role English plays in modern Russia and in other East European societies. You may find the following references useful:

Proshina, Zoya G. 2005. Russian Englishes. Introduction. *World Englishes* 42:4, 437–438.
Proshina, Zoya G. and Brian P. Ettkin. 2005. English-Russian language contacts. *World Englishes* 42:4, 439–444.
Ter-Minasova, Svetlana G. 2005. Traditions and innovations: English language teaching in Russia. *World Englishes* 42:4, 445–454.

Sources

TEXTS

[1]   The interview stems from own data collection conducted at the Collaborative Research
        Centre on Multilingualism in Hamburg in January 2008. We are grateful to the interviewee
        for consenting to publish the interview.

[2]   Mey, Reinhard. 1985. M(e)y English Song. In: *Hergestellt in Berlin*. Intercord. Reproduced
        with Permission of Edition Reinhard Mey.

[3]   The interviews stem from own data collection conducted at the *Landesexzellenzcluster*
        on Linguistic Diversity Management in Urban Areas in Hamburg on January 10, 2012. We
        are grateful to the interviewees for consenting to publish the interviews.

PICTURES AND FIGURES

European flags: © Isabel Peters. Hamburg, 2009.

French-speaking engineer: © Isabel Peters. Hamburg, 2012.

Stereotypical German: © Isabel Peters. Hamburg, 2009.

Notes: © Isabel Peters. Hamburg, 2009.

Russian food: © Julia Davydova. Hamburg, 2011.

Russian church: © Julia Davydova. Hamburg, 2011.

Russian tea party: © Julia Davydova. Hamburg, 2011.

Russian spaces: © Julia Davydova. Hamburg, 2011.

Drawings of Russian students © Isabel Peters. Hamburg, 2012.

REFERENCES AND FURTHER READING

Berns, Margie. 2005. Expanding on the Expanding Circle: where do WE go from here?
        World Englishes 24:1, 85–93.

Melchers, Gunnel and Philip Shaw. 2003. *World Englishes (The English Language Series)*.
        London: Arnold (Hodder Headline Group), 178–191.

Mukherjee, Joybrato and Marianne Hundt (eds.). 2011. *Exploring Second-Language
        Varieties of English and Learner Englishes. Bridging a Paradigm Gap (Studies in
        Corpus Linguistics)*. Amsterdam/Philadelphia: John Benjamins.

Schneider, Edgar W. 2011. *English around the World. An Introduction*. Cambridge:
        Cambridge University Press, 211–227.

[i]   McBee, Susanna. 1985. English: out to conquer the world. *U.S. News & World
        Report*, February 18, 1985. In: Engel, Georg, Rosemarie Franke, Armin Steinbrecher,
        Dieter Vater, Gerhard Weiß, and Egon Werlich (eds.), *Britain and America. Traditions
        and Change*. Berlin: Cornelsen, 237–238.

[ii]   Crystal, David. 2003. *English as a Global Language*. Cambridge: Cambridge
         University Press, 61.

[iii]   Mesthrie, Rajend and Rakesh M. Bhatt. 2008. *World Englishes. The Study of New
         Linguistic Varieties (Key Topics in Sociolinguistics)*. Cambridge: Cambridge University
         Press, 12, 14, 17, 18, 19.

[iv]   Schneider, Edgar W. 2007. *Postcolonial English. Varieties around the World*.
         Cambridge: Cambridge University Press, 144.

[v]   "Alsou." Wikipedia. Wikipedia Foundation Inc., 2012. <http://en.wikipedia.org/wiki/
         Alsu>, February 24, 2012.

[vi]   "Vladimir Posner." Wikipedia. Wikipedia Foundation Inc., 2012. <http://en.wikipedia.
         org/wiki/Vladimir_Posner>, February 24, 2012.

[vii]   Mühlau, Peter, Monika Kaliszewska, and Antje Röder. "Polonia in Dublin. Preliminary
         report of survey findings. Report No. 1. Demographic overview." Trinity College
         Dublin. <http://www.tcd.ie/sociology/news/assets/Polonia%20in%20Dublin%20
         Report%20I%5B1%5D.pdf>, March 14, 2012, 6–7.

[viii]   "Магазин одежды в Хабаровске оштрафован за рекламу на английском языке".
         AmurMedia.ru, 2012. <http://amurmedia.ru/news/economics/25.07.2011/164474>,
         March 08, 2012.

[ix]   Kortmann, Bernd. 2005. *English Linguistics: Essentials*. Berlin: Cornelsen, 155–186.

[x]   "Ze masters of ze vorld!" *The Sun Online* [London], July 31, 2007. <http://www.
         thesun.co.uk/sol/homepage/sport/125030/Ze-masters-of-ze-vorld.html>, October 05,
         2009.

[xi]   "Das sollten Sie noch mal checken: Schein-Anglizismen, die von Engländern nicht
         oder falsch verstanden werden." *Focus Online* [München], July 07, 2008. <http://www.
         focus.de/kultur/leben/focus-listen-das-sollten-sie-noch-mal-checken-_aid_316409.
         html>, October 05, 2009.

[xii]   Knapp, Robbin D. 2008. "Robb: Invented English Words in German."
         humanlanguages.com. <http://www.humanlanguages.com/rlerfeng.htm.>, February
         29, 2012.

[xiii]   "Englisch, das so kein Englisch ist: Scheinanglizismen und ihre Hintergründe."
         english-study.de, September 04, 2010. <http://www.english-study.de/2010/09/04/
         englisch-das-so-kein-englisch-ist/>, February 29, 2012.

[xiv]   "False Friends in German." about.com. <http://german.about.com/library/blfalsef.
         htm>, February 29, 2012.

Conclusion and outlook

Our book has offered you an empirical-inductive introduction to eight important varieties of English by means of authentic and illustrative examples: Irish, Scottish, British, American, Australian, Indian, Nigerian, and South African English.

To be sure, this introduction could neither do full justice to the overarching internal complexity of these varieties nor to the diversity of the English language as a whole. We highlighted the expansion of English and its undeniable status as a global lingua franca in Chapter 1 and returned to this topic again at the end of the book in Chapter 9. There, we illustrated the ways in which English has even become an important means of communication in regions where it did not play a significant historical role, such as Russia and France.

In the chapters discussing the individual varieties, we saw that these varieties of English can differ from one another along different lines such as geography, ethnicity, and social class, as well as for historical reasons. We observed, for example, that mainly historical reasons are responsible for the differences between British and American standard English, while geographic distance can explain the differences between Southern and Northern English dialects. With regard to the social dimension of language, we noted that particular social groups may use particular language varieties. Cases in point include Valleytalk and Estuary English. Furthermore, these

various parameters often interact: We have seen that sociohistorical reasons are responsible for different ethnicities in South Africa being associated with different varieties of English, as these ethnicities were strictly separated from each other during the era of Apartheid.

To find out more about the sociohistorical background and particularities of these varieties, we refer you to other comprehensive handbooks offering detailed descriptions of the phonological and morphosyntactic inventories of these varieties. Valuable handbooks discussing a number of varieties include Britain (2007), Burchfield (1994), Hughes, Trudgill, and Watt (2005), Kachru, Kachru, and Nelson (2006), Kortmann et al. (2004), Milroy and Milroy (1993), Peters, Collins, and Smith (2009), Mesthrie and Bhatt (2008), Schneider (2007, 2011), and Schreier et al. (2010), to mention a few. Many of these handbooks (e.g. Kortmann et al. 2004) also provide descriptions of numerous varieties that we could not discuss here for reasons of space, but that are currently the focus of much linguistic research, such as Singapore, Philippine or New Zealand English.

Even from the limited number of varieties discussed in the present book, you might have noticed that some interesting similarities exist between different varieties of English. We noted, for example, that both American and Irish speakers often replace the present perfect with simple past forms in contexts in which this would not be admissible in standard British English. In the respective chapters on India, Nigeria, and the expanding circle varieties, we also saw that these speakers of English often replace the *th*-sounds /θ, ð/ with other sounds such as /t, d/ or /s, z/. This is not a coincidence, and we can indeed observe many similar features across even seemingly unrelated varieties. Such features are often called 'Angloversals' or even 'Vernacular Universals'. Examples of Angloversals include negative concord, i.e. the occurrence of more than one negative form in a clause without cancelling out the negative meaning (e.g. *He did**n't** do **nothing** about it* 'He didn't do anything about it'), the lack of inversion in yes/no questions (e.g. *You like it?* 'Do you like it?') and the use of *me* instead of *I* when used in coordinate subjects (*You and me have to go* 'You and I have to go' (Szmrecsanyi and Kortmann 2009).

If you are further interested in the analysis of a specific linguistic feature, for example for a term paper, you can also begin to explore different varieties of English by starting with a certain feature that interests you. In order to do so, you can consult books that offer a feature-based approach to varieties of English such as Bauer (2005) and Siemund (forthc.), which introduce and discuss certain morphosyntactic features and examine their prevalence and distribution across varieties of English. Furthermore, you can also consult eWAVE, the **E**lectronic **W**orld **A**tlas of **V**arieties of English (Kortmann and Lunkenheimer

2011), which can be accessed at http://www.ewave-atlas.org/. This database offers you interactive world maps, surveys, and distribution profiles of 235 non-standard morphosyntactic features from 74 varieties of English and is a suitable starting point for any variationist study.

If you wish to conduct an empirical analysis of a certain feature yourself, the best way to do this is by means of a corpus study. A corpus can be defined as "a collection of texts when considered as an object of language or literary study" (Kilgariff and Grafenstette 2003: 2). Corpora often consist of different types of both spoken and written language and attempt to represent different modes of discourse, registers, and degrees of formality. The International Corpus of English (ICE) is a particularly valuable resource (cf. http://ice-corpora.net/ice/) for the analysis of varieties of English. The ICE corpus consists of several subcorpora, each of which contains roughly one million words and represents a distinct variety of English. There are components depicting Irish, Indian, British, Canadian, Jamaican, and Singapore English, to mention but a few. Some of these subcorpora can even be downloaded directly from the website.

As a corpus itself is merely a collection of text files, you need an additional tool, a so-called concordancing program or simply concordancer, in order to actually search the corpus. A concordancer is a search program that helps you to find words, phrases or simply search strings in a corpus and is actually quite similar to a web search engine such as Google, though it enables you to perform much more sophisticated queries. A concordancing program well-suited for beginners is *AntConc* (Anthony 2012), as it is freeware, easy to handle, and is available for all common software platforms such as Windows, Linux, and MacIntosh. This program as well as many helpful tutorials can be downloaded from Laurence Anthony's website http://www. antlab.sci.waseda.ac.jp/antconc_index. html. However, many other good concordancing programs are also available.

Another possibility to conduct empirical corpus studies without having to obtain concordancing software and copies of the respective corpora is to use online corpora. Mark Davies' website at Brigham Young University (http://corpus.byu.edu/) provides free online access to versions of the British National Corpus (Davies 2004–), with over 100 million words, as well as to the Corpus of Contemporary American English (Davies 2008–), which currently consists of more than 425 million words.

For additional general introductions to corpus linguistics and linguistic methodology, you may also consult Biber, Conrad, and Reppen (1998), Gries (2009), Meyer (2002), Mukherjee (2009), Tagliamonte (2012), and Wray and Bloomer (2006).

With this book, we hope not only to have increased your awareness of the linguistic diversity in the Anglophone world, but also to have aroused your interest in the regional and social differentiation as well as the ever increasing global expansion of the English language.

REFERENCES AND FURTHER READING

Anthony, Lawrence. 2012. *AntConc (3.2.4)* [Computer Software]. Tokyo, Japan: Waseda University. Available from http://www.antlab.sci.waseda.ac.jp/, January 17, 2012.

Biber, Douglas, Susan Conrad, and Randi Reppen. 1998. *Corpus linguistics: Investigating Language Structure and Use.* Cambridge: Cambridge University Press.

Bauer, Laurie. 2005. *An Introduction to International Varieties of English.* Edinburgh: Edinburgh University Press.

Britain, David (ed.). 2007. *Language in the British Isles.* Cambridge: Cambridge University Press.

Burchfield Robert W. (ed.). 1994. *Cambridge History of the English Language.* Vol. 5. *English in Britain and Overseas: Origins and Development.* Cambridge: Cambridge University Press.

Davies, Mark. 2008–. *The Corpus of Contemporary American English: 425 million words, 1990–present.* Available online at http://corpus.byu.edu/coca/, January 17, 2012.

Davies, Mark. 2004–. *BYU-BNC. (Based on the British National Corpus from Oxford University Press).* Available online at http://corpus.byu.edu/bnc/, January 17, 2012.

Gries, Stefan Th. 2009. *Statistics for Linguistics with R: A Practical Introduction.* Berlin/New York: Mouton de Gruyter.

Hughes, Arthur, Peter Trudgill, and Dominic Watt. 2005. *English Accents and Dialects: An Introduction to Social and Regional Varieties of English in the British Isles.* London: Hodder Arnold.

Kachru, Braj, Yamuna Kachru, and Cecil L. Nelson (eds.). 2006. *The Handbook of World Englishes.* Malden/Oxford/Carlton: Blackwell.

Kilgariff, Adam and Gregory Grafenstette. 2003. Introduction to the Special Issue on the Web as Corpus. *Computational Linguistics* 29:3, 333–347.

Kortmann, Bernd, Edgar Schneider, Kate Burridge, Rajend Mesthrie, and Clive Upton (eds.). 2004. *A Handbook of Varieties of English,* 2 Vols. Berlin/New York: Mouton de Gruyter. (+ CD-ROM).

Kortmann Bernd and Kerstin Lunkenheimer (eds.). 2011. *The Electronic World Atlas of Varieties of English [eWAVE].* Leipzig: Max Planck Institute for Evolutionary Anthropology. http://www.ewave-atlas.org/, January 10, 2012.

Mesthrie, Rajend and Rakesh M. Bhatt. 2008. *World Englishes: The Study of New Linguistic Varieties.* Cambridge: Cambridge University Press.

Meyer, Charles F. 2002. *English Corpus Linguistics: An Introduction.* Cambridge: Cambridge University Press.

Milroy, James and Lesley Milroy (eds.). 1993. *Real English: The Grammar of English Dialects in the British Isles.* London: Longman.

Mukherjee, Joybrato. 2009. *Anglistische Korpuslinguistik: Eine Einführung.* Berlin: Erich Schmidt Verlag.

Peters, Pam, Peter Collins, and Adam Smith (eds.). 2009. *Comparative Studies in Australian and New Zealand English: Grammar and beyond*. Amsterdam: John Benjamins.

Schneider, Edgar. 2007. *Postcolonial English: Varieties around the World*. Cambridge: Cambridge University Press.

Schneider, Edgar. 2011. *English around the World: An Introduction*. Cambridge: Cambridge University Press.

Schreier, Daniel, Peter Trudgill, Edgar Schneider, and Jeffrey P. Williams (eds.). 2010. *The Lesser-Known Varieties of English: An Introduction*. Cambridge: Cambridge University Press.

Siemund, Peter. forthc. *Varieties of English: A Typological Approach*. Cambridge: Cambridge University Press.

Szmrecsanyi, Benedikt and Bernd Kortmann. 2009. The morphosyntax of varieties of English worldwide: a quantitative perspective. *Lingua* 119:11 (Special issue "The Forests behind the Trees", ed. by Nerbonne, John and Franz Manni), 1643-1663.

Tagliamonte, Sali. 2012. *Variationist Sociolinguistics: Change, Observation, Interpretation*. Malden/Oxford/Chichester: Wiley-Blackwell.

Trudgill, Peter and Jean Hannah. 2002. *International English: A Guide to Varieties of Standard English*. London: Arnold.

Wray, Alison and Aileen Bloomer. 2006. *Projects in Linguistics: A Practical Guide to Researching Language*. London: Hodder.

...ean **Creole** spoken on the is-
...ds.

... unit in morphology, a build-
... word to which other units such
...d suffixes are attached. For in-
...ord *hardship* consists of the base
...ch the suffix -*ship* is added (see
... **suffix**).

...n Indo-Aryan language from the
...pean language family, one of the
...anguages in India. It is the official
... of the state of West Bengal.

...al: involving the use of two languag-
...also **monolingual**, **multilingual**).

...ualism: varying degrees of mastery of
...nguages that are accounted for in terms
...guistic, social, and psychological fac-
...such as age and context of acquisition,
...ural orientation, and domains of use.

...lama: an English-based Melanesian
...dgin, one of the three official languages of
...anuatu, a state in the Southwest of the Pa-
...ific Ocean.

...orrowing: words in a language or variety
originating from a different language (or
variety). For instance, the word *sputnik* has
found its way into English from Russian to
refer to a specific type of spacecraft.

Boston English: a variety of English spoken
in the city of Boston and in eastern Massachusetts. It is non-rhotic featuring some phonological elements that make it similar to
Received Pronunciation. Boston harbours
some highly prestigious schools of tertiary
education such as Boston University, Har-
vard University, and M.I.T. (Massachusetts
Institute of Technology).

Brighton English: is associated with the city
of Brighton and Hove, East Sussex, located
on the southern coast of England. The city
hosts a well-known public school for girls,
Roedean, and the University of Sussex
founded in 1961.

British Creole: a variety of English that
emerged as a result of contact between Caribbean **Creoles** and urban vernaculars spoken
in Britain.

C

Central Kanuri: a Saharan language from
the Nilo-Saharan language family, one of the
official languages in Nigeria.

Chicano English: a variety of English spoken by the immigrant population from Mexico in the United States.

clipping: a strategy of word formation
whereby the number of syllables in a word
is reduced to produce a shorter variant. For
instance, the word *advertisement* is shortened
to *ad* in English.

Cockney English: a variety of English associated with working class speech in London.

code-switching: a practice of using more
than one language concurrently by bilingual
speakers.

coinage: creation of new words or phrases;
new words and phrases.

colloquial: (of words and phrases) informal,
pertaining to informal speech.

colloquialism: a word or a phrase used in informal speech as opposed to formal speech.

community language: a language spoken
by a group of people sharing a set of cultural
values or a religion.

compound: a word (a noun, a verb or an adjective) created through the juxtaposition of
two or more words or its parts. Compounds
can be hyphenated, written as one word or

Glossary of linguistic t

A

accent: distinct features of pronunciation i.
a language variety (see also dialect).

Adamawa Fulfulde: a language from the
Niger-Congo language family spoken in
West Africa, including Nigeria; one of the of-
ficial languages of Nigeria.

adjective: words modifying nouns and noun
phrases (e.g. *a green house*, *a menacing figure in the dark*).

adverb: words modifying verbs, adjectives,
and other adverbs whose meaning relates to
time, space, manner, and quality. English adverbs frequently end in *-ly* (e.g. *She is nicely
dressed.*), although many are simple words,
not specifically marked (e.g. *They work hard
every day. Her smile is very beautiful.*).

African-American Vernacular English: an
ethnic variety, or an ethnolect, spoken by the
population of African descent in the United
States.

Afrikaans: a language developed from a historical variety of Dutch that is now spoken in
South Africa.

Anglo-Celtic: (of people) stemming from
Great Britain and Ireland. The term is par-
ticularly salient in locations boasting robust
British and Irish diasporas such as Australia,
New Zealand, Canada, and the United States.

Anglophone: related to the English-speaking
world and culture.

Appalachian English: a regional variety of
English, or a dialect, spoken in the region of
Appalachia lying between New York in the
North and Mississippi in the South.

Arabic: a Semitic language from the Afro-
Asiatic language family spoken in North

o
po
defi.
aspe
the int
or an a
tion, an e
and compl
habitual (the
is in progress
just begun (the
to tense, aspect
an event or an a
also **tense**).

Assamese: an Indo-
Indo-European langua
national languages in I
language of the state of A

Australian accents: thre
accents: **Cultivated Austr**
with upper class speech, **Ge.**
an associated with speech of th
population, and **Broad Australi.**
people from the lower socioecon
Australianisms: distinct lexis of .
English.

Australian Vernacular English: a.
mal, non-standard type of speech spok
the working class of Australia and those
ing in rural areas.

B

Bajan: a Caribl
land of Barbad

base: a centra
ing block of a
as prefixes a
stance, the w
hard to wh
also **prefix**

Bengali:
Indo-Eur
national
language

bilingu
es (see

biling
two la
of li
tors
cult

Bis

Pi

V

c

written separately (e.g. *lop-sided*, *micro-wave*, *top manager*).

connotation: a meaning that a word possesses in addition to its primary meaning (see also **denotation**). These meanings are often culture-specific. For instance, the primary meaning of the word *dove* is 'a specific type of bird'. In many cultures, however, the word *dove* has a secondary meaning and stands for 'peace'.

consonants: speech sounds emerging as a result of a partial or complete stop of the air flow in the mouth. To give examples, the letters <b>, <c>, <d>, etc. all stand for specific types of consonants (see also **diphthong**, **vowel**).

conversation: a type of speech involving two or more people.

Creole: a language arising in situations involving contact between groups of people that do not share a common language. In contrast to Pidgins, Creoles are characterised by more elaborate grammars and vocabulary and are employed in many different contexts and situations including communication in the family (see also **Pidgin**).

D

denotation: the primary meaning of a word. For instance, the primary meaning of the word *lotus* is 'a specific type of plant'. This is its denotation. The secondary meaning of the word *lotus* can be described as 'awakening' and 'spiritual growth'. This is its connotation (see also **connotation**).

dialect: distinct phonological, morphosyntactic, and lexical features of a language variety spoken in a particular region (e.g. Lancashire dialect). It is quite possible to speak the standard dialect of a language with a regional accent. However, one hardly ever hears someone speak a regional dialect of a language with a standard accent (see also **accent**).

dialogue: a verbal exchange between two or more people.

diphthong: a type of sound consisting of two vowels. These vowels are considered inseparable in this type of sound. The vowel sounds in the words *line*, *bake*, and *stroke* are all diphthongs (see also **consonant**, **vowel**).

discourse: a unit of language organisation longer than a sentence.

Dutch: pertaining or related to the culture and language of the Netherlands; a West-Germanic language from the Indo-European language family.

E

Edo: a Benue-Congo language from the Niger-Congo language family, one of the official languages in Nigeria.

Efik: a Benue-Congo language from the Niger-Congo language family, one of the official languages in Nigeria.

English: a West-Germanic language from the Indo-European language family.

Estuary English: a sociolect spoken by the middle class in England.

expanding circle, the: a set of countries which recognise the importance of English as a means of international, academic, and business communication (see also **inner circle**, **outer circle**).

expression: a (set) combination of words.

F

finite verb: a verb form marked for tense, person, number, or mood.

first language: the language that one learns before all other languages (see also **mother tongue, native language**).

formal: (of language) associated with social occasions that are official, highly constrained, and consistent with recognised rules and requirements.

French: a Romance language from the Indo-European language family.

G

German: a West-Germanic language from the Indo-European language family.

grammar: a set of rules that accounts for word and sentence formation in a language.

Gujarati: an Indo-Aryan language from the Indo-European language family, one of the national languages in India. It is the official language of the state of Gujarat.

H

Hausa: a Chadic language from the Afro-Asiatic language family, one of the official languages in Nigeria.

Hiberno-English: also known as Irish English, this variety of English is spoken in Ireland.

Hindi: an Indo-Aryan language from the Indo-European language family, the official language of India. It is also the official language of the states of Bihar, Rajasthan, Haryana, Delhi, Himachal Pradesh, Madhya Pradesh, and Uttar Pradesh.

Home Counties, the: the area surrounding London that comprises the Southeast, some parts of East Anglia, most of the Eastern Southwest, and most of the Central East.

I

idiomatic: distinctive, typical of a particular language or its dialect.

idiosyncrasy: peculiarity.

Idoma: a Benue-Congo language from the Niger-Congo language family, one of the official languages in Nigeria.

Igbo: a Benue-Congo language from the Niger-Congo language family, one of the official languages in Nigeria.

indigenous: originating from a particular place; native, local.

inner circle, the: a set of countries in which English is the first, and in most cases the only, language of the dominant social group (see also **expanding circle**, **outer circle**).

intonation: a distinctive pattern or distinctive patterns of rising and falling tones characterising connected speech of a particular language.

Irish Gaelic: a Celtic language spoken in Ireland. As it is the national language of the country, it is taught in schools.

K

Kannada: a Dravidian language, one of the national languages in India. It is the official language of the state of Karnataka.

Kashmiri: an Indo-Aryan language from the Indo-European language family, one of the national languages in India. It is the official language of the state of Jammu and Kashmir.

Konkani: an Indo-Aryan language from the Indo-European language family, one of the national languages in India. It is the official language of the state of Goa.

L

language: a rule-governed system of communication, both oral and written, shared by people with a common cultural background.

lexeme: a word or a combination of words conveying a discrete meaning; a vocabulary unit.

lexical: belonging to the vocabulary of a language.

lexis: all the words of a given language (see also **vocabulary**).

Liberian Settler English: a variety of English spoken in Liberia, West Africa. This variety is largely based on English spoken by African-Americans who returned to Liberia in the 19th century.

lingua franca: a language shared by a group of people speaking different, mutually unintelligible languages.

linguistic: pertaining to the study of language.

linguistics: the study of language.

M

malapropism: a misuse of words that, while sounding similar, often produce a humorous effect. For instance, an absent-minded reporter may write down: 'A serial woman killer was known for her vivacious character', mistaking the word *vivacious* for *vicious* and thus prompting a smile on the reader's lips.

Malayalam: a Dravidian language, one of the national languages in India. It is the official language of the state of Kerala.

Mandarin: a Sino-Tibetan language; the official language of China and one of the four official languages in Singapore.

Marathi: an Indo-Aryan language from the Indo-European language family, one of the national languages in India. It is the official language of the state of Maharashtra.

misnomer: an inaccurate way of naming or describing something.

monolingual: involving the use of one language (see also **bilingual**, **multilingual**).

mother tongue: a first language learnt by a child (see also **first language, native language**).

multilingual: involving the use of more than two languages (see also **bilingual, monolingual**).

multilingual setting: an environment, a context or a situation involving the interaction of more than two languages.

N

national language: a language associated with the identity of a large group of people populating a territory or a country.

native language: a language acquired naturally from early childhood (see also **first language, mother tongue**).

native speaker: a person who acquires a language or languages naturally as their first language(s). It is, in fact, quite possible to be a native speaker of more than one language. For instance, children from transnational marriages often learn to speak two languages from birth and grow up bilingual.

Ndebele (isiNdebele): a language of the Bantu-speaking Ndebele people populating the Limpopo and Mpumalanga provinces in South Africa.

negation: a pattern in language whereby a proposition or an assertion about a state of affairs is denied (e.g. *I go to school every day.* vs. *I don't go to school every day.*).

Nepali: an Indo-Aryan language from the Indo-European language family, one of the national languages in India. It is spoken in Nepal and in the areas between Nepal and India.

Newfoundland English: a dialect spoken in the Northeast of Canada incorporating features from the western parts of England and Ireland.

Nigerian Pidgin English: a variety of Afro-Caribbean English Lexifier **Creole** spoken by over 50 per cent of the entire population in Nigeria.

non-native speaker: a person that began learning a language some time after acquiring their first language. For example, a vast majority of Indian English speakers are non-native speakers of English.

non-rhotic: used to describe a phonological rule of a variety whereby the *r*-sound following a vowel, as in *car*, *arm*, etc. is not pronounced (see also **rhotic**).

noun: a word designating a state (e.g. *happiness*), a process or an activity (e.g. *running*), an animate or an inanimate object (e.g. *man*, *vase*), or a phenomenon (e.g. *magnetism*).

O

object: in linguistics, a noun, a noun phrase or a pronoun designating a referent at which the action expressed by a verb is directed (**direct object**, e.g. *He wrote a letter*.). A noun, a noun phrase or a pronoun indicating a benefactor of an action expressed by a verb is an **indirect object** (see also **subject**). Indirect objects are often marked with the help of the prepositions *to* and *for* in English (e.g. *John gave the book to Mary*.).

official language: a language that is legally recognised in a country and is used for administrative, executive, legislative, and judicial functions.

Oriya: an Indo-Aryan language from the Indo-European language family, one of the national languages in India. It is the official language of the state of Orissa.

outer circle, the: a set of countries in which English is recognised as an official or a co-official language. In these countries, English also plays an important role in education and is frequently used as a means of communication between different ethnic groups (see also **expanding circle**, **inner circle**).

P

participle: a language form typically derived from the verb. In English it is built with the help of the suffix *-ing* (the **present participle**) and *-ed* (the **past participle**).

patois: a non-standard variety of a language spoken in a particular area, a dialect.

Pedi (Sepedi): a language of the Bantu-speaking Pedi people populating the Limpopo province in South Africa.

perfect: a language category typically indicating completion of an action, an event or a situation. English distinguishes between three forms of the perfect: the **present perfect** (e.g. *have/has written*), the **past perfect** (e.g. *had written*), and the **future perfect** (e.g. *will have written*).

phonetics: the field of linguistics exploring speech sounds, their acoustic characteristics, and articulatory properties. Phoneticians are concerned with the classification of concrete sounds as well as their adequate description with the help of an extended inventory of symbols known as **phonetic alphabet**.

phonology: the study of sounds as mental representations. Phonology explores the sound systems of specific languages and asks whether or not the substitution of a given sound through a different sound results in a change of word meaning or not. For instance, the words _bitch_ and _beach_ differ from each other with respect to the high front vowels /ɪ/ and /iː/, both of which are phonemes in English.

phrase: a combination of words forming clausal constituents. We can identify **noun phrases** (e.g. _Mary's mother_), **adjective phrases** (e.g. _extremely upset_), **verb phrases** (e.g. _had been singing_), and **prepositional phrases** (e.g. _in the house_) in English.

Pidgin: a form of language characterised by a simple grammar and reduced vocabulary that oftentimes emerged as a result of interaction between Europeans and indigenous population groups. In contrast to Creoles, Pidgins do not normally have native speakers, exhibiting restricted domains of use such as trade, interaction with tourists, and military activities (see also **Creole**). So-called **extended Pidgins** are spoken in a wider array of social contexts, including communication amongst indigenous speakers that do not share a common language.

prefix: a unit of word formation attached to the front of a word changing or modifying its meaning. For instance, the prefix _re-_ changes the meaning of the verb _do_ in _re-do_ (see also **base, suffix**).

progressive (aspect): a type of aspect indicating that an action, an event or a situation is in the process of unfolding (see also **aspect**). In English, it is formed with the help of the finite forms of the verb _be_ and the present participle, e.g. _is calling, are waiting,_ (see also **finite verb, participle**).

pronoun: a word employed in place of a noun or a noun phrase. In English we differentiate between **personal pronouns** (e.g. _I,_ _you, he,_ etc.), **possessive pronouns** (e.g. _my, her, their,_ etc.), **demonstrative pronouns** (e.g. _this, that,_ etc.), **reflexive pronouns** (e.g. _myself, yourself, himself,_ etc.), **reciprocal pronouns** (_each other, one another_), **interrogative pronouns** (e.g. _who/whom, whose, what, which,_ etc.), **relative pronouns** (e.g. _who/whom, whose, what, that, which,_ etc.), and **indefinite pronouns** (e.g. _some, any, much, many,_ etc.).

pronunciation: a manner in which a particular language sound is produced.

Punjabi: an Indo-Aryan language from the Indo-European language family, one of the national languages in India. It is the official language of the state of Punjab.

Q

question tag: an expression or phrase allowing the speaker to turn a statement into a question (e.g. _You are going home, aren't you?_).

R

reduplication: a morphological process whereby a new linguistic item is created by means of (partial) word repetition. A word can be repeated exactly as it is (e.g. _bye-bye_). Oftentimes it is, however, modified (e.g. _nitty-gritty_).

rhotic: used to describe a phonological rule of a language variety whereby the _r_-sound following a vowel, as in _car, arm,_ etc. is pronounced (see also **non-rhotic**).

Received Pronunciation (RP): an accent associated with the upper class from southern England. This accent is often taught as a target accent to non-native speakers of English.

Russian: a Slavic language from the Indo-European language family.

S

Scottish Gaelic: a Celtic language spoken in Scotland. It is associated with the Scottish national identity and culture. Because of the overwhelming dominance of English in the region, this language is currently endangered.

Scottish English: a variety of English native to Scotland.

Scots: an historical variety of English related to Northern Old English dialects.

schwa: a vowel reduced in its length and quality because it occurs in unstressed positions. For instance, <e> in *often* is a schwa sound.

second language: a language that a speaker learns after acquiring their first language (see also **first language**).

Sierra Leone Krio: an English-based **Creole** spoken in Sierra Leone, West Africa. This Creole is used as a lingua franca of the country and is spoken natively by ten per cent of the population.

Sindhi: an Indo-Aryan language from the Indo-European language family, one of the national languages in India. It is spoken in urban areas of western India.

slang: an informal type of speech used by a particular social group such as teenagers, gangsters, etc.

Solomon Islands Pijin: an English-based **Pidgin** spoken on the Solomon Islands. It is not an official language of the country although it is widely used as a lingua franca in urban areas. In rural areas, local languages occupy a more prominent position.

Sotho (Sesotho): a Bantu language from the Niger-Congo language family spoken in South Africa.

South African Indian English: a variety of English spoken in South Africa. It emerged when indentured labourers from India, who came to South Africa in the 19th and early 20th century, shifted to English.

standard English: English associated with educated native speakers, which traditionally serves as a target for non-native speakers (see also **native speaker**, **non-native speaker**).

stress: a way of emphasising a particular part of a word.

subject: in linguistics, a noun, a noun phrase or a pronoun designating a referent that is the agent of the action expressed by a verb. For instance, in *John built a house* the subject of the sentence is *John* (see also **object**).

suffix: a unit in morphology attached to the end of a word. The major function of suffixes is to produce lexical items belonging to a different class of words or to produce a new grammatical form of the lexical item. When added to the adjective *happy*, the suffix *-ness* produces the noun *happiness*. When added to the noun *son*, the suffix *-s* produces the plural form *sons* of this noun (see also **base**, **prefix**).

Swati (siSwati): a language of the Bantu-speaking Swati people populating Swaziland and the Mpumalanga province in South Africa.

Swiss German: varieties of German belonging to the Alemannic dialect family spoken in Switzerland.

syllable: a word unit minimally consisting of a vowel sound, often found in combination with one or more consonants.

syntactic: related to the word order of a language.

T

Tamil: a Dravidian language, one of the national languages in India. It is the official language of the state of Tamil Nadu.

Telugu: a Dravidian language, one of the national languages in India. It is the official language of the state of Andhra Pradesh.

tense: a grammatical category whose function is to place a situation, an event or an action on the time axis at (around), prior to or after the moment of utterance. It is different from aspect, which describes the internal structure of a situation, an event or an action (see also **aspect**).

term: a conventionalised way of naming (or referring to) objects and phenomena; a label, a definition (e.g. *an academic term*).

Tok Pisin: a **Creole** spoken as a first and a second language in Papua New Guinea. Together with English and Hiri Motu, it is one of the official languages of the country.

transcript: (recorded) speech that has been written down.

translation: the process of conveying a meaning or a message from one language into another.

Tsonga (Xitsonga): a language of the Bantu-speaking Tsonga people inhabiting the Transvaal area in South Africa.

Tswana (Setswana): a language of the Bantu-speaking Tswana people spoken in South Africa.

U

Ulster Scots: a variety of Scots spoken in Northern Ireland.

Urdu: an Indo-Aryan language from the Indo-European language family, one of the national languages in India. It is the official language of the state of Jammu and Kashmir.

V

Valley Girl Talk: a variety of English originally spoken by middle and upper-middle class young females from the San Fernando Valley in Los Angeles.

variety: a distinct form of language spoken in a particular region (a dialect), in a particular time period (an historical variety) or by a particular ethnic or social group (an ethnolect / a sociolect).

variation: a process whereby two or more language forms compete with each other for expressing a similar meaning.

Venda (Tshivenda): a language of the Bantu-speaking Venda people spoken in northeastern parts of South Africa.

verb: a word designating an action (e.g. *snap*), an activity or a process (e.g. *run*) or an event (e.g. *occur*). Some verbs also refer to states (e.g. *be*, *exist*, etc.) and mental perceptions (e.g. *see*, *think*, *hear*, etc.).

vernacular: unmonitored and spontaneous speech reserved for casual situations.

vocabulary: all the lexical items of a particular language (see also **lexis**).

vowel: sounds produced without any stop of the air flow in the mouth. To give an example, the letters <a>, <e>, <i>, etc. all stand for specific types of vowels (see also **consonant, diphthong**).

W

word: a language unit; spoken or written.

X

Xhosa: a Bantu language from the Niger-Congo language family spoken in South Africa.

Y

Yiddish: a Germanic language originating in the Jewish communities of Central and Eastern Europe that is heavily influenced by Hebrew and some Slavic languages.

Yoruba: a Benue-Congo language from the Niger-Congo language family, one of the official languages in Nigeria.

Z

Zulu: a Bantu language from the Niger-Congo language family spoken in South Africa.

IPA tables

IPA consonants

	Bilabial	Labial-dental	Dental	Alveolar	Palato-alveolar	Retroflex	Palatal	Velar	Uvular	Glottal
Nasal	m	ɱ	n			ɳ		ŋ	ɴ	
Plosive	p b		t d			ʈ ɖ	ɟ	k g	q ɢ	ʔ
Fricative		f v	θ ð	s z	ʃ ʒ		ç	x ɣ	χ	ħ
Approximant				ɹ		ɻ	j	ɰ		
Trill				r					ʀ	
Tap, flap				ɾ		ɽ				
Lateral approximant				l		ɭ		ʟ		
Lateral flap				ɺ						

The vowels of Modern English

RP vowels   front ⟵ central ⟶ back

beat	/iː/
bit	/ɪ/
pen	/e/
pan	/æ/
cut	/ʌ/
dark	/ɑː/
spot	/ɒ/
sport	/ɔː/
pull	/ʊ/
pool	/uː/
bird	/ɜː/
about	/ə/

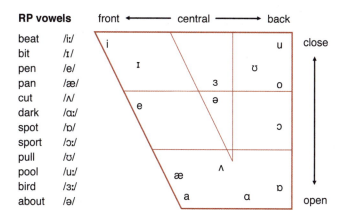